HOW TO LIVE TOGETHER

European Perspectives: A Series in Social Thought and Cultural Criticism

European Perspectives

A Series in Social Thought and Cultural Criticism

Lawrence D. Kritzman, Editor

European Perspectives presents outstanding books by leading European thinkers. With both classic and contemporary works, the series aims to shape the major intellectual controversies of our day and to facilitate the tasks of historical understanding.

For a complete list of books in the series, see pages 221–222.

HOW TO LIVE TOGETHER

Novelistic Simulations of Some Everyday Spaces

Roland Barthes

Notes for a lecture course and seminar at the Collège de France (1976–1977)

Translated by Kate Briggs

Text established, annotated, and introduced by Claude Coste

COLUMBIA UNIVERSITY PRESS   NEW YORK

Columbia University Press wishes to express its appreciation for assistance given by the government of France through the Ministère de la Culture in the preparation of this translation.

Columbia University Press
Publishers Since 1893
New York   Chichester, West Sussex
cup.columbia.edu
Copyright © 2002 Éditions du Seuil
English translation copyright © 2013 Columbia University Press

Library of Congress Cataloging-in-Publication Data
Barthes, Roland.
    [Comment vivre ensemble: simulations romanesques de quelques espaces quotidiens. English]
    How to live together : novelistic simulations of some everyday spaces / Roland Barthes.
        p. cm.
    Includes bibliographical references and index.
    ISBN 978-0-231-13616-7 (cloth : acid-free paper) —
    ISBN 978-0-231-13617-4 (pbk. : acid-free paper)
    1. Philosophy, Modern—20th century.   2. Philology.   3. Literature—History and criticism.   I. Title.

B804.B36513 2012
100—dc23

                                                2012021328

CONTENTS

"Form is costly, Paul Valéry would answer when asked why he did not publish his lectures at the Collège de France. Yet there has been a whole period, that of triumphant bourgeois writing, when form cost about the same price as thought." These are the opening lines of "Style as Craftsmanship," an article first published in *Combat* on November 16, 1950, and later reprinted in *Writing Degree Zero*.[1]

At the time, along with and in contradistinction to Sartre and Blanchot, Barthes was exploring the possibility of an ethics of literature, one that would be neither terrorism nor nihilism but a responsibility of form. He was not to know that one day he would be teaching at the Collège de France and that the question of whether or not to publish his own lecture courses would arise. Yet it is clear from the reference to Valéry that it was first and foremost a personal ethics that Barthes sought to edify, not a moral treatise for his contemporaries. Far from a list of prescriptions or summations, that ethics would indeed involve a great deal more than intellectual commitment: it was in a certain sense *a treatise on style*.

We all know that in literature (as in other fields) there are no such things as last wishes. Whenever, out of naivety or remorse, a writer decides to leave last-minute instructions, it is only so that they will be disobeyed—which is always what happens. Thus, when the issue of publishing Barthes's "Lecture Courses at the Collège de France" arose, it was never going to be a matter of producing some kind of testament, or of acting out of pious loyalty to the dead. Rather, the aim was to conceive of the publication within the broader logic of Barthes's oeuvre, of the thinking that guided his work and the ethics that has always been both its object and its guardian. Those reflections on Valéry thus came quite naturally to mind at the start of the project: a veritable *mise en abyme* of the young Barthes at the heart of the posthumous Barthes.

The first principle of this edition—which is almost an axiom—is that Barthes's lecture courses at the Collège de France could not be and should not be *books*. Accordingly, two hypotheses were rejected at the outset: to rewrite the lecture courses, which would have made them look like a written production, or to publish a transcription of the recorded oral version, which would have turned them into artifacts.

Both hypotheses had their own logic. It is not difficult to see what prompted the rejection of the first. For a disciple to rewrite the Master's speech only makes sense, and can only be justified, in exceptional cases: when, after the Master's death, it is a matter of fulfilling a specific editorial demand, of annexing a space of potential elucidation onto an obscure doctrine or, indeed, of uniting disciples and readers through the transmission of the doctrinal message via a posthumous collection of books. Such a project would clearly have made no sense in relation to Barthes, who was a man of the book, for whom teaching was a secular and profane practice and whose books contained the essence of what he wanted to impart in and of themselves. Moreover, in those instances when Barthes did attempt to turn a seminar into a book (*S/Z*, *A Lover's Discourse*) the result was not in any sense a written prolongation of the teaching, but a new object.[2]

The second hypothesis—to transcribe the oral version of the lecture courses—was rejected for different, more profound reasons: reasons furnished by Barthes himself and that pertain to the relationship between the spoken and the written; in other words, that touch on the very question of the *ethos* of the work. In an early text (written in 1959) apropos of the publication of a round-table discussion on the *Nouveau Roman*, Barthes writes:

> It is still possible to hear a writer speak (on the Radio, for example): his breath, the manner of his voice always has something to teach us; but to then convert that speech converted into writing, as if the order and the nature of languages were of no importance . . . , is nothing other than to produce a bastard and meaningless writing that possesses neither the arresting distance of the written thing, nor the poetic pressure of the spoken thing. In short, the sole purpose of the round table is to extract the worst of speech from the best of writers: discourse. Now, writing and speech cannot be interchanged and nor can they be conjoined because between them there is quite simply something like a challenge: writing is constituted by a rejection of all other kinds of language.[3]

An oral lecture course is clearly not as vacuous as a round-table discussion, but it carries within it the very fatality of speech: its contingency, its ephemeral and transitory nature, its irreversible continuity, its verbal fluctuations, opposing it to the necessary, delimited, recursive, durable and flowing, discontinuous and cadenced written object. What's more, beyond even those oppositions, beyond the triviality that sets around all speech preserved in print, there is what Barthes considers the defining feature of writing: "Writing is precisely that contradiction that turns the failure of communication into a secondary communication, speech for others but speech without the other."[3]

The decision not to rewrite or to provide a "rewritten" transcription of Barthes's lecture courses was not, however, simply a matter of principle, informed by Barthes's doctrine of the book. If both hypotheses were rejected, this had just as much to do with the particular nature of the lecture courses themselves and with their material and singular status within Barthes's intellectual trajectory.

The lack of overlap between Barthes's written production and his teaching practice grew more apparent with his election to the Collège de France in 1977. While heading a small seminar at the École pratique des hautes études, Barthes had on occasion been tempted to turn a particular course into a book. But once at the Collège that possibility was no longer considered: here, no trace of the Socratic gatherings of the past remained, nothing to incline Barthes to preserve his lectures.

At the Collège de France, the lecture courses no longer played an explicitly foundational role in Barthes's thinking, nor a genealogical one in relation to his oeuvre. This was also likely to be due to the period of personal transformation that Barthes was experiencing at the time.

Those circumstances will not be gone into at any length here—other than to note that, in a roundabout way, Barthes himself sets out the reasons his discourse appears to be steadily de-theorizing itself in the lecture courses (to the disappointment of his audience): "We are in an active phase of 'healthy' deconstruction of the 'mission' of the intellectual: this deconstruction can take the form of a withdrawal but also of a jamming, of a series of decentered affirmations." A little further on in the course on the Neutral, he adds: "pleasure in substituting an irenic knowledge (perhaps obsessional: reification, inventory) for a battle of ideas."[4]

Indeed, what characterizes the lecture courses and makes nonsense of the idea of rewriting them in order to give them the appearance of a work, or indeed of transcribing them with a view to endowing them, as in a simulacrum, with the self-importance of a book, is the practice of a kind of systematic *understating* of the aim of the course: a practice that on occasions is so pronounced that some sessions seem to consist in Barthes simply reading aloud from his working notes.

Even the very structure of a lecture course—which, rather than the development of a discourse or the trajectory of a logic or a thought process, is organized around what Barthes calls *traits* (presented in either alphabetical order or according to a mathematics of the aleatory)[5]—was designed to radically suspend the possibility of Barthes's words acquiring any doctrinal function. Lecture courses followed one after another over a period of three years in the order described; that is to say, in no order: sorts of "chapters" of unequal size and length, like extended or succinct "index cards": index cards that are comprehensive to a greater or lesser degree, personal to a greater or lesser degree, inspired by the field of knowledge opened out by the topic of the course: "Living-Together," "The Neutral," "The Preparation of the Novel."

On Barthes's part there is a double movement that can appear contradictory. On the one hand, the desire to produce a *course*, that is to say, to willingly engage with all that can be somewhat off-putting about the positive exploration of a field of knowledge. Yet, on the other, and concomitantly, the refusal to exploit that knowledge, to develop it into a personal phenomenology as had been his practice in previous years. The result is that the courses can seem disappointing.

That disappointment is not only something Barthes anticipated but also, in a certain sense, something he sought. Clearly, the notion of disappointment is not to be understood in the usual sense but rather—to be fully Barthesian—in accordance with a *bathmology*, that is to say a science of degrees. There is an astute saying that Barthes used to attribute to Gide: not even a God could adopt "I disappoint" as a motto. The point is that disappointment has many virtues and our understanding of it should not be on the banal mode of failure, or at any rate that it inscribes itself within a dialectic of effects that takes us outside the realm of the measurable.

That disappointment also manifests itself in other ways, even in the very theme of the lecture course—for instance, in a very explicit manner on the subject of "Living-Together." The question underpinning the course could be summarized as follows: "Is it possible to have an idiorrhythmic group? Is it possible for a community of beings to exist with no *Telos*, no Cause?" The response is clearly negative. And that negativity, since what we are dealing with is a lecture course without beginning or end—without order, as we said—is always already there, serving almost to invalidate the very object of the research inquiry from the start. It is therefore as if negativity were ultimately the real object of the course—as if that were its truth.

In this regard, one could reflect on Barthes's mode of negative deconstruction and its very different treatment of question of Community—now a very topical issue in a number of academic writings.[6] One could then get a measure of the strange negativity that came to serve as a kind of paradoxical method in Barthes's work. More than a method, an asceticism, in which we see Barthes quietly attaining to that *degree zero,* that abeyance, that narrow corner of thought where speech seems capable of avoiding the forms of mystification (of alienation) specific to the intellectual: the mystification of mastery, the mystification of persuasion, the mystification of "theory," the alienation of status, the alienation of domination and conflict. Barthes's quasi-absence with respect to his speech serves as a means of deserting the field of academic or intellectual discourse—that of someone who always has something to say—in a quiet attempt to adopt the marginal position of a discrete subject, someone who seems content to do no more than point to sites of knowledge, to delimit, to classify, to list possible dossiers, to effect a kind of philological deviation from his theme—and to do so amidst the hopeless disorder of an arbitrary alphabetical or mathematical sequence of unconnected fragments drawn from an encyclopedia in progress.

Yet if disappointment is in some sense consubstantial with the object, the form, the protocol, and even the detail of Barthes's three lecture courses at the Collège de France, disappointment can also be said to be bound up with the very act of giving a lecture. An act that it would seem Barthes no longer expected anything from.

The lecture course is a production with no other aim or existence than to be delivered. As Barthes himself makes clear in the first session on the Neutral: "We'll have to hold onto the unsustainable for thirteen weeks: after that, it will fade."[7]

It was therefore evident that Barthes's lecture courses should not be made into posthumous books. It was evident that the physical existence of Barthes's lecture courses should be in the form of an *archive of the lecture courses* and that any editorial intervention that did not stem from that axiom would be erroneous.

The subtitle of each volume, "Notes for a Lecture Course at the Collège de France," is a very precise description of what the reader is presented with: the "text" that Barthes would use as the basis of his lecture each week at the Collège.[8] If the word "text" appears between quotation marks, it is precisely because these notes are closer to what one might call an *infra-text*, that is to say a state of discourse that comes before the text but whose rudimentary, abridged, miniaturized, reduced, concentrated, elementary, sometimes outlined or virtual character is entirely bound up with the tension of its future delivery, in the anticipation or the project of its actualization.

The organizing principle of each volume of lecture and seminar notes is the course session, since that was the true rhythm of the reading,[9] a rhythm that Barthes would retrospectively inscribe on his manuscript by marking the date and time where he had left off that day and where he would take up again the following week.

As for the "text" of the lecture course itself, the principle adopted here was to intervene as little as possible. The symbols that Barthes uses—for instance, to condense a logical construction [→, ≠]—have been retained, although we have completed abbreviations where they are a matter of a habitual shorthand (such as *R.C.* for *Robinson Crusoe*) and corrected punctuation where it is too muddled.

Where Barthes's written argument is too obscure, we also took the liberty of paraphrasing the overall sense of the passage in a footnote to spare the reader an unnecessary enigma. We took advantage of the wide margins in the Traces écrites series: the bibliographical references that Barthes uses for the quotations are inscribed here, appearing at the same place on the page as in the manuscript itself. It should be added that the rare passages that Barthes crossed out have been retained but are identified as such in footnotes that indicate where the deleted passage begins and ends. When a session is prefaced by remarks relating to letters received or the argument from the previous week, these remarks appear in italics. Finally, the editors' interventions in the text of the course are indicated by square brackets ([]). Occasionally, Barthes breaks off a quotation to make a point; these interventions are indicated by angle brackets (<>).

The footnotes are in the traditional philological style, essential in a text that is occasionally allusive. As far as possible, quotations, proper names, expressions in foreign languages (particularly from Ancient Greek, which we chose to transliterate in Latin characters), place names, and historical events are identified and explained in the notes, which the inclusion of a complete bibliographical index saves from being too repetitive. References to other texts or books by Barthes are to the new edition of the *Oeuvres complètes*, published in five volumes in 2002, and appear in the following form: OC 1, OC 2, etc.[10] In addition to the index of names and places, we have included an uncommented index of concepts, which appear in alphabetical order. When Barthes refers to an old or unlocatable edition of a text, our footnotes indicate a more accessible one.[11]

A short preface contextualizes the lecture course and highlights its most salient features.

Éric Marty

On March 14, 1976, following a recommendation made by Michel Foucault, the committee of professors elected Roland Barthes to Chair of Literary Semiology. The new professor would teach at the Collège de France until his death in the spring of 1980. The uncertain trajectory of Roland Barthes's career has often been noted: an academic with no *agrégation* qualification, a singular researcher who had spent much of his working life either abroad (Romania, Egypt, Morocco) or in the margins of the French university system. Barthes's meandering path culminated in a prestigious setting; even so, his election, secured by just a single vote, serves as a reminder of the intellectual and institutional resistance that has so often stalled the advancement of a singular thinker . . .

Barthes delivered his Inaugural Lecture on January 7, 1977. On January 12, he began delivering his lectures before the diverse audience of the Collège de France. The lecture notes preserve the trace of the proximity between those two dates. The first sessions often refer back to the Inaugural Lecture and ask to be read as its direct and immediate application. In keeping with the rules of the Collège de France, the professor was required to do twenty-six hours of teaching, which could be divided between the lecture course and the seminar as he saw fit. The lecture course, entitled "How to Live Together: Novelistic Simulations of Some Everyday Spaces," took place every Wednesday during term-time, from January 12 to May 4, 1977, working out as one hour of teaching per week. Barthes also held a parallel weekly seminar entitled "What is it to hold forth? Research on invested speech," to which outside speakers were invited.[1] Barthes's contribution to the seminar, which examines the "intimidations of language," consists in a general introduction ("Holding Forth") and an analysis of "Charlus-Discourse." As the notes for the last session indicate, a small change was made to the timetable: Barthes planned to divide his teaching hours equally between the lectures and the seminar, setting aside thirteen hours for each. In the end, fourteen sessions were given to the lecture course and twelve to the seminar.

Conditions in the lecture halls were far from comfortable, as the sound recordings attest. Due to the crowds of people wanting to attend—out of intellectual enthusiasm, worldly curiosity, or the lure of the latest fad—the Collège was obliged to offer a live broadcast of the professor's speech in an adjacent lecture hall. The first session in particular suffered a number of interruptions: the retransmission not working, the irritated amusement of the students, having to send out for a technician, Barthes's own embarrassment at the many technical failings. While those problems were quickly resolved, conditions remained poor for the rest of the year.

It is not easy to give a date to the labor of preparation. When did Barthes first conceive of his lecture course? Were all the handwritten notes drafted in advance of the first session? Although we cannot be sure, it would appear that most of the lectures were ready by early January. Barthes had the habit of working on his teaching for the coming year over the summer months spent in his house in Urt, in the Basque country. There are several passages with temporal indicators in the notes that suggest that progress from conception to the delivery of the lectures suffered occasional interruptions: the anecdote of the bad mother (dated December), an allusion to the *Ring* cycle at Bayreuth (summer 1976), receiving a letter from a reader following the publication of an article in *Photo* (in the spring of 1977). That is more or less it. When he presents the organization of the year as a series of "traits," Barthes concedes that their order was not yet definitively fixed, allowing us to suppose that chance would play a role in how his teaching developed. That uncertainty did not have any great impact on the course and can be set against the fact that the contours of each session were very clearly delimited. Barthes would always mark where he had left off by writing the day's date in his notes. The decision was taken to title each session with the date that Barthes inscribed within the body of his text.

Until now, the only knowledge a reader may have had of Barthes's first lecture course at the Collège de France was the course summary drafted by the professor. Published in the Collège de France yearbook and reprinted in the third volume of the *Oeuvres complètes*, those very condensed pages remain the best possible introduction to Barthes's work. Conserved at the Institut de la mémoire de l'édition contemporaine (IMEC), the archives of "How to Live Together" are comprised of two different types of material support: the text of the lectures itself and Barthes's index cards. The largest archive is the handwritten manuscript of the lecture notes. It comprises ninety-two single-sided, numbered pages, written in a crowded hand, with a certain number of interlinear additions, some of which are numbered. The first pages of notes were often expanded upon in the form of additions that were then stapled or stuck on. Those additional texts offer an occasional clarification (on Bachelard's conception of the imaginary, for instance) or propose a longer excursus (on Benveniste's analysis of the word "rhythm") . . . The editorial decision was taken to incorporate those additions into the main text—which proved simple to achieve. As regards the seminar on "Holding Forth," only Barthes's introductions are conserved in the archives, numbering some thirty pages in total.

The manuscripts, drafted clearly in blue ink, are not difficult to read. The literal comprehension of the text, however, required some further effort. Barthes did not write up his lectures and his notes should on no account be compared to a text destined for publication. Yet nor does Barthes's work present itself as a mere outline from which to improvise. The lecture notes, which get progressively more structured as the sessions go on, represent very different stages in the drafting process. Following after syntactically constructed passages, or complete paragraphs, are pure enumerations, lists of words. But even if the manuscript abounds in ellipses (of verbs and causal links), necessitating a continual adjustment of the brain and the eye, it nevertheless remains comprehensible.

Sound recordings exist of almost all of the sessions (only the last thirty minutes of the last lecture, delivered on May 4, are missing). Those recordings are naturally an extremely rich resource, and in the preparation of this edition of the notes they served two purposes. In the first case, the sound recording expands on and explains a written note that in certain instances would have been clear to the professor (who was using the notes as an aide-memoire) but obscure to a reader for whom the text was not written. A literal transcription of what Barthes said in the lecture is provided as footnotes wherever the oral formulation serves to elucidate the manuscript. Also included as footnotes are clarifications and elaborations that the spoken delivery affords the written text. Those additions and asides provide insight into Barthes's future projects (a seminar on Sartre and the origins of language) as well as his intellectual practices. Whenever a learned word ("irenic") or an obscure reference is indicated in the manuscript, when delivering the lecture Barthes would always be sure to repeat or to reformulate the written word and propose a more familiar alternative.

The researcher disposes of a collection of index cards offering insight into the workings and the trials and errors of intellectual labor. Those index cards, which are likewise conserved and numbered at the IMEC, are organized into three envelopes. The first two (running from numbers 1 to 50 and from 51 to 100) comprise a collection of pieces of paper, cut to size, in alphabetical order: comments, examples, and citations are classified by theme or by key word ("Dances," "Demons," "*Discretio*," "Writing [and reading]," etc.). The contents of the third envelope are not ordered in any way and comprise unclassified index cards, loose sheets of notes, and a number of pages of bibliography. Included among those pages is a list of "books read" that appear marked with an asterisk in the general bibliography to this edition. That library, comprising at least fifty books, some of which were read in their entirety, while others were merely consulted, attests to the care with which Barthes documented his preparation. The index cards also show the evolution of a dynamic research project: some of the works that appear frequently in the preparatory papers virtually disappear in the lecture course (Xenophon's *Oeconomicus*) or are given less importance (*Pot Luck*); conversely, other texts become more forceful or receive a different treatment (the love story in *The Magic Mountain* fades into the background as Barthes focuses solely on the sociability of the sanatorium). Quotations from some of those index cards in the footnotes gives the reader insight into the elaboration of the course.

Along with the summary of the lecture course and the seminar that Roland Barthes wrote himself for the Collège de France yearbook, two indexes (one of proper names, the other of key ideas) and a glossary of Greek terms have been provided.

So it was that at the peak of his renown, Barthes left "*École*" {primary school} for "*Collège*" {secondary school}—as he jokingly remarks in "Holding Forth." At the École pratique des hautes études, the last seminar dealt with the lover's discourse, a labor of two years that produced *A Lover's Discourse: Fragments*. Barthes's status and audience may have changed with the move from the seminar to the lecture course (he was now addressing a wider public), but his work did not undergo a sudden mutation. The last class session at "*École*" ended on an opposition—borrowed from Nietzsche—between "Method" and "Culture." It is with that same opposition that Barthes opens the long "Introduction" that takes up the first two sessions of the lecture course at "*Collège*." Moreover, the writing of *A Lover's Discourse* and the preparation of the lecture course were undertaken at more or less the same time, somewhere between the summer of 1976 to the winter of 1977, providing a different link between the past and the present.

More importantly, both the object and the title of the lecture course ("How to Live Together") make it very clear that the lecture format would not mark the end of an ethical enquiry (how to conceive of the relationship between the subject and the other) or a moral one (on the condition that we invest the word with a concrete and practical dimension).

Inseparable on an institutional and intellectual level, the seminar and the lecture course enter into a play of opposition and complementarity. It is the job of the seminar to present the dark side of Living-Together, while the lecture course presents the brighter side, eagerly embarking on a quest for social utopia.

Barthes describes language as the very space of sociability in all of his work, whether it is a matter of exercising its power through words or of freeing oneself from the code through literature. In the seminar on the intimidations of language, Barthes tries to define that "discourse" that each of us sustains our whole lives and that only death manages to interrupt, the discourse that constitutes us and whose aim is often to subdue our interlocutors. "To Hold Forth," Barthes notes, is to assert yourself through your words and your body. "To Hold Forth" is to manifest the hysteria that haunts the whole of Barthes's oeuvre, that infatuation of a subject intoxicated by his own imaginary, that theatricalization of the self that Sartre called "bad faith." By choosing Andromache's speech to Hermione as the first example and analyzing the rhetoric of the victim facing her executioner, Barthes gestures back to *On Racine* with its "techniques of aggression" taken to their extreme within the contained world of the tragedy, where people speak in order to save themselves from death.

The second example concerns "Charlus-Discourse," the passionate discourse to which Charlus, in the guise of a disappointed lover, subjects the narrator in *The Guermantes Way*. Always attentive to the strategies of language, Barthes proposes a preliminary sketch of this "science of the unique being" he dreamt of in *Camera Lucida*. "Charlus-Discourse" is not the prototype of a general discourse of seduction, but rather the unique encounter between an intractable subject and an intractable speech—thus making its particular functioning an apt topic for investigation. As a means of indexing all of its particularities (a singular discourse delivered by a singular individual), Barthes has fun creating a whole series of concepts or pseudo-concepts, such as the "exploseme" (figure of anger) or the "strategeme" (figure of the ruse).

In contradistinction to the preoccupations of the seminar, the lecture course is a more positive enquiry, sustained throughout by the energy of a "fantasy." In his inaugural lecture, Barthes claimed the right to a "fantasmatic" teaching, a research project that accepts that it will be compromised by the affect of the researcher but manages to avoid descending into confession or egotism nevertheless (in that regard, there is very little biographical content in lecture course). But for the fantasy to take recognizable form and for the research enquiry to open out depended on the encounter with a particular word. It was while reading Jacques Lacarrière's *L'Été grec* that Barthes came across the word that would uncover a latent fantasy of sociability: that word was "idiorrhythmy."

Composed of *idios* (particular) and *rhuthmos* (rhythm), the word, which belongs to a religious vocabulary, refers to any community that respects each individual's own personal rhythm. "Idiorrhythmy" names the lifestyle of certain monks of Mount Athos, who live alone and yet are dependent on a monastery; at once autonomous and members of a community, solitary and integrated, idiorrhythmic monks partake of an organization that falls somewhere between the eremitism of the early Christians and institutionalized coenobitism. The religious origins and practice of the word prompts Barthes to study forms of communal life, chiefly Oriental monasteries where the rules and organization are far more flexible. Once again, it is the individual's difficult and complex relation with Power (or powers) that interests Barthes. Struck by the historical overlap between the development of coenobitism and the establishment of Christianity as the religion of the State, Barthes endeavors to look beyond occidental monachism. Moving from West to East, and from East to Far East, Barthes expands his corpus to include the Buddhist monks of Ceylon, who in a sense serve as a counterexample to the interventionism of the Christian churches, which were increasingly intolerant of idiorrhythmic structures . . . Analogous to the opposition between the West and Japan that he developed in *Empire of Signs*, the lecture course sees Barthes opposing Saint Benedict's Rule to the "lenient" Buddhism of the Ceylon monks.

Thanks to the work of metaphor, the word "idiorrhythmy" opens out onto other fields of application and investigation, beyond that of religion. Without directly linking it to monastic life, in Barthes's lecture course "idiorrhythmy" also names any attempt to reconcile collective life with individual life, the independence of the subject with the sociability of the group. Opening his corpus up to the profane world, Barthes selects five literary texts that in some degree engage with "idiorrhythmy" in its broader sense. Working with texts from very different cultures, Barthes mobilizes the effects of emphasis, contrast, and nuance in order to arrive at a more precise definition of a notion that is never dealt with directly by the various authors. While Palladius's *Lausaic History*, with its picturesque description of eremitic life in the eighth century, draws us back into the world of religion, the other texts clearly pull in the other direction. Thomas Mann's *The Magic Mountain* for the very particular sociability of the sanatorium, Émile Zola's *Pot Luck* for the strict hierarchy of the bourgeois apartment building, Daniel Defoe's *Robinson Crusoe*, and André Gide's *The Confined Woman of Poitiers* for the counterexample of Living-Alone: each one of the texts makes a small contribution to the exploration of a lifestyle that Barthes dreams of turning into life-art. In addition to the main corpus, there are a number of one-off references (to Xenophon, Le Corbusier, etc.) as well as frequent references to Proust, whose presence is increasingly felt (Aunt Léonie at the center of his childhood home . . .). From the first lecture course (*How to Live Together*) to the two that followed (*The Neutral* and *The Preparation of the Novel* in particular), *In Search of Lost Time* gradually emerges as the key reference in Barthes's last years of productivity.

The intellectual trajectory accompanying that quest for idiorrhythmy bears little resemblance to our habitual idea of what constitutes a lecture course at the Collège de France. Barthes accumulates scraps of knowledge, multiplies scholarly references and borrowings from Ancient Greek, but his bits and pieces of learning, which for the most part are drawn from secondary sources, are never made to function as arguments in and of themselves. In his long "Introduction" to the course, Barthes sets out the stakes and the approach of an atypical research project. If, citing Nietzsche and Deleuze, Barthes starts by setting up an opposition between "Method" and "Culture," it only to make clear his preference for the second option. If method means proceeding directly towards a precise goal, permitting no wandering off course or bifurcation, then Barthes prefers culture or *paideia*; in other words, the curved line, fragmentation. As in *A Lover's Discourse: Fragments*, the lecture course is organized into a sequence of "traits" (the new name Barthes gives to "figures"), that succeed one another in alphabetical order—the only order, as Barthes reminds us, capable of circumventing the constraints of the thesis and the ruses of chance.

"We are merely opening a dossier . . . ": Barthes often uses this phrase to introduce or round off a new section of the course. As well as working counter to the implacable nature of dialectical argument, the use of the "trait" is also a refusal to expand or develop. In the form of an embryonic thought, a mere sketch, at times a purely descriptive approach, each of the "traits," the "dossiers," stop short of comprehensiveness so as to enable a degree of personal investment on the part of the auditors. Accepting that the price he may have to pay is banality, Barthes stops himself from being overly learned for fear of being shut up in method. By inaugurating a quest that it is for others to undertake, by articulating the singularity of the research project and the plurality of the directions in which it could be pursued, Barthes transposes the idiorrhythmy that inspired both the content and the shape of his lecture course into the intellectual and pedagogical domain.

Curious about different fields of knowledge (but never letting himself get intoxicated by erudition), Barthes looks less to science than to the novel: the novels of Thomas Mann or Daniel Defoe, of course, which he discusses in his own manner, but also the dreamt-of novel he was inclining toward, whose "Preparation" would preoccupy the last two years of his teaching at the Collège de France. The novel as utopia prompts a "novelistic" renewal of Barthes's writing and teaching. Presenting his lecture course as "Novelistic Simulations of Some Everyday Spaces," Barthes experiments out loud with a form of the novelistic at the edges of the novel: the novel with no narrative. Barthes is not telling us a story. The sequencing of the traits makes this very clear: the course is structured according to theme ("Akedia," "Anachoresis," "Animals," "Athos," "Autarky," etc.) not narrative, where any metonymy is excluded by the arbitrary nature of the alphabetical order. But what remains when we write or speak a novel with no narrative? What might the "novelistic" dimension to the course consist in? The word "simulations" directs us toward *mimesis* for an answer. Like the novel it anticipates, the novelistic postulates reality as the referent of all representation. "That's exactly it!" cries Barthes when discussing Thomas Mann's novel: between his own experience of tuberculosis and Hans Castorp's experience in *The Magic Mountain*, it is the same reality that effects a rapprochement between life and literature.

The word "simulations" also directs us toward the "maquette," to that imaginary and yet at the same time very real construction that a novelist will sketch out before writing begins. A space habitable by fiction, the "maquette" is the novelistic décor that comes before the novel. In his "Introduction," Barthes puts a great deal of emphasis on the dynamic function of that spatial simulation; each of the texts he discusses corresponds to a particular space that pertains in some way to the sociability of Living-Together: Palladius's desert, the Confined Woman's bedroom, the apartment building in

Pot Luck, Robinson Crusoe's island—a list to which Barthes also adds the monasteries of Mount Athos or Ceylon. When considered in the light of the novelistic nature of the lecture course, the research project deals in spaces, and "simulation" becomes description. In these "maquettes" transformed into intellectual decors, objects and characters inhabit the spaces and open them up to temporality. As Barthes writes in the trait titled "Event," Robinson Crusoe gets less interesting when the cannibals arrive, and less again when he returns to Europe—in other words, whenever the novel starts reading like an adventure story. The event has its place in the "maquette," but in the singular, or in the disorder of fragmentation: events that are extended, disaccorded, insignificant, that avoid both the prospect of narrative and of justification. Like all novelists, Barthes shows more than he tells, short-circuiting a train of thought before it becomes too abstract, before the "maquette" becomes a symbol. For Barthes, the fantasmatic "scenario" amounts to the "scene," where the ambiguity of the word refers as much to the space of the theatre as the action that takes place on it . . . The novelistic dimension to Living-Together emerges in spaces full of objects (flowers, waste, tables, chairs, cowls . . .) where we are presented with the ordinary gestures of often extraordinary characters (a stylite, a confined woman, a shipwrecked man . . .).

Seeking a new Abbey of Thélème, a perfect accord between solitude and community, Barthes's lecture course proceeds in opposition to two countermodels: the couple (the lover's discourse made conjugal), and the crowd, whether indifferent or aggressive, whose hyperbolic figure is the school of fish. Poised between those two unwanted extremes, Barthes sets out to establish a morality of tact, where geographical space and social space merge around the theme of distance. The whole lecture course is in this question: What distance must I maintain between myself and others if we are to together construct a sociability without alienation, a solitude without exile? As one might expect, the lecture course offers no response. Barthes had planned to devote the final session to a utopia of Living-Together, but in the end gave up the idea. He gives a number of reasons why: lack of enthusiasm, the difficulty in imagining an idiorrhythmic life that would be an end in and of itself, the necessarily collective dimension of any utopia, the awareness that only the written form is capable of *taking account of* the fantasy. The failure of utopia—which is not the failure of the lecture course—is also hinted at by the increasing significance, session after session, accorded to *The Confined Woman of Poitiers*. Initially presented as equivalent in importance, Barthes sets the supporting texts to work: *Pot Luck* fades into the background as Gide's text slowly makes its presence felt. The passion for shutting oneself away, the omnipresence of waste surrounding an individual who has herself become a waste product, gives the lecture course a peculiar tone, in which shock mingles with sympathy, tenderness with disillusionment. Mélanie—the Confined Woman—and Aunt Léonie, who is present in so many of the traits, both speak, together and singly, of the disquieting fascination for a withdrawal into the self that only the novelistic imagination and novelistic writing will redress. Mélanie, described as a creator of language (a "logothete"), Aunt Léonie, a distant portent of the narrator's own creative sequestration, indirectly serve to present literature as the only successful idiorrhythmy, as the harmony to come between a writer's solitude and the community of his readers.

ACKNOWLEDGMENTS

For their indispensable expertise, I would like to thank: Louis Bardollet, Ridha Boulaâbi, Michèle Castells, Benard Deforge, Philippe Derule, Carole Dornier, Giles Faucher, Brigitte Gauvin, Dominique Gournay, Azzedine and Suzanne Guellouz, Nicole Guilleux, Anne-Élizabeth Halpern, Corinne Jouanno, Michèle Lacorre, Marie-Gabrielle Lallemand, Jean-Claude Larrat, Nathalie Léger, Bruno Leprêtre, Sophie Lucet, Alain Schaffner, Jürgen Siess, Andy Stafford, Gerald Steig, Pascale Thouvenin, and Serge Zenkin.

Alice Guillevin, of the Department of Ancient Languages at the University of Caen, transliterated the Ancient Greek in this edition. I would like to warmly thank her for her expertise, her availability, and her patience.

Claude Coste

Toward the end of the first session of this lecture course, as part of his long introduction to the central, productive notion of "idiorrhythmy," Roland Barthes recounts a scene viewed from his window. He sees a mother walking along with her small son; the boy is holding one of her hands, while she pushes an empty stroller out in front of them with the other. What strikes Barthes about the mother and son—strikes him enough, that is, to make a note of both what he saw and the date (December 1, 1976)—is their manner of walking "together": "She walks at her own pace, imperturbably; the child, meanwhile, is being pulled, dragged along, is being forced to keep running, like an animal. . . . She walks at her own pace, unaware of the fact that her son's rhythm is different. And she's his mother!" (p. 9) How to walk together (how to live together) in such a way that recognizes and respects individual rhythms? The briefly observed scene stages the conflict between two apparently incompatible walking speeds. As such, Barthes presents it as characterizing the question of idiorrhythmy—and the preoccupations of the lecture course—in "a specific, localized manner." In the oral delivery of the lecture, Barthes elaborates further: "It's when two different rhythms are put together that profound disturbances are created." (p. 178, n. 39).

Always (at least) one step behind the pace of original publication, the rhythm of translation is inevitably different to that of production. The timings of translations, that is to say how quickly or slowly they follow on from the original work and the order in which they appear, can invent new chronologies for an author's body of work, repattern the rhythm of an intellectual output, and contribute to shaping its reception in a new context. Elizabeth Bruss's account of the history of the translations of Barthes's work into English in the period 1963 ("Criticism as Language") to 1978 (*A Lover's Discourse: Fragments*), is especially alert to the phenomenon of what, in the same session, Barthes calls "disrhythmy."[1] While there was a degree of spacing between Barthes's publications in French in his lifetime—ten years between *Le degré zéro de l'écriture* (1953) and *Eléments de sémiologie* (1964–65), for instance—Bruss notes that in English the "pattern of an entire career has been telescoped, even rearranged, under the pressure of translation."[2] Her point is that in the mid- to late 1970s Barthes's oeuvre arrived in English "all at once": *Writing Degree Zero* and *Elements of Semiology* both appeared in English in 1967, allowing them to be read together in a way that simply was not possible in French. The kind of acceleration effected by translation can indeed create profound disturbances.[3] However, due to the frequency with which this occurs, registering those effects cannot simply be a matter of correcting false impressions. One of the issues that Barthes is deeply interested in here is how books can be productively read together, and we are not necessarily helped in this process by the steer that the calendar gives us (see p. 6)—that is, from the chronological order in which books were produced, published, and translated. The remarkably heterogeneous corpus that Barthes compiles and examines in this lecture course is testament to the way that reading—*actual* reading, the kind that defies the logic of periodization that structures academic disciplines—works: books of all kinds, traditions, and historical periods are variously pored over or merely dipped into; unlikely volumes are set alongside and made to walk in step with one another, obliging us to rethink what we mean when we speak of contemporaneity.[4]

Translation can be speedier than the original pace of production; it can also, of course, be much slower. Barthes's "Inaugural Lecture" at the Collège de France, delivered on January 7, 1977, appeared in English in 1982.[5] *How to Live Together*, the lecture course which began five days after that declaration of intent and can be considered its "direct and immediate application" (see Claude Costes's preface to this volume, p. xvii), now appears in translation some thirty-five years after the event. The lag is in large part due to the complexities of posthumous publication: the three lecture courses only appeared in French in 2002–3, a delay with its own consequences and frustrations.[6] But those issues do not explain the resequencing that has occurred in English: of the three lecture courses, the second appeared first (*The Neutral*, translated by Rosalind E. Krauss and Denis Hollier and published in 2005), then the third (*The Preparation of the Novel*, published in 2010), now followed by *How to Live Together*, the first. To account for the often strikingly haphazard and unsystematic history of what gets translated when and by whom, one might cite the availability and willingness of translators, the speed at which they work, and the nature and length of the texts they are translating. One might also look to *The Preparation of the Novel*, where Barthes pays close attention to the kinds of interruptions and life demands that can determine rhythms of production and publication.[7] Those factors certainly came to bear on the pace and sequence of the translation of the Collège de France notes. But so, too, did what Barthes identifies elsewhere in *The Preparation of the Novel* as a happy, albeit insufficiently examined, phenomenon: we do not all feel the same way about the same books.[8] In keeping with the basic enabling principle of Barthes's pedagogical enterprise ("the subject is not to be repressed"),[9] one further, if on many accounts wholly unsatisfactory explanation for the sequence of the translations is this: for me, well before the opportunity to translate *How to Live Together* arose, the last lecture course took precedence because it is the one I encountered first and, perhaps as a consequence, it is the one I still love the most.[10]

Translating the notes out of order has had some impact on the process itself: what seemed a brief, obscure reference to painting technique in *The Preparation of the Novel*, for example, came to be clarified by working closely on *How to Live Together*, where the process of adding touches or daubs of color figures that of discerning the contours of a notion or field of knowledge. The most immediate consequence for the reader is that she now has access to Éric Marty's important account of the project of preparing the lecture and seminar notes for publication, shortened to a "notice" in the subsequent volumes.[11] In his introduction, Marty meditates at length on the peculiar textual status of the notes *as notes*: this is writing written with a view to being read aloud, in anticipation of its eventual actualization in speech (see p. xiv). That peculiarity determined the approach to translation adopted here. As in *The Preparation of the Novel*, the aim has been to give some sense of that anticipation of an oral performance as well as to reproduce Barthes's own "non-arrogance": his concern to produce an unpretentious discourse that does not intimidate its audience, that is careful not to lecture *at* anyone, but instead invites us to collaborate in its elaboration.[12]

Qu'est-ce que tenir un discours? is the title of the seminar that ran parallel to the lectures; it also presents a challenge to translation. The idiomatic expression *tenir un discours* can simply mean to make or deliver a speech, but also to have or hold to a position or point of view; indeed, the session of the seminar proceeds by breaking the expression down into its constituent parts before considering the whole (*tenir, discours, tenir un discours*). Two solutions presented themselves: either to identify an English expression that was similarly idiomatic but not altogether equivalent (since Barthes makes a case for taking an idiomatic expression as the starting point for a broader inquiry, see p. 143) or to explicate the expression for the reader in such a way that at least makes it clear that the seminar will be dealing with "discourse," a term that is already a part of a Barthes vocabulary in English (*Qu'est-ce que tenir un discours?* followed the year after the 1974–76 seminar held at the École pratique des hautes études that produced *A Lover's Discourse: Fragments*). In the end, the decision was taken to translate the title of the seminar as *What is it to hold forth?* and to vary that translation with the more literal "to sustain a discourse" wherever necessary. According to the *Oxford English Dictionary*, "to hold forth" can mean to keep up, to maintain, to go on with, to continue your course. Barthes is interested in exploring the proposition that we each take the same line our whole lives, repeat the same arguments, uphold the same positions, interrupting ourselves only to pick up where we left off. To hold forth can also mean, more commonly, to preach, to speak publicly, to harangue, to lecture *at* in precisely the way Barthes wants to avoid in his own teaching. Finally, it can mean to proffer, to set forth, to exhibit or display; as the seminar progresses, it becomes clear that for Barthes *tenir un discours* is not just a verbal phenomenon. It is possible to hold forth by lounging across two seats and ostentatiously peeling an orange in a crowded train carriage, for example, or—more endearingly—by devouring a copious breakfast with visible gusto while the man who loves you looks on (see p. 151).

ACKNOWLEDGMENTS

I would like to thank Diana Knight for her patient and rigorous reading of the manuscript of this translation and her many invaluable corrections and suggestions; Claude Coste for his support and generous responses to my questions; Eftichis Pirovolakis for his help in reviewing and translating the glossary of Greek terms; Anna-Louise Milne for her careful reading and discussion of my translation of the seminar. Any remaining infelicities or translation errors are my own.

Kate Briggs

HOW TO LIVE TOGETHER

Introduction

Method and *paideia*

A fantasy: idiorrhythmy

Monachism

Works

Greek network

Traits

Traits

AKÈDIA / AKEDIA

ANACHÔRÈSIS / ANACHORESIS

ANIMAUX / ANIMALS

ATHOS / ATHOS

AUTARCHIE / AUTARKY

BANC / SCHOOL

BÉGUINAGES / BEGUINAGES

BUREAUCRATIE / BUREAUCRACY

CAUSE / CAUSE

CHAMBRE / ROOM

CHEF / CHIEF

CLÔTURE / ENCLOSURE

COLONIE / COLONY

COUPLAGE / PAIRING

DISTANCE / DISTANCE

DOMESTIQUES / SERVANTS

ÉCOUTE / HEARING

ÉPONGE / SPONGE

ÉVÉNEMENT / EVENT

FLEURS / FLOWERS

IDYLLIQUE / IDYLL[1]

MARGINALITÉS / MARGINALITIES

MONÔSIS / MONOSIS

NOMS / NAMES

NOURRITURE / FOOD

PROXÉMIE / PROXEMICS

RECTANGLE / RECTANGLE

RÈGLE / RULE

SALETÉ / DIRTINESS

XÉNITEIA / XENITEIA

UTOPIE / UTOPIA

BUT WHAT ABOUT METHOD?

INTRODUCTION

METHOD?

As I begin this new lecture course, I have a Nietzschean opposition in mind, one that Deleuze adeptly brings to light (pp. 101–4):[2] *method / culture*.

Method

Presupposes "the goodwill of the thinker," "a 'premeditated decision.'" In actual fact, "a means by which we avoid going to a particular place, or by which we maintain the option of escaping from it (the thread of the labyrinth)."[3] Indeed, in the so-called human sciences—positive semiology included—method (I myself have been taken in by it):[4]

Deleuze

1. A manner of proceeding toward a goal, a protocol of operations with a view to achieving an end; for example: a method for decoding, explaining, describing exhaustively.

2. The idea of the straight path (that wants to head toward a goal). Now, paradoxically, what the straight path actually marks out are the places the subject doesn't want to go to: it fetishizes the goal as a place and, as a result, by ruling out all other places, it enters into the service of a generality, a "morality" (a Kierkegaardian equation).[5] The subject, for instance, renounces what he doesn't know of himself, his irreducibility, his force (to say nothing of his unconscious).

Culture

Nietzsche (≠ humanist, irenic meaning) = "violence undergone by thought," "a training undergone by thought through the action of selective forces, a training that brings the whole unconscious of the thinker into play"[6] = the *paideia*[7] of the Greeks (they didn't speak of "method"). "Training," "force," "violence": those words are not to be taken in the highly charged sense. It would be necessary to go back to Nietzsche's idea of force (here's not the place to go over it again) as the engendering of a difference: a person can be placid, civilized even! and still situate themselves within *paideia*. For me, culture as "training" (≠ method) evokes the image of a kind of *dispatching*[8] along an eccentric path: stumbling among snatches, between the bounds of different fields of knowledge, flavors.[9] Paradoxically, when understood in this way, as the registering of forces, culture is hostile to the idea of power (which is in method). (Will to force ≠ will to power).

Here, then, as a hypothesis at least, it's a matter of culture, not of method. Don't expect anything on method—other than in Mallarmé's sense of the word:[10] "fiction": language reflecting on language. → The practice of culture = an attentiveness to forces.[11]

Now, the first force I'm able to investigate, to interpolate, the one I can see is at work within myself, even through the illusions of the imaginary: the force of desire or, to be more precise (since it's the point of departure for our research): the figure of the fantasy.

FANTASY

Cf. Inaugural lecture on fantasmatic teaching. To elaborate (each year) a research inquiry from a fantasy. Science and fantasy: Bachelard: the intrication of science and the imaginary (eighteenth century). But Bachelard's moralism: the basis of science is said to be the decantation of fantasies.[12] Without disputing that (it could be said that no separating out occurs, rather the superimposing of fantasy and science), let's be clear that our starting point will be somewhat prior to that decanting process. → The fantasy as the origin of culture (as the engendering of forces and differences).

Before stating my original fantasy explicitly (nothing indecent), a word on the fantasmatic force of Living-Together in general. Some remarks:

1. I'll not be dealing with the Phalanstery (or only intermittently), despite the fact that the Phalanstery clearly = the fantasmatic form of Living-Together. A word, nevertheless. In Fourier, the fantasy of the Phalanstery doesn't spring from the oppression of solitude but, paradoxically, from a fondness for solitude: "I like being alone." The fantasy isn't a counternegation, it's not the site of a frustration experienced as its opposite: eudemonic visions coexist without contradicting each other. Fantasy: an absolutely positive scenario that stages the positives of desire, that knows only positives. In other words, fantasy isn't dialectical (clearly!). Fantasmatically speaking,

there's nothing contradictory about wanting to live alone and wanting to live together = our lecture course.

2. Still apropos of Fourier: utopia is rooted in a certain day-to-day existence. The more vivid the subject's everyday life (to his own mind), the more potent (the more elaborately detailed) the utopia: Fourier is a better utopianist than Plato.[13] So what was everyday life like in Fourier's utopia? Two of Fourier's commentators (Armand and Maublanc)[14] pinpointed it exactly—while a third (Desroche) was outraged by it (misguidedly, of course): "The phalanstery is a paradise conjured up by an old habitué of tables d'hôte and brothels for his own personal use." Tables d'hôte, brothels (or similar sorts of places): excellent utopian material.

3. Further evidence of the fantasmatic force of Living-Together: living together "harmoniously," cohabiting "harmoniously"; it's what fascinates most about other people, what can inspire the most envy: couples, groups, families even, getting along well together. It's myth (illusion?) in its most basic form: the right sort of material for a novel. (We'd have no families at all there weren't one or two that got along well together!)

4. I said: the fantasy is not the contrary of its rational, logical opposite. But it's possible for fantasy to contain counterimages, negative fantasies within itself (opposition between two fantasmatic images, two scenarios—not between an image and reality). For example:

a. Being shut up for all eternity with those irritating people sitting at the next table in a restaurant = hellish image of Living-Together: the *huit clos*.

b. Another horrible fantasy of Living-Together: being an orphan and then discovering you have a commoner for a father, a rotten family: *Alone in the World*.[15] (→ Living Together: discovering you have a "good" father, that you come from a "good" family: a Sovereign Good-Family? From the perspective of analysis, this is the ultimate fantasy! the *Familien-Roman*.[16]

5. As a fantastical digression, this: it goes without saying that we'll be thinking of Living-Together as an essentially spatial fact (living together in the same space). But in its most basic form Living-Together is also temporal, and here we need to tick this box: "living at the same time as . . . " "living in the same time as . . . " = contemporaneity. For example, I can truthfully say that for twenty-seven years, Marx, Mallarmé, Nietzsche, and Freud lived together. What's more, it would have been possible to orchestrate a meeting in some Swiss town or other, in, say, 1876, giving them an opportunity—the ultimate sign of Living-Together—to "talk together." Freud would

Desroche, p. 51

Mallarmé: 1842–1898
Marx: 1818–1883
Nietzsche: 1844–1900
Freud: 1856–1939
1856–1883

have been twenty at the time, Nietzsche thirty-two, Mallarmé thirty-four, and Marx fifty-six. (We might wonder which one of them is the eldest now). The point of that fantasy of concomitance is to alert us to what seems to me to be a very complex, insufficiently studied phenomenon: contemporaneity. Who are my contemporaries? Whom do I live with? It's no use asking the calendar—as our little chronological game makes clear. Unless it's only now that they're becoming contemporaries? Something to be explored further: the effects of the directional lines of chronology (cf. optical illusions). Perhaps we'd come up against this paradox: an unexpected link between the contemporary and the untimely[17]—like the encounter between Marx and Mallarmé, Mallarmé and Freud around the table of time.[18]

MY FANTASY: IDIORRHYTHMY

A fantasy (at any rate, what I call a fantasy): a resurgence of certain desires, certain images that lurk within you, that want to be identified by you, sometimes your whole life, and often only assume concrete form thanks to a particular word. That word, a key signifier, is what leads from the fantasy to its investigation. To mine the fantasy through snatches of knowledge = research. The fantasy is thus mined like an open quarry.

For me, the fantasy wanting to be identified [had] nothing to do with the topic of the last two years (the "Lover's Discourse").[19] Then, it wasn't a matter of mining a fantasy (≠ Living-Together). It's not a case of Two-People-Living-Together, of a pseudo-conjugal Discourse succeeding (by some miracle) the Lover's Discourse.[20] [It's] a fantasy of a life, a regime, a lifestyle, *diaita*, diet. Neither dual nor plural (collective). Something like solitude with regular interruptions: the paradox, the contradiction, the aporia of bringing distances together— the utopia of a socialism of distance (apropos of strong, ungregarious ages such as the Renaissance, Nietzsche speaks of "a pathos of distance").[21] (All this is still very imprecise).

Now, it was in the course of a chance reading (Lacarrière, *L'Été grec*)[22] that the fantasy encountered the word that would set it to work. On Mount Athos: coenobitic convents + monks both isolated from and in contact with one another within a particular type of structure (I'll describe the features of that structure later on) = idiorrhythmic clusters. Where each subject lives according to his own rhythm.[23]

The Twilight of the Idols, p. 64

1. Let's be clear that a fantasy requires a setting (a scenario) and therefore a place. Athos (where I've never been) conjures a mix of images: the Mediterranean, the terrace, the mountain (in the fantasy, we erase; in this case, the dirtiness, the faith). Basically, it's a landscape. I can picture myself there, standing on the edge of a terrace, the sea in the distance, the coarse white plaster on the walls, with two rooms for my own use and two more close by for a few friends + somewhere to come together for synaxe[24] (the library). A very pure fantasy that glosses over the difficulties that will come to loom like ghosts (this: somewhat the topic of the lecture course). "Idiorrhythmy," "idiorrhythmic": this was the word that transmuted the fantasy into a field of knowledge. Through that word, I gained access to things that can be learned. Which is not to say that I was able to learn them: bibliographically speaking, my research has often been disappointing. For example, I learned virtually nothing from the monastic forms of idiorrhythmy, Beguinages, the Solitaries of Port Royal, or small communities (I'll come back to this)—I'll also come back to the predominance of religious models.

2. *Excursus*: a reminder of Benveniste's important article on the notion of "rhythm" in *Problems in General Linguistics*, vol. 1, chap. 27.[25] *Rhuthmos*: usually related to *rhein*[26] (morphologically speaking, this is correct, but only as a result of a deplorable semantic shortcut, which Benveniste demystifies): "the regular movement of the waves"! Now, the history of the word: entirely different. Origins: in ancient Ionian philosophy;[27] for the creators of atomism, Leucippus, Democritus, it was a technical term. Prior to the Attic period, *rhuthmos* never meant "rhythm," it was never applied to the regular movement of the waves. The actual meaning is rather: a distinctive form, a proportioned figure, an arrangement; very close to and yet very different from *schema*. *Schema*: a fixed, fully developed form that's set down like an object (statue, orator, choreographical figure). *Schema* ≠ form, the instant it's assumed by something moving, mobile, fluid, the form of something that lacks organic consistency. *Rhuthmos* = the pattern of a fluid element (a letter, a *peplos*,[28] a mood), an improvised, changeable form.[29] In atomism, one manner in which atoms can flow; a configuration without fixity or natural necessity: a "flowing" (the musical, that is to say, modern meaning: Plato, *Philebus*).[30]

For us, that etymological reminder is important:

1. Since *rhuthmos* is by definition individual, idiorrhythm is almost a pleonasm: the interstices, the *fugitivity* of the code, of the

manner in which the individual inserts himself into the social (or natural) code.

2. Has to do with subtle forms of way of life: moods, unstable configurations, phases of depression or elation; in short, the exact opposite of an inflexible, implacably regular cadence. It's because rhythm acquired a repressive meaning (I refer you to the life-rhythm of a coenobite, or a phalansterian, whose activities are scheduled to the nearest quarter of an hour) that it was necessary to add the prefix *idios*:[31]

$$idios \neq \text{rhythm,}$$
$$idios = rhuthmos.[32]$$

In its original setting (Athos), idiorrhythmy merely indicates the proportions of the fantasized community—and therein lies its advantage, its enabling force (for me). Proportions = an ontology of the object. Architecture. Enlargement: Cézanne / De Staël.[33]

For the fantasy is in fact = a clear, powerful, unwavering projector that isolates the brightly lit stage whereupon desire installs itself, leaving either side of the stage in shadow:

1. The couple. Perhaps there are such things as idiorrhythmic couples? That's not the issue. A fantasy that's expressly uninterested in the inevitable fixture of the bedroom, in the cloistering and the legality, the legitimacy of desire won't be investigating the setting of the couple. The apartment, with its focus on the bedroom, can't be idiorrhythmic. In the same way as the Linguistics Society—when it was founded, putting it into the statutes themselves—took the decision not to accept papers on the origins of language, we could decide not to talk about couples (or only talk about couples in the context of larger groups, in outdoor settings). In addition: the Family-System blocks any experience of anachoresis, of idiorrhythmy. In modern-day "communes,"[34] the commune falls apart from the moment family groups are reestablished—due to the conflict between sexuality and the law.

2. On the other side of the stage, likewise in shadow: macro-groupings, large communes, phalansteries, convents, coenobitism. Why? By which I mean: Why doesn't the fantasy encounter these larger forms? It's obvious: because their structure is based on an architecture of power (I'll come back to this) and because they're openly hostile to idiorrhythmy (historically speaking, it's for precisely this reason, in opposition to idiorrhythmy, that such structures get established—that they have been established). I refer you to the

fundamental inhumanity of Fourier's Phalanstery: with its *timing*[35] of each and every quarter hour, it's the exact opposite of idiorrhythmy: barracks, boarding schools.

Again: what we're looking for is a zone that falls between two excessive forms:

- — an excessively negative form: solitude, eremitism.
- — an excessively assimilative form: the (secular or nonsecular) *coenobium*.[36]
- — a median, utopian, Edenic, idyllic form: idiorrhythmy. Note that as a form it's very eccentric: it never really caught on in the Church (on Mount Athos, through *disaffiliation*); in fact, the Church always resisted it (Saint Benedict and the Sarabaites,[37] monks living in groups of two or three, the satisfaction of desires). What's more, psychoanalysis has never really engaged with the question of "small groups." It's either the subject in his familial straitjacket or the crowd (with the exception of Wilfred Ruprecht Bion's *Experiences in Groups*, 1961;[38] very specific: groups in a hospital setting; not an especially lucid book). In sum: neither the monastery, nor the family, the idea being to eschew those grand repressive forms.

To bring this introduction to idiorrhythmy to a close, I shall present a trait that seems to me to characterize the problem in a specific, localized manner. From my window (December 1, 1976), I see a mother pushing an empty stroller, holding her child by the hand. She walks at her own pace, imperturbably; the child, meanwhile, is being pulled, dragged along, is forced to keep running, like an animal, or one of Sade's victims being whipped. She walks at her own pace, unaware of the fact that her son's rhythm is different. And she's his mother! → Power—the subtlety of power—is effected through disrhythmy, heterorhythmy.[39]

MONACHISM

The forces by which the fantasy attains to or opens out onto culture: don't act in a straightforward manner, are subject to unforeseen tensions. Example: the fantasy of a free life lived among just a few other people → the idiorrhythmy of Mount Athos. → Identifying the themes, the traits, the structures of that form that might in turn shed light on contemporary issues. Not general, cultural, sociological issues (for example, communities or communes), but idiolectical issues: things I see happening around me, in my friends' lives, things that apply to me. You might expect: the direction of our research will be that of an affective psychology, the relation to other people, to the other.

But at this point it actually takes an unexpected detour: the crystallizing word—Athos—sets me reading. Sets me delving into in a handful of novels (for there are a great many novels about couples but not very many about small groups) + a more systematic approach: readings on monastic life ("life" in the sense of *diaita*). Now, those readings prove compelling, even if I'm not sure what fantasy they concern (they definitely concern a fantasy, not a signified: there's been no conversion to monastic spirituality). → An already unsettling investment in monastic material.

Then there's yet another tension: the fantasy visibly recoils from coenobitism. The reading adventure turns away from Western coenobitism, from the Benedictine model (sixth century) and starts getting interested in precoenobitic forms: eremitic or semianachoretic forms (idiorrhythmy); in other words, in Oriental monachism (Egypt, Constantinople). And it's in this way that we work our way back to Athos.

Apropos of which, I'd like, once and for all, to get us clear on a few dates (see p. 11).

Notice how everything was played out in the fourth century. The date certainly looks impressively meaningful. Coenobitism, as a liquidation of anachoritism (eremitism, semianachoretic, and idiorrhythmy were considered dangerous marginalities, resisting integration into a power structure), is directly contemporary (along with Saint Pachomius) with the shift that lead to Christianity, a persecuted religion (martyrs), acquiring the status of State religion, that is to say, with the shift from No-Power (or Dis-Empowerment) to Power. The year 380, the date of Theodosius's edict, is perhaps the most important one in the history of our world (and the most occulted: for who remembers it?): collusion between religion and power, the creation of new marginalities, the division of the East and West → Occidentocentrism (the triumph of coenobitism).

Diocletian	275–305	End of the third century	Anthony in the Desert[a]	Eremitism
Conversion of Constantine	313	Beginning of the fourth century	Anachorites around Anthony (Sinai)	Semianachoritism Idiorrhythmy
	314	Beginning of the fourth century	Pachomius founds coenobitism[b]	
Christianity, religion of the State	380	End of the fourth century–fifth century	Saint Augustine: conversion	The rule of Saint Augustine
Theodosius's edict			Stylites	
Division into East / West (death of Theodosius)	395			
	534	Sixth century	Saint Benedict on Mount Cassin	Western coenobitism
		Tenth century[c]	*Laura*[d] founded on Mount Athos	

[a]Index card 173: "Draguet xviii. Pères du désert. Some: live alone, as hermits. Others, more frequently: live together in colonies of anachorites: the advantages of a small degree of communal living. Pachomian (coenobitic) system."

[b]Index card 145: "Pachomius": Ladeuze 273. Monastic costume:
– sleeveless linen tunic
– belt
– tanned goat hide
– a short cape and hood
– a travelling coat
– bare feet, sandals for outdoors only
All monks:
– two hoods, two tunics + an old one for working and sleeping in
– clothes they're not wearing that day: stored in the communal cloakroom
– all look after their own clothes: together, they wash and dry them at an appointed time.
– origin? Egyptian priests?
– trimmed hair (Pachomius's worship of Serapis?)
[c][Oral: "This doesn't really belong in the table."]
[d]Laura (Latin): laure, medieval monastery.

INTRODUCTION
(continued)

You'll therefore find a lot of references to monachism (in its semi-anachoretic and Egyptian, Byzantine form). I hope this won't prove too tiresome—since you're clearly under no obligation to share in this secondary cultural fantasy with me. Apropos of which, I must make the following clear: it's possible to have a theory (in this sense new) of reading (a kind of anti-philological reading). Reading that dispenses with the signified: reading the Mystics without God or where God is a signifier[1] (whereas God = the ultimate signified, since in good theology he signifies nothing other than himself: "I am who I am").[2] Think what would happen if we were to generalize a method of reading exempted from the signified, from all signifieds. One example (among others): imagine if we were to read Sartre without the signified "commitment."[3] What this would give rise to is a sovereign reading—sovereignly free: all forms of reading's superego would fall away, for the law always springs from the signified in that the signified is what's presented and received as final. The effects of this exemption from faith—in whatever form it presents itself (political faith included, now the substitute for religious faith for the entire intellectual caste)—are for the moment incalculable, almost intolerable. For what it's a matter of lifting, outmoding, trivializing are the generators of guilt. It's therefore a matter of working at non-repression: it's less repressive for us to speak of monks having no faith ourselves than not to speak of them at all.

WORKS

Alongside monachism, we shall also be examining materials drawn from a literary corpus.

Novels are simulations, that is to say fictional experimentations on a model, the most classical form of which is the maquette. The novel implies a structure, an outline (a maquette) through which topics, situations are let loose. As far as I can recall, there's no such thing as a novelistic maquette for idiorrhythmy (if you know of one, let me know). But almost all novels contain bits and pieces of material pertaining to Living-Together (or Living-Alone): little snatches of simulation, like a very clear, fully realized detail that all of a sudden catches your eye in an otherwise muddled painting (this is precisely the spatial organization, the topology of *An Unknown Masterpiece*).[4]

I have thus selected a few works from which I've extracted the material concerning Living-Together. My choice is entirely subjective, or rather entirely contingent. It has to do with the kinds of texts I read, with my memories. The anarchism of my sources is justified by the eviction of method in favor of *paideia*. Besides, we shan't be reading these works "in and of themselves" (cf. *Werther*).[5] There'll be some cross-fertilization, some *marcottage*[6] from one work to another.

Stretching things a little bit, so they're clear in our minds, each of the selected works can be said to correspond broadly to a problem-space of Living-Together and Living-Alone, its paradigmatic opposite (the maquette in a novel: very important space. Balzac always sets out the maquette). But that's not to say that the novels will be dealt with thematically, with reference to that topographical theme: the work shall shatter into "traits" (I'll come back to this in a moment):

Naturally, there could be other traits drawn from different works. What's more, the works I've selected may not, in the end, furnish us with very many traits = the vagaries of research. The systematic ("systematic readings") gradually breaks down, is disappointed—the non-systematic flourishes, proliferates. Yet something direct has to be put in place in order for the indirect, an unforeseeable to emerge. That's how *paideia* advances, as distinct from method.

Work	Space (Maquette)	Remarks
Gide: *La Séquestrée de Poitiers* (Gallimard, 18th edition, 1930); "The Confined Woman of Poitiers" in *Judge Not*, trans. Benjamin Ivry (Urbana: University of Illinois Press, 2003).	The Room (single, not comfortable), *cella*,[a] *kellion*[b] (there's even a photograph).	The story of a news item, 1901: Gide chose to simply present the documents (it's a very powerful narrative). Mélanie is discovered, aged fifty-one, in indescribable filth—which is nevertheless described in great detail—in a bedroom of a well-to-do bourgeois house in Poitiers.

		For more than twenty-five years, she'd been kept on her bed, locked up in her bedroom with the windows and shutters closed, by her mother, Bastian de Chartreux, widow of the dean of the arts faculty, who at the time of the discovery was seventy-five years old. Pierre Bastian, the brother, a former subprefect of Puget-Théniers, and the maidservants were fully aware of Mélanie's sequestration. It's the suitor of a new maid who alerts the police. Mélanie is taken to hospital, her mother is arrested, and her brother questioned. The mother dies in prison; the brother is dis-charged. The case is an ambiguous one: it is not clear whether Mélanie herself—who is "mad" according to the usual criteria—had not chosen her confinement. →"Judge Not'" says the title of the collection. Mélanie = the ultimate anachorite, albeit without faith ("madness" in its place?).
Defoe: *Robinson Crusoé (Vie et Adventures de Robinson Crusoé)* (Pléiade); *Robinson Crusoe: Complete and Unabridged* (London: Penguin, 1994).	The Hideout	Novel published in 1719, based on the true story of Alexander Selkirk, whose captain left him behind on the island of Juan Fernandez as punishment, to be picked up in 1709 (Caribbean Sea). Robinson Crusoe, born in 1632, leaves England in 1651. A novel very much engaged with the politics of its time. Robinson Crusoe: capitalist, colonizer, slave trader.[c] Having lost everything (sort of shipwreck-bankruptcy, all he's left with is a knife), gets back on his feet, colonizes and populates his island, becomes its governor, etc. Part 1 (the part we're interested in, before the adventures in Europe): Robinson Crusoe alone (in time, with Friday).

		Now, this concerns Living-Together, not only because here we're dealing with its opposite term (solitude), but because Robinson Crusoe has to contend with a problem of adaptation analogous to the problem of Living-Together: objects, nature = human beings. Nature: he's obliged to live with other forces, a game of resistance and complicity. For example: fearful of lightning, he divides up his gunpowder and hides it in different places: cf. prudent apportioning of his affections (Selkirk dancing with the young goats).[d] As a general rule, in relations with objects or animals: intelligence, self-interest, prudence, foresight, tenderness, followed by cruelty (he kills and eats the kid he'd wanted to tame, 63). Last,[e] a curious tautology: *Robinson Crusoe*, an epic tale of solitude, enjoys the mythic status of a novel conceived for the express purpose of enriching the experience of solitude: "the book you'd take to a desert island"! Malraux:[f] along with *Don Quixote* and *The Idiot*. Philarète Chasles, on the banks of the Ohio, p. xiv.[g]
Pallade (Palladius): *Histoire lausique* (A. Lucot, 1912); *Palladius: The Lausiac History*, translated by R. T. Meyer (New York: Newman Press, 1964)	The Desert.	In Greek: dedicated to Lausius, a chamberlain at the court of Theodosius II = anecdotes relating to Egyptian, Syrian, and Palestinian monks. Palladius, 363–425, Bishop of Helenopolis, in Bithynia (on the Euxine Sea in northwest Asia Minor). Travels in Egypt—to Alexandria and the Nitrian Desert (388–99). Often delightful, innocent humor. Rich in "traits" (= signifiers).

Thomas Mann: *La Montagne magique* (trans. Fayard, 1931);[h] *The Magic Mountain*, trans. H. T. Lowe-Porter (London: Vintage, 1999)	The Hotel.	Of course it's in fact a sanatorium-hotel. That designates a fairly well-defined space of Living-Together: sanatorium-hotel (cruise ships, possibly even Club Med!) = hotel-style Living-Together. Very striking structure: bedrooms + a room for socializing; intense, short-lived relationships, etc. Thomas Mann's stay in Davos in 1911 (for his wife's cure). Written: 1912–13. Published in 1924. Story: 1907–14. Counterpart to *Death in Venice*: the seduction of illness and death. I described my relationship to this book in the inaugural lecture:[i] *a.* projective (because: "that's exactly it"), *b.* disorien-tating, but in a chronological sense.[j] 1907/1942/the present moment, because it means my body is historically closer to 1907 than to the present day. I'm the historical witness for a work of fiction. A book I find very poignant, depressing, almost intolerable: a very palpable investment in human relationships + death. Belongs to the category of the Heart-rending. → I felt out of sorts on the days I spent reading it—or rather rereading it (I'd read it before my illness but had only a vague recollection of it).
Zola: *Pot-Bouille* (Fasquelle, 2 vols.); *Pot Luck*, translated by Brian Nelson (Oxford: Oxford University Press, 1999).[1]	*The (bourgeois) Apartment Building.*	1882: Octave Mouret: son of Mouret de Plassans, future hero of *The Ladies' Paradise* and brother of Serge, of *The Sin of Father Mouret*. = the dark side of bourgeois Living-Together.

[a]*Cella* (Latin): cell
[b]*Kellion* (Greek): storeroom, cellar.
[c][Oral: Barthes states that Defoe's novel calls for a "Lukascian" or "Goldmannian" analysis].

[d]In *A Cruising Voyage Around the World*, Captain Woodes Rogers describes how he brought the sailor Alexander Selcraig (or Selkirk), who had been abandoned for four years and four months on the island of Jean Fernandez, back to England. An extract of this narrative can be found in the Pléiade edition of Robinson Crusoe: Daniel Defoe, *Vie et Aventures de Robinson Crusoé*, in *Romans*, vol. 1, trans. Pétrus Borel, preface François Ledoux (Paris: Gallimard, Bibliothèque de la Pléiade, 1959, introduction, appendix 1). Barthes is referring to the following passage: "He likewise tamed some kids; to divert himself would now and then sing and dance with them and his cats." From Woodes Rogers, *A Cruising Voyage Around the World* (London, 1712).—tr.

[e]Paragraph crossed out in the manuscript.

[f]See François Ledoux's preface: "In the words of one of André Malraux's characters: in this day and age, for someone who has experienced life in prison or a concentration camp, only three books remain true: *Robinson Crusoe*, *Don Quixote*, and *The Idiot*." This is a reference to A. Malraux's *The Walnut Trees of Altenburg*, trans. A. W. Fielding (Chicago: University of Chicago Press, 1992), pp. 89–90.

[g]A point that François Ledoux makes in his preface to the Pléiade edition of *Robinson Crusoé* that Barthes is using: according to Philarète Chasles, one of the colonizers of Ohio took great comfort from reading Defoe's novel.

[h]Barthes is in fact using the 1961 edition.

[i]Barthes, "Inaugural Lecture, Collège de France," pp. 477–48.

[j]With respect to the present day.

[k]On Brian Nelson's decision to translate Pot-Bouille as Pot Luck see his translator's introduction, p. vii.—tr.

GREEK NETWORK

So, two sets of materials: monachism (oriental monachism) + a few works of literature. I should consider a third grid—one that in truth derives from the first but at another terminological, "glottic" (≠ factual) level: a network of Greek words that served to identify (to crystallize) the problems of Living-Together within oriental monachism.

There are quite a number of them (thirty or so). I'll introduce them as we go along.[7] To give you an example of what I mean by a Greek network, here's a small portion of it: Living-Together is structured by three basic states (structured = attaining to a paradigm, a meaning):

— *Monosis*:[8] a solitary life (and a celibate life: *monachos*)[9] = Anthony's system.
— *Anachoresis*:[10] a life lived at a distance from the world = idiorrhythmy in its nascent form.
— *Koinobiosis*:[11] the conventional form of communal life = Pachomius's system.

Two energies, two forces, two orderings traverse each of those three states:

— *Askesis*:[12] the systematic organization {*dressage*} of space
                                     of time
                                     of objects
—*Pathos*:[13] affect colored by the imaginary.[14]

Why prioritize a Greek network? Why not be French, like everyone else? Why make things complicated, convoluted, why dress up in some pseudo-erudite garment? (Sempiternal reproach; still made even today, January 6, in response to an article in the journal *Photo*:[15] Why don't you speak the language "everyone else" speaks?)

Cf. Inaugural Lecture:[16] that several languages should be conveyed in and by our own idiom is a good thing:

1. First, a point of fact: an idiom isn't monolithic, homogeneous, pure. An idiom = a patch-work, a rhapsody (there's nothing more absurd than the diatribe against *franglais*:[17] the particularity of an idiom inheres—for better or for worse—in its syntax, not in its vocabulary.)

2. Next: more than one language exists because more than one desire exists. Desire seeks out words, taking them wherever it finds them; what's more: words themselves engender desire, and what's more besides: words obstruct desire. In French, there's no felicitous word to express the complex of a wholly solitary life or the specific shape of monastic life. Pluri-language (within an idiom) is a luxury but, as always, for desire it's no more than a basic requirement: thus, as with any linguistic theft, the right to it is to be insisted upon and defended.

Evidently, in addition to, or underlying, those principles, there are some further technical justifications (techniques of meaning):

1. The transfer of sets of connotations: "solitary life" does not connote a system of rules, it isn't a semantic "being" (≠ *monosis*: connotes the rule of *monachos*).

2. The Greek word pinpoints a concept that serves simultaneously as an origin, an image and defamiliarizes.

3. The Greek word generalizes and emphasizes. It acts as a summary, a compendium, an ellipsis—and in this respect ensures a productive unfolding (= etymological inventiveness). More generally, a dossier to be opened: on the concept-words from one language that get inserted into another idiom. In psychoanalysis, Freud's German words gave rise to a sort of baroque *knowledge*, to disputes over how they should be translated (*Trieb*),[18] in other words to a mode of inquiry that works at the level of the signifier—always preferable to working at the level of the signified.

4. Last: philology (or pseudo-philology) is slow-going. To have recourse to Greek words = not to be in any particular hurry; besides, when the point is to let the signifier expand and spread like a fra-

grance, that slow pace is sometimes necessary. In today's world, any technique that entails slowing down: something progressive about it.

TRAITS

That's all for the material. Now for the mode of presentation. Point of departure (and of incessant returns, of verification): the (idiorrhythmic) fantasy. Now, fantasy = scenario, but a scenario in bits and pieces, always very brief = just a glimmer of the narrative of desire. What's glimpsed is very sharply contoured, very brightly lit, but all of a sudden it's gone: a body I catch sight of in a car as it goes round a bend, before it plunges into the shadows. The fantasy = an unruly projector that picks out fragments of the world, of science, of history—of experiences—in an abrupt, discontinuous fashion.[19] The dis-cursive is therefore not of the order of demonstration, persuasion (it's not a matter of setting out an argument, of convincing someone of a belief, a position)—but of a "dramatic" order, in the Nietzschean manner: *who*, rather than *what*.[20]

Nietzsche[21] again—via Klossowski, p. 32: "The suppression of the *true world* was also the suppression of the *apparent world*—and also entailed the suppression of the notions of *conscious* and *unconscious*—the *outside* and the *inside*. We are nothing more than a succession of discontinuous states in relation to *the code of everyday signs*, and about which *the fixity of language* deceives us. While we depend on this code we imagine our continuity, but in fact we live only discontinuously. But these *discontinuous states* merely relate to the way we use, or do not use, the fixity of language: to be *conscious* is to use it. But, when we fall silent, how are we ever to know what we are?"[22]

Very beautiful, very important passage. What he's saying (at least, this is what I infer from it): it's a matter of fracturing the fixity of language and drawing closer to our fundamental discontinuity ("We live only discontinuously"). To be sure, the fragmentary nature of discourse (as a result of the pressure exerted by the fantasy) is a feature of language, it's a false discontinuity—or an impure, attenuated discontinuity. But since we have to make some concessions to the fixity of language, this, at least, is the smallest possible one.[23]

From now on, this lecture course must consent to take the form of a series of discontinuous units: traits. I didn't want to group those traits into themes (though perhaps I shall at some point?). It's increasingly my belief (even though social, academic usage always requires it) that to do so involves a kind of hypocritical manipulation of index cards, turning each one into a rhetorical "topic for discussion," a *quaestio*.[24] It's like a deck of cards. Take note: the game (*game*)[25] is normative, it wants to resist, prevail over the disorder of the given, it thinks of chance as disorder. Likewise for index cards: you endeavor (as in any *game* of cards) to put them back into suits, into families (as ever): all the hearts, all the spades, etc., four of a kind, three of a kind, flushes. But our method—the one we're adopting here—involves shuffling the cards and dealing them in the order in which they appear. For me, now, whenever I'm working, any thematic grouping of traits (of index cards) always makes me think of Bouvard and Pécuchet's question: Why this, why that? Why here, why there? = An automatic distrust of associative ideology (which is an ideology of the ordered presentation). The cardplayer's motto: "I cut the deck," I react against the fixity of language.

And yet, to write discontinuously (in fragments)—OK, it's possible, people do it. But to speak in fragments? The (cultural) body resists it; it requires transitions, linking phrases. *Oratio = flumen*: it's what Latin discourse, the *contio*, trains us to do (or used to, at any rate).[26] This problem: came up once before apropos of the figures of the Lover's Discourse. There the solution was to use an artificial sequence, a non-transitional order (leaving its discontinuity thoroughly exposed): the alphabet;[27] it's the only option (other than pure chance; but, as I said: the danger of pure chance is that it can be just as effective at producing logical sequences). I'll be using the same method this year for my "traits." But because the traits identified are far less developed, far shorter than the figures of the Lover's Discourse, there's every chance that the discontinuity will be even more conspicuous (and offensive).

This method of the traits is clearly bound up with a certain politics (cf. Inaugural Lecture): a politics that seeks to deconstruct metalanguage.[28]

These traits, often slight, often discontinuous. Again, I shall present them in alphabetical order, as a way of taking full responsibility for the fact that I'll not be linking them to an overall idea, or at least not for the moment. I'm aware that this might give the tiresome impression of flitting from one topic to another, of dispersion—especially since some of the traits, in their abruptness, will seem to be only indirectly related to Living-Together: to circle around it, but often at a distance.

I think I've now sufficiently, not justified, but accepted responsibility for a mode of presentation that consists in circling, so to speak, above the topic ("Living Together") often at quite a great height—not knowing whether I'll ever be able to land on it. For this is research-in-progress. I truly believe that for a teaching relationship to be effective the speaker should know only slightly more about the topic than the listener (sometimes, on certain points, less: this is the process of exchange). Research, not a Lecture.

AKÈDIA / AKEDIA
Acedy

Draguet, p. xxxvi

The feeling, the state of a monk who disinvests in asceticism, who can no longer bring himself to invest in it (≠ who loses his faith). It's not a loss of belief; it's a loss of investment. Depressive state: melancholy, lassitude, sadness, boredom, loss of heart. Life (spiritual life) seems monotonous, aimless, impossible to bear, futile: the ascetic ideal has been obscured, it has no appeal. Cassien (*Institutions*, 10):[29] "< . . . > what the Greeks called *Akedia*[30] and what we might call boredom or anxiety of heart (*taedium sive anxietas cordis*)." Phenomenon that comes up fairly often in stories of oriental ermetism. (Cassien: Italian, 360–335. Lived in Egypt. Two monasteries in Marseille.)

Akedia: prostration < *kedeuo*:[31] to care for, to take care of, take an interest in. Whence the opposites: *akedeo*:[32] to be unconcerned (effectively the loss of investment); *akedestos*:[33] abandoned; *akedes*:[34] negligent, neglected. We must pay close attention to the permutations of the active and the passive. To abandon (the object invested in) = to be abandoned (active = passive; trace of the logic of affect: "a child is being beaten").[35] In *akedia*, I'm both the subject and the object of abandonment: whence the feeling of being blocked, trapped, at an impasse.

It's a state (of decline as the result of a blockage) that's closer to *aphanisis* (notion introduced by Jones:[36] state of non-desire, the fear of non-desire) than to castration (to the fear of castration). = Complex of words: *aphanisis, taedium*,[37] *fading*[38](the fading-out of desire, hence of the subject), "standstill"[39] {*point mort*} (after years in the sanatorium, Hans Castorp comes to a standstill {*le point mort*}: he no longer has any investment in illness, death itself), he's "on the verge of suicide" (very different from "Suicide,"[40] cf., *A Lover's Discourse*). It can originate in a violent desire, but one that's never satisfied so eventually fades away. But instead of

The Magic Mountain, p. 626

fading into "wisdom," it leaves a kind of residue behind: a dull hopelessness.

Robinson Crusoe, or rather Selkirk the sailor, gives a very good description of that process: "When those Appetites <needs> were satisfied, the Desire of Society was as strong a Call upon him, and he appeared to himself least necessitious when he wanted everything; for the Supports of his Body were easily attained, but the eager Longings for seeing again the Face of Man during the Interval of craving bodily Appetites, were hardly supportable. He grew dejected, languid, and melancholy, scarce able to refrain from doing himself Violence < . . . >"[41]

I'm providing these references to Hans Castorp and Robinson Crusoe because I want suggest that acedy is not exclusively linked to the monastic state. We're not monks and yet we're interested in acedy. Acedy has a specific relation to a form of "asceticism," that is to say to the practice (in the etymological sense)[42] of a particular lifestyle.[43] What's at stake in acedy isn't belief, an idea, the option of faith (acedy isn't a "doubt"), it's no longer having any investment in a way of life. Acedy: the repeated, extenuated, insistent moment when you find you've had enough of your way of life, of your relationship to the world (to the "worldly"). I can wake up in the morning, see the schedule for the week unfolding before my eyes, and feel hopeless. It's repetitive, it goes round and round: the same old tasks, the same old meetings, and yet there's no investment whatsoever—irrespective of the fact that, when viewed separately, the different bits of that schedule are endurable, sometimes even pleasant.

The amorous experience of acedy ≠ the hopelessness of love (not being loved, being left, being broken up with, etc.) isn't a matter of acedy. The specificity of acedy is that it involves a loss of investment. Acedy is the mourning of investment itself, not the thing invested in. In reality, disinvestment in the loved object: can be a liberation (free at last, free from alienation!) but can also be a source of distress: the misery of not being loved. Acedy: what's mourned is not the image, it's the imaginary. It's what's most painful: you experience all of the pain and yet are deprived of the secondary gain that is playing it up for effect.

The relation between acedy and Living-Together? Historically, a notion with a particular link to eremitic asceticism: painful disinvestment in the asceticism of solitude → the eremite reenters the world. Coenobitism: in that it entails the monk's integration into a strong communal structure, was probably conceived—at least in part—as a means of combating acedy. Acedy (modern acedy): no longer being capable of investing in other people, in Living-with-several-other-people and yet at the same time being incapable of investing in solitude. → Throwing it all away, but without even somewhere to throw it: waste without a waste bin.

At the end of the last session, some of you → made a few remarks, a few suggestions, provided some additional references relating to what was said.

It's something I value: a productive practice in that it's collaborative rather than progressive. This lecture course (especially with its traits) = a checkerboard of boxes, a topos. I begin by setting out the boxes, then—to a greater or lesser extent—I fill them in. But it goes without saying that those boxes can be filled in by other people. → So long as they relate to the topic, that is to say, so long as they're neither laudatory (redundant) nor corrective, I shall try to incorporate your remarks into each lecture. A bit like exchanging letters with my audience.

On the idiorrhythmic novel?

1. Goethe's Elective Affinities
2. A novel by Simone Jacquemard[1]

Idiorrhythmy: due to the aspirated rho[2]
On acedy:

1. In Search of Lost Time: *dead point {point mort}, before time is regained. On the train = acedy, because he has ceased to invest in writing.→ Reversal, not through or toward worldliness, but through Time being Regained (arrival at the Guermantes' party).*

2. kedeia:[3] burial → akedia:[4] mourning without an object (I said: it's more a matter of mourning the feeling than the object). The apogée of desolation: death with no sepulture.

ANACHÔRÈSIS / ANACHORESIS

ana:[5] distancing (in an upward direction); *chorein*:[6] to go back up to a distant place.

= act or state, or concept (a word ending in -*sis*)[7] of separation from the world that's effected by going back up to some isolated, private, secret, distant place.

HISTORICALLY

A tendency to retreat (≠ towns): already present among the pagans.

Festugière, I, p. 41

Anachorite: announces he's retreating from the world. Takes up residence in a cabin or a cell (*kellion*) that may or may not be attached to a monastery (Athos) where he'll live alone or in the company of one or two monks.

Décarreaux, p. 20

Anachoresis is not a matter of absolute solitude, but rather of this: a way of reducing one's contact with the world + individualism (individualistic asceticism):

Amand, p. 40

1. Retreating from the world. End of the third, beginning of the fourth century, sharp rise in anachoresis (Anthony: Pharaoh's tombs, then oasis, the Egyptian mountains). Fleeing the State, the taxman, military service + forms of independence whose aim is to reduce the amount of contact one has with society, to protect oneself from it.

2. Everyone organizes themselves as they see fit: private prayer + manual labor (basket-making, weaving, braiding), accompanied by chanting.

3. ≠ Eremitism: possibility of two or three people living together. Attached to a monastery (Orient and Mount Athos). Anachorites visit one another. The elders offer bits and pieces of advice on how to temper eccentricities. Everyone comes together on Saturdays for synaxe (communal prayer).

METAPHORICALLY

Anachoresis: its foundational act is to break away, the abrupt jolt of departure. The distancing has to be symbolized in some way. Anachoresis = an action, a line, a threshold to be crossed.

Robinson Crusoe,
pp. 50–51, 60

For example, symbolically, Robinson Crusoe: is wrenched from the world by the shipwreck. In a single stroke, he's deprived of all his companions (only "three of their hats, one cap and two Shoes that were not fellows" can be seen floating on the surface of the sea). After thirteen days, the ship sinks = his last remaining link to the world is broken (the world will resurface later on in the form of cannibals).

Colerus, *Life of Spinosa*,
p. 38

Secular anachoresis: at the end of his life, Spinoza retires to Voorburg, near The Hague. To begin with, he takes lodgings in a boarding house; but decides he is spending too much money; he rents a room in someone's home (so he can eat what he likes). True anachoresis because he would sometimes go downstairs to converse with his hosts. He lived "a very retired Life, according to his fancy."[8]

The notion of anachoresis needed to clarified for three reasons:

1. Historically: the template for idiorrhythmy in that it represents a collective-individualistic structure.

2. Anachoresis = any fantasy involving a moderate form of retreat. The calming image of Spinoza. Anachoresis: an individual's solution to the crisis of power. I flee, I reject power, the world, systems; I want to create a life-structure that isn't a life-system. Whence the symbolic act of breaking away: *anachorein*[9] = to reject power, to object to power (even if only to other people as power)

3. It's possible to have a contemporary version of (secular) anachoresis. In today's world: gregariousness, alienation, forms that are pregnant with power. → Dreams, fantasies, acts of distancing. Would often contain the metaphor of being wrenched from the world (Robinson Crusoe): "realizing" your assets and buying a sheep farm in the Ardèche. Less specifically: going off to live in the country (a theme in mass culture; the advertising campaign for Gervais—due to the cows),[10] isolating yourself, retaining just one or two points of anchorage {*points de capiton*}[11] with the world: a balanced form of anachoresis (there are some crazy ones).

ANIMAUX / ANIMALS

Festugière, I, p. 46

By chance: alphabetical contiguity + thematic connection between anachoresis and animality. Let's consider two contrasting movements, one after the other: 1. from beast to man: Robinson; 2. from man to beast: excessive forms of religious anachoresis.

1. ROBINSON CRUSOE

Robinson Crusoe, p. 46

Robinson Crusoe starts out from a state of nature, or thereabouts: all he has is a knife, a pipe, and a bit of tobacco. He then proceeds to work his way through each phase of civilization: sleeps in a tree → raft → objects → hut, etc. → becomes ruler of the (inhabited) island.

This ascendency from animal to man runs in parallel to another, symmetrical movement: the domestication of animals:

Robinson Crusoe, p. 58

1. Man and animal are equals. Taming a wild cat: "she sat very composed and unconcerned, and looked full in my face, as if she had a mind to be acquainted with me." The equality is so perfect, Robinson Crusoe tracks her as he would a man-enemy. In the face of the cat's indifference, Robinson Crusoe tosses her a bit of biscuit.

Robinson Crusoe, pp. 77–78

2. After maiming a goat, Robinson Crusoe tames it. Process of domestication: the goat is tamed, Crusoe conceives of a mode of systematic domestication that will supply him with food once he's no longer able to hunt (when his gunpowder and shot are all spent). First phase of domestication.

3. Second phase of domestication: anthropophilia. The animal is made to live commensally with man = a substitute for man (≠ a food supply):

Robinson Crusoe, p. 110

a. Substitute for language: the parrot. Robinson Crusoe captures one, so they can "speak." After many years of training → the parrot calls Robinson Crusoe very familiarly by name. = To solicit a familiar *You*? To create someone who says *You* to you? It's possible to fetishize an object by turning it into a person, a God, a term of interpellation: the parrot in *A Simple Heart*.[12] But it's not possible to solicit a familiar *You* from an object. Whence the irreplaceable nature of Robinson Crusoe's parrot: through the fact of hearing his own name, Robinson doesn't lose sight of the fact that he's a human being.

Robinson Crusoe, p. 113

b. Substitute for affect: a young goat ("half-starved"). "As I continually fed it, the creature became so loving, so gentle and so fond that it became from that time one of my domestics and would never leave me afterwards." Domestic: a humble, non-aggressive presence. = How urban domestication operates nowadays.

Robinson Crusoe = all the major types of relation between man and animal. Accession to humanity: the acquisition of power over things (tools), over animals (domestication). The last phase of this "humanization" is the most interesting: deriving affect from power, creating an affective power, using power as a means to receive affect. Man is truly born in Robinson Crusoe—with the story of the young goat.

As a digression, this offers a good basis for understanding the anthropological phenomenon of domesticating animals (the domestication of plants is another matter). Diderot: "You know how one likes to talk about what one has just learned" (*Letter on the Deaf and Dumb*).[13]

Ruffié, p. 108 *sq.*, "De la biologie à la culture"

Man = a harsh alternative to how natural selection operates on wild species; speeded-up selection focused upon a few valuable characteristics.

The species of wild animal must to be predisposed to anthropophilia (to living commensally with man):

1. Capacity for impregnation, for *imprinting*.[14] A very young wild animal can sometimes form an attachment to man: the subordination-dominance relation is established very quickly. A wolf cub captured at birth and raised by man will behave like a dog. Impregnation: conditional upon the very first hours of life, upon what or who the animal sees first (≠ a puppy that spends the first three months of its life in the wild: irreversibly wild). *Imprinting*: Robinson Crusoe and the kid. (*Imprinting*: affect as conduit of the imprinting process?)

2. Capacity for being trained (quick, conditioned reactions).

3. Affective capacity.

4. Biologically capable of coping with life in captivity.

Phases

1. In the Palaeolithic period: hunters would take live animals back to their homes and keep them as a supply of fresh meat = Taming (man and animal cohabiting) → domestication, if they're able to reproduce in captivity → maximum degree of *imprinting*.

2. Selection by man: sorting according to type → breeds selected for specific purposes (different breeds for meat, milk, labor, etc.) Decline in polymorphism.

History

The first domesticated animal: the dog, originally a cross between the European wolf and the Asiatic wolf. 10,000 B.C. (hunting and gathering): wolves trailing man to feed off the remains of the hunt (cf. rats in big towns). Dogs alter the hunting strategy. Promote the emergence of livestock farming.

Mutton, goat	6700 B.C.
Pork	6500
Beef	6000 → Farmers (supplies of fodder)
Horse	3000
Poultry	Bronze Age (2000 B.C.), dependent on men becoming settlers.
Rabbit	Ninth century A.D. From North Africa, via Spain. Hunting for sport. Middle Ages = a fish for Lent.[a]

[a]As Barthes explains orally, rabbits were classed as fish.

Ecological risk: from overselection, causing other species to die out, relying too heavily on just a few breeds (France, 1939: twenty-one breeds of cattle ≠ 1972: seven; donkeys are now in the process of becoming extinct). Should a disaster befall one of those breeds there'd be no genetically feasible alternative → risk of famine. The world of domestic animals = extremely fragile.[15]

2. ANACHORITES

Anachoresis and animality ≠ *Robinson Crusoe* (animal desired by man) = man desiring, drawn to, fascinated by animality. To specify three forms:

1. Animals = nature. Animals ≠ society. Anachoresis = a literal return to nature = to animality. Brahmanic India = forest-dwelling hermits, *Hulobioi*[16] = inhabit the forests in the way animals do. Christian anachorites, especially in Syria, fourth century (several radical, idiosyncratic forms): Grazers (grass, roots, leaves, no cooked food); Dendrites:[17] nest in trees, birds (cf. *Robinson Crusoe* and *The Swiss Family Robinson*).[18] From *living as* we attain to *being* (a psychotic passage from comparison to metaphor): the anachorite *is* an animal. Acepsimus walks "on all fours" (he gets himself put into iron shackles): a shepherd mistakes him for a wolf and just misses killing him with his "slingshot." Another: Thalelus gets a squirrel's cage built for himself, with a wheel inside. He's discovered "curled up in his cage, his knees up against his chin," reading the Gospels. He's turned himself into a squirrel.

Draguet, p. 43–44

2. Animals = Evil. Demons figured in animal form, a vast theme. Anthonian theme: demons entering Saint Anthony's cave: snakes, lions, bears, leopards, bulls, wolves, aspics, scorpions: all the "wild beasts." Their figurative profusion in painting. Animality = infra-nature: aggression, fear, greed, flesh: man without law. Lascault.[19] Baltrušaitis.[20]

Draguet, p. 58

3. Animals = nature inverted, redeemed. Conduits of miracles (inversion of their basic animal nature): lions burying Paul of Thebes, a lion bringing Simeon his meal of dates (cf. Elijah being fed by the raven). The inverted animal: the theme of the *impossibilia* (*adunata*)[21] in the Middle Ages. Excesses, the World Turned Upside Down: the association of two incompatible things as a metaphor for a world turned upside down. Virgil: the wolf being chased by a flock of sheep;[22] the donkey playing the lyre;[23] etc.

Curtius, p. 117 *sq*.

Le Millénaire du mont Athos, p. 173

A less extreme version of the "good animal": the affectively humanized animal. A much-noted practice: hermits who choose to live with a domestic animal. A way of attenuating solitude without the risk of sin? Not necessarily! Saint Gregory: the hermit is deemed to be overly fond of his kitten; receives a supernatural warning to grow less attached to it—although not to deprive himself of it entirely.[24] An aporia typical of love: How is it possible to love someone just a little bit?

Animality / Humanity: circular theme. The animal can occupy any one of the boxes in this paradigm:[25]

Good	Bad	Neither the one nor the other	Both
Kids Kittens Domestic animals, a food supply and useful	Demons	Nature	"Inverted" animals, whose untamed animality has been conquered

ATHOS / ATHOS
Mount Athos

I shall group the key aspects of religious idiorrhythmy under this trait—since it has a particular historical connection to the place.

HISTORY

Décarreaux, p. 23

An exemplary episode, generative model of the idiorrhythmic structure: around Pispir (the desert to the south of Alexandria): Anthony (who, according to myth, lived as a total hermit, albeit in phases) starts offering instruction to the ascetics who'd gathered around him → the beginnings of an idiorrhythmic organization.

They all: spend five days of the week alone—three or four to a hut at most, but as a rule no one is properly acquainted with anyone else; wholly solitary activities. On Saturday afternoons and Sundays, come together in a central spot: church, for prayer, to sell their baskets and mats, and stock up on palm fibres, salt, and bread. No leader; just an "elder," a model, "*guru*": Anthony.

Athos: initially, a scattering of hermitages = "natural," "unregulated" idiorrhythmy; by definition, what's never discussed, what

Encyclopaedia Universalis

falls outside historiography. As always: like all forms of marginality, eremitism is socially intolerable. → 963 (tenth century) Saint Athanasius founds the Great Laura, the first coenobitic monastery = foundation of Athos. After that, an even spread of *coenobia*[26] (in the north) and idiorrythmic semianachoritism (in the south).

Décarreaux

1430: Fall of Thessaloniki → Turkish rule → the strict regime becomes more lenient, idiorrhythmy spreads → seventeenth century: idiorrhythmy adopted by all the major monasteries.[27]

Encyclopaedia Universalis

Today, Athos is in decline[28] (7,000 monks in 1912 → 1,500). Nine idiorrhythmic monasteries (eight Greek + one Serbian). The biggest and the wealthiest: idiorrhythmic. (Athos: Athonite federation of monasteries, governed by a council, under Greek protection, 1912).

CONCLUSION: (a) ambivalence of idiorrhythmy: strict, pure, impoverished asceticism ≠ comfortable, free, relaxed asceticism. (b) The point is that it's not a matter of tension, but of marginality (cf. *infra* "Power"). Athos = mystical bent (*hesynchastes*:[29] the "silent ones"; the rhythm of prayer based on the cadences of respiration and the heart; Byzantine pneumatology).

SPACE

Encyclopaedia Universalis

North Athos: large monasteries. Mediterranean forest, no she-goats.[30]

Décarreaux, p. 51

South Athos: rocky desert: hermitages and *skites*[31] (masculine or feminine depending on whether you speak Russian or Greek < *asketerion*:[32] ascetery in Huysmans.)[33] *Skites* = a few disciples gathered around a master they elected themselves; *skite* = generic term for ascetic idiorrhythmic settlements.

More specific forms:

Décarreaux, p. 53

1. *Kelliotes*[34] < *kellion* = home to four or five monks, under the supervision of an elder + chapel. For the most part, subsist by tilling the fields.

2. *Lauriotes* < *laura*, Laure. Generic term for the monasteries on Mount Athos. But it's a broad term that can refer to several different forms:

Le Millénaire du mont Athos, pp. 112, 170

a. A transitional *coenobium*, where monks prepare themselves for solitude (three or four years).[35]

b. A community of around twelve people. Here, again, the phenomenon is defined by its scale.[36] More than in strict eremitism; less than in a monastery. Eremitism tempered with coenobitism:

Décarreaux, p. 19

ordo eremiticus, ordo eremiticae vitae[37] (Sadian convent; Sainte-Marie-des-Bois).[38]

3. A kind of monastic village. Contiguity of idiorrhythmies. Today: small apartments with a private chapel (cf. Carthusians:[39] two rooms + a small chapel). Possessions are allowed. Sorts of apartment blocks, bourgeois dwellings for erstwhile prelates: *kathismata*.[40] Vestige of luxury → modest comfort.

CONCLUSION. Here, once again (cf. "History"): the lability of forms (integral to the very principle of idiorrhythmy). Differences in scale depending on: (a) the degree of concentration, (b) the number of participants, (c) "economic standing" (poverty → wealth).

SESSION OF FEBRUARY 2, 1977

Reminder:

From February 9: Lecture, Room 8.

Idiorrhythmic novel: Simone Jacquemard: L'Éruption du Krakatoa ou Des chambres inconnues dans la maison *(Seuil, 1967).*

Robinson Crusoe → the first language (the familiar You). A vast dossier, but also a futile one. One day we'll see where it fits in. Myths of the origins of language.[1]

On Athos. I said: in decline; 7,000 in 1912 → 1,500 monks in 1972. Since then, there appears to have been a revival: 300 new monks—through transfers from other monasteries. Spiritual revival—but especially in the coenobia. *It goes without saying that what's resisted, neglected, rejected, marginalized to the point of extinction is idiorrhythmy. I was thus in the process of giving a brief account of how idiorrhythmy functions on Mount Athos. A bit of diachrony: from 963 to the present day, constant vacillation between the coenobitic structure and the idiorrhythmic structure, which has always been ambivalent. As we'll see, at times it's been very ascetic and at others very lenient; at times very poor, and others very wealthy, comfortable; at times hard-working, at others idle, etc. → In ethical terms, an unclassifiable phenomenon, possibly because it's always been implicitly linked to a mystical experience. And mysticism is the* atopia[2] *of the Church as society.*

ATHOS / ATHOS
(continued)

WAY OF LIFE

Diaita:[3] this is the properly idiorrhythmic approach.

Principle: each monk is free to live at their own particular rhythm.

Labor: unequal. Some are idle.[4]

Intellectual level: receive more teaching than coenobites. A kind of throwback to the philosophical schools of Ancient Greece.

Décarreaux, p. 50
Décarreaux
Décarreaux
Lacarrière, p. 40

Constraints:

Décarreaux, p. 50

a. Liturgy: no liturgical constraint (optional prayers), with the exception of complines, and on some of the main feast days.

b. Fasts and abstinences: some allowances made.

c. Once a year, all idiorrhythmics engage in a communal act by eating a meal together (a very ancient anachoretic custom that predates Christianity; the Therapeuts; the Essenians).[5]

Encyclopaedia Universalis

CONCLUSION: A flexible conception of constraint. No rules; merely a few "suggestions." → Mobility (cf. the other conclusions) and flexibility: it's always possible to lean more toward communal living or complete solitude.[6]

OWNERSHIP

Here, the same alternation, the same ambiguity, the same reversal, the same ir-relevance (despite ownership being of the utmost relevance to how lives are structured).

Décarreaux

1. Originally: idiorrhythmy = eremitism or semianachoritism; total poverty. Egyptian anachorites: a very small-scale wickerwork industry; enough to buy bread.[7]

2. Athos, end of the fourteenth century. Relaxation of the rules → idiorrhythmy through leniency. → Tolerance of certain practices: coenobites are permitted to work a piece of land and to keep the revenue for themselves, to live out their own marginal version of land ownership.

3. New reversal: to alleviate the community's expenses, monks are permitted to manage and live within their own individual means, whether their own earnings or financial support received from a wealthier monk.

Décarreaux, p. 50

4. Whence two categories of idiorrhythmic:

— the wealthy: those with a private income;

— those who have no revenue of their own: the *paramikri*, often employed by the rich → A social divide is automatically reinstated.

CONCLUSION. This leniency around questions of ownership, clearly: a sensitive issue for all forms of monachism; underscores the doctrinal marginality of idiorrhythmy. Ambivalence: proves that it's not a structure based on privilege in the strict sense (cf. the *Ancien Régime*), on injustice—simply that it's indifferent to the anti-money law, to the super ego of poverty (cf. Fourier and money versus Marx, Freud, Christians).[8]

POWER

Décarreaux

Décarreaux, p. 19

Idiorrhythmy = generalized fluctuation ≠ a stable point: its relationship to power.[9] → From the solitary hermit to communities of *lauriots*,[10] all idiorrhythmic constellations: operate outside a superior's control. It's not the way of life that distinguishes idiorrhythmy from coenobitism; rather the true dividing line is the degree to which they're dependent on a power (the abbot). Coenobitism = power.

The very first structures: if there was a "polariser": it was an elder; an example to follow, not a chief.[11]

Modern structures: *coenobium*: monarchic power ≠ idiorrhythmic structures. Collegiate:[12] assembly + college (six members) renewed through cooptation or in the event of death (cf. the Solitaires of Port-Royal project and Buddhist monks). → Managers (one year): epitropes.[13]

CONCLUSION: The single stable element: a negative relationship to power. Once again, what we're dealing with is: a consubstantial relationship between power and rhythm. Before anything else, the first thing that power imposes is a rhythm (to everything: a rhythm of life, of time, of thought, of speech). The demand for idiorrhythmy is always made in opposition to power. Think back to the mother and her child:[14] she imposes her own walking pace, generates a disrhythmy. And recall the distinction that we made: rhythm ≠ *rhuthmos*. Idiorrhythmy: a means of safeguarding *rhuthmos*, that is to say a flexible, free, mobile rhythm; a transitory, fleeting form, but a form nonetheless. Cf. in music, metronomical rhythm ≠ *rhuthmos*. *Rhuthmos* = *swing* (qualitatively speaking, rhythm isn't musical). Whence: the antithetical category of power = music, so long we're defining it as *rhuthmos*—not as "rhythm." *Rhuthmos*: a rhythm that allows for approximation, for imperfection, for a supplement, a lack, an *idios*: what doesn't fit the structure, or would have to be made to fit. Remember Casals's formulation: rhythm[15] is delay.[16] Now, only a subject (*idios*) can "delay" rhythm—that is to say, bring it about.[17]

AUTARCIE / AUTARKY

(Often, a "trait": hastily described; a scanty dossier. But remember: what we're doing is marking out boxes; to be filled in at some later stage and/or by each one of us. Even if it's being badly or sketchily filled in for the moment, I feel strongly that the box still needs to be put in place. Hence: the intuition that there's a box <a trait>: autarky of the group, group-life on itself and by itself.)

The Magic Mountain, p. 428

The Magic Mountain: Hans Castorp pays a visit to his cousin Joachim; only intends to stay for a few days as a visitor, a tourist, but will remain there for seven years. Similarly, the uncle who visits the sanatorium to see how Hans is getting along and is at once terrified and fascinated by illness: he finds himself being lured into discovering he's ill too and should remain there. The uncle escapes without warning. → The group exerts a fascination over all those who visit it. This is confirmed in personal relationships: anything that's perceived as a group draws us in, through a kind of vertigo.

But what's the fascination of the "small group" (the gang, the sanatorium)? The state of autarky (*autarkeia*:[18] self-sufficiency, contentedness) = plenitude. It's not the emptiness that draws us in, it's the fullness or, if you prefer, the intuition that there's a vertiginous vacuity to the plenitude of the group. It's this that Hans's uncle finds fascinating and it's this that he'll abruptly take flight from: a day densely packed with sick people immersed in the Living-Together of the sanatorium: 434.

The Magic Mountain

Autarky: a structure made up of subjects, a little "colony" that requires nothing beyond the internal life of its constituents.

Autarky: strong intradependence + zero extradependence. Independence marks the boundary, and so gives the definition, the mode of being of the group. A group in a state of autarkic Living-Together → a sort of smug pride, a self-satisfaction (in the Greek sense of the word) that's fascinating to someone looking in from the outside.

Material autarky → feeling of self-contained existence. For example: Nemo and the *Nautilus*. Nemo thinks of the sea as an autarkic environment, that is: as a being with its own boundaries that he sees no need to overstep; he has absolutely no recourse to land, to mankind. The sea provides him with all he needs: clothes, food, lighting, heating, energy—even cigars (p. 109)[19] → Nemo's pride (= No one[20]—other than himself). The first hermits rarefied their basic requirements (food) to such an extent that they inclined toward autarky (no doubt: mats ← → bread;[21] but among the ultramarginals: raw herbs). Incidentally, it was because of this risk of pride that eremitism was stamped out. And at the same time: attraction, fascination. As a form of material and spiritual autarky, it glittered, it drew people in.

Sanatorium: a wholly autarkic milieu; this includes the intradependence of affects; affective plenitude. All the affects you want can be found in the sana; you don't need the outside world. Once the structure (the Living-Together) is established, it's ever-lasting; it runs on and on—like a homeostat. (It will take the war of 1914 to interrupt it for Hans). For the visitor: repulsion and attraction. Fascination: death; not because it's a place where people die, but because it's never-ending.[22]

BANC / SCHOOL

Encyclopaedia Universalis,
"Territory"

Here we have what appears to be the perfect image of Living-Together, one that would appear to effect the perfectly smooth symbiosis of what are nevertheless separate individual beings. I'm referring to a school of fish: "a coherent, massive, uniform grouping: subjects of the same size, the same color, and normally of the same sex all moving in the same direction in a synchronized fashion."[23]

Clearly: one should never seriously compare traits of animal ethology with traits of human sociology, never infer one order from the other (because between the two there's always at least this separating them: language). Of course, there are parallels, especially between the two groups: invertebrates and vertebrates. Each group culminates (on the axis of intelligence) in a more "successful" order, characterized by an aptitude for Living-Together: insects (animal societies) and homines (human societies). Even so, they're still not comparable: human society ≠ insect society. Insect society: has its basis in a series of innate behaviors. ≠ Men: intelligence that's individual rather than specific;[24] connections are often learned: it's what we call "culture."[25] Ethology: supplies images, not explanations.

Image of the school ≠ extremely banal myth of an anthill-society. Which is: generalized, universalized bureaucratic training (this has nothing to do with specific regimes: the mass culture of capitalist societies = a version of the anthill society; television = an extension of the ant-hill). ≠ The school: collective, synchronized, abrupt shifts in tastes, pleasures, fashions, fears. The school: a more terrifying image than that of the anthill. Anthill: the equalization of individuals, the mechanization of social functions. ≠ School: the canceling of subjects, the training of affects, which are wholly equalized.[26]

Indeed, school: how schools of fish make love. During the spawning season: a school of male fish will swim above a school of females. As the mass of eggs floats up to the surface it passes through the school of males, which then release their sperm → reproduction without contact, pure species with no subjects. Erotic paradox: bodies are pressed against each other and yet they don't make love. The more idiorrhythmy is foreclosed, the more Eros is excluded. Idiorrhythmy: dimension constitutive of Eros. → Proportional, direct relationship between the particular rhythms, the aerations, the distances, the differences of Living-Together and the plenitude, the richness of Eros. → Toward an erotics of distance: an idea not unrelated to Tao. Idiorrhythmy: protects the body in that it keeps it at a distance in order to safeguard its value: its desire.

BÉGUINAGES / BEGUINAGES[27]

Encyclopaedia Universalis
Encyclopaedia italiana
Dictionnaire de spiritualité

Concern us because = an Occidental attempt to create an idiorrhythmic space within Catholicism—which, generally speaking, has been hostile to idiorrhythmy, favoring purely coenobitic monachism. → Differs in various ways from Oriental, Athonite idiorrhythmy.

HISTORY

In their phase of expansion (thirteenth, fourteenth century), and in the normative and normal sense of the term (as we shall see, to begin with it had a suspect, heretic, marginal inflection), beguinages = urban religious organizations; individuals dedicated to living a religious life who withdraw from ordinary society and wear distinctive dress. Primarily: women, but also *Beghini*, particularly at the start.

Thirteenth-fourteenth century: the institution flourished in Holland—but also in France, Germany, Spain . . .

Fifteenth-sixteenth century: died out in Holland and (partially) in France (the last remaining ones were eradicated at the time of the Revolution). ≠ Numbers increased in Belgium (with a strict disciplinary regime).

Today: Belgium: twelve convents (Grand Convent in Ghent), four hundred Beguines.

SPACE

Idiorrhythmy: as always, the importance of spatial organization.

More or less the same structuring principle as in the Athonite laures. The very principle of the idiorrhythmic space ($\neq$ phalansteries, monasteries, communities): small houses, hermitages inhabited by two or three people: *curtes*;[28] built in the precincts of a church + near a hospital and running water. That beguinal quarter (a separate parish): high walls, its doors kept open in the daytime. Has its own cemetery. (= urban phenomenon.)

WAY OF LIFE

Structuring principle: somewhere between religious life and secular life. But with stricter rules than in Oriental idiorrhythmy:

1. Monastic inflections: three key principles of the coenobitic institution: (a) stability (residency); (b) chastity, not for life, but for the duration of the stay in the beguinage; beguines: *continentes*[29] (cf. the Albigeois);[30] (c) obedience (to a superior: *Magistrae, Marthae*[31] and, overseeing them all, a Mother Superior: the "Grand Dame" + poor woman's clothing: a black robe and white headdress).

2. Secular inflections: no religious vows; occasional visits and outings (but always closely regulated and closely supervised; no worldly meetings); no canonial hours (importance of *timing*[32] in idiorrhythmy), but seven *Pater noster*.

3. In sum, a quasi-monastic life (austere rules). The idiorrhythmy is in the *timing*, which is fairly flexible + the fact of having permission to go outside (even if seldom granted) + it wasn't a life commitment (absence of vows). A very rigid idiorrhythmy, strongly inflected by law, a paradoxical idiorrhythmy (paradoxical according to our criteria) since it's trying to operate under the command of a power: *magistrae*.

SOCIO-ECONOMICS

Here, once again, we're dealing with the ambivalence of idiorrhythmic groups, which throughout history have always oscillated between wealth and poverty.

In the Middle Ages, intake resulted from two sets of historical circumstances:

1. The Crusades, eliminating all the husbands, produced a sharp increase in the number of widows, a surplus of women. → Wealthy

ladies choosing to withdraw from society. → Living-Together: offers the protection of the group to disadvantaged individuals (cf. retirement homes).

2. The precarious situation of the urban working classes who sought shelter within the precincts of a monastery and then want to join some kind of religious protective organization.

Whence three types of community:

1. The richest women (those with a source of income). Begging was obviously prohibited.

2. Poor women, living off benefactors' donations (basically equivalent to the university grant in bourgeois regimes). Begging likewise prohibited.

3. Poor women, with no benefactor: would beg + would be employed by a beguine (cf. Athos), or manual labor: washing, bleaching, lacework (following the veto on the importation of English wool).

POWER

Always the same problem with idiorrhythmy: the tension between power and marginality.

Origins of the *Beghini*: fairly obscure (like the word itself: several etymologies). It seems that to begin with (twelfth century) *Beghini* was the name of the Albigensians *(Albigensis)* of Cologne, and had an offensive connotation = heretic. Beghins or beghards: share a number of traits with the Albigensians: exaltation of abstinence, a horror of vows, public beating of the breast + it being forbidden to sleep without a nightshirt on! (A key clause in religious rules. A warning to those of you who don't wear pajamas in bed—quite a number nowadays!)

Beghins then acquires a feminine form: *continentes*, chaste women. (Remember: historically, chastity: the first Christian vow, not obedience or poverty). Produced virgins. The first churches.[33]

Those ill-favored (heretical) origins were later forgotten, normalization → the all-female religious organizations we've been discussing. The Church's power over marginality: (1) through its obedience to a Superior, (2) through the serving priest, who was initially Cistercian, then later Dominican or Franciscan, (3) through the tendency among pensionnaires—as a means of avoiding suspicion—to join the third order or follow the Rule of Saint Augustine (rule for semireligious men and women).

CONCLUSION. Clear differences with respect to Oriental idiorrhythmy, whether Antonite or Athonite, the stamp of Roman legalism:

1. Austerity: weighed down by rule.
2. Hierarchy and control.
3. More focused on charity (helping others in society) than on mysticism → a very domesticated form of idiorrhythmy.

SESSION OF FEBRUARY 9, 1977

Two books relating to the course have been brought to my attention:

1. Idiorrythmic novel: Les Enfants terribles *by Cocteau = the room, but the shared room (whereas shortly we'll be looking at the single room,* kellion, cella*).*

2. On life in the sanatorium before chemotherapy, a novel other than The Magic Mountain: Les Captifs *by Joseph Kassel, around* 1920.[1]

BUREAUCRATIE / BUREAUCRACY

Unregulated idiorrhythmy (Egypt, Anthony): not structured in any way. The sole communal activities: the weekly prayer, the direct exchange of labor (mats) for bread. That unregulated state can be precisely characterized by the absence of bureaucracy, no state power, not even in embryonic form, absolutely no reified, institutionalized, objectified relay between the individual and the microgroup.

Ladeuze, p. 296

Birth of coenobitism: the immediate and concomitant emergence of a bureaucratic apparatus, albeit just the beginnings of one. Executive agents: whoever was in charge for that week, the "*semainier*"[2] (the Rule of Saint Pachomius and the Rule of Saint Benedict).

St. Benedict, chap. 35

Bureaucratism: a vigilant deity lying in wait for the merest hint of an idiorrythmic grouping, swooping down upon it the moment it starts to "take":

— Athos: *skites* (generic term for all idiorrhythmic groupings: masculine or feminine, depending on whether you speak Russian or Greek: < *asketeron*; ascetery,[3] in Huysmans). The college delegates the running to its representatives, the epitropes.[4]
— Around about the 1920s, the desire for communes (in the modern, secular sense). In USSR, in the years immediately following the October Revolution, a kind of "sexual revolution" (laws passed on divorce, abortion, unmarried couples, commune). Wilhelm Reich (1925) describes the difficulties experienced by one commune: some friends who are about to grad-

uate, finding it impossible to return to their families, set up home on the second story of a big house. → The little obstructions that can stall everyday life (not doing the washing up, making noise at night, etc.) → meetings, never-ending discussions → commissions. The commission is the fatal and absurd outcome of all meetings (the circle: meeting → commission → report → filing cabinet). Commissions for every aspect of daily life: the Tea Commission, the Soap Commission, the Toothpaste Commission, the Clothes Commission, etc. Reich: "As far as its organization was concerned, then, the commune took over the form of state government, i.e., government by 'commission.'"[5]

Let's note, without resolving it, the veritable aporia (impasse) that an idiorrhythmic structure generates—one that wants to remain as such. The satisfaction of basic needs → the agents in charge of meeting those needs:

— either there's a gradual delegation of power, a tacit creation of posts: Commisioners; the major risk that they will crystallize into a real power,
— or rotation (everyone takes a turn: the *semainiers*); no power, but chaos, frictions, conflicts: legacies and handovers. (The problem is how to substitute rule for law).

CAUSE / CAUSE

Let's remind ourselves once again: idiorrhythmics = small, flexible groups of several individuals who are attempting to live together (within a certain proximity to one another), while each preserving his or her *rhuthmos*. Question: What brings them together?

Let's make a distinction between the motive, the determination (objective), causality, cause (with a small "c"), in a word: the why; and the end, the goal, the object (the idea) that fascinates, attracts, directs, and activates a tropism, the Cause (with a capital "C"), in three words: the for-what-purpose, the *Telos*.[6]

Here we're opening the box of the *Telos* that (because we shall want to exploit the term's ambivalence) we're calling Cause: Cause / cause and Cause / Thing (the Thing invested in, the Thing we obsess over. Charcot, Freud: it's always the Thing, the genital Thing: the "Thing").[7] Determination ≠ Objective.

CHRISTIANITY

Christian clusters: What's the ultimate goal of communal life? Vast dossier. The *Telos* is straightforward: joining together: the path to perfection, to sainthood. The Christian's sole aim (Saint Augustine): to become a saint. Saint Benedict, as a student, fleeing Rome and retreating to Enfide, near Tivoli, to practice asceticism. There, he founds a colony of ascetics: living in society, but united by the desire for perfection. The *Telos* = Perfection (*coenobium*: space of three vows: chastity, poverty, obedience). But, historical determination: the individual subject is governed by a hierarchically structured power (which starts off by: curtailing eccentricities, individual bouts of madness) > *coenobium*: a way of containing religious excesses.)

Festugière, I, p. 17

Schmitz, I, p. 17

Why the small groups, why these organizations with idiorrhythmic tendencies? What is the *Telos* (within the sphere of Christianity)?

1. *Orient:* "true" idiorrhythmy. While there are some economic justifications (nominal exchange of services: basketwork / bread, Athos), the *Telos* is essentially mystical: not to achieve perfection, but to "breathe," to join together (Byzantine pneumatology; hesychasm). In reality: a contemplative *Telos*. Idiorrhythmy: a simple, practical way of organizing the solitude of eremitism.

2. *Occident:* has always resisted idiorrhythmy. It's the exact opposite: the contemplative *Telos* is consigned to monasteries. Vatican II: contemplative institutions ≠ apostolic institutions (action, *preaching* the Gospels out in the world). Fraternal communities (monks / brothers)[8] ≠ spiritual families: charitable acts (example: the Visitandines, Beguinages, the third orders). Spiritual families: organizations operating under the Rule of Saint Augustine.[9] Excellent literary example: Balzac, *L'Envers de l'histoire contemporaine.*[10] In an old house near Notre Dame Cathedral, a group of charitable men live together under the supervision of Madame de la Chanterie; *Telos*: to do good works.

Pléiade, VII

OTHER SORTS OF *TELOS*

The *Telos* of all microgroups (with idiorrhythmic tendencies) is most often expressed by some vague term, a mana-word[11] (pseudo-hippy communities:[12] "happiness"). Examples of two different sorts of *Telos*:

1. Sanatorium (*The Magic Mountain*). Let's repeat the distinction I was proposing between determination (causality) and *Telos* (what draws people in, the common goal that fascinates, that's invested in).

Putting sick people together; objective cause: on the face of it, to protect society from contagion, to exploit a taboo, send people away + the standardization (hence profitability) of health care. The ostensible goal = to preserve life. But the goal that's invested in, that fascinates, the Cause, the *Telos*, is Death.

a. It is the theme of the book: a fascination with Death (≠ *Death in Venice*).[13]

b. Death = they all think about it, but it's taboo: fascination. The object of an imperfect foreclusion: the indirect, an intriguing category. The presence of Death is indicated by a series of indirect, domestic, "silly" signs: the oxygen canisters outside the doors of the *moribundi*;[14] death as form of housekeeping (cf. the idea of dressing a corpse).

The Magic Mountain, p. 106

c. A curious but very real dialectic between Illness (= Death) and illnesses. Illnesses (with the exception of tuberculosis): on the side of life (of struggles, of worries). Now, in the sanatorium, those other sorts of illnesses = denied. "It is not advisable to fall ill up here; you aren't taken any notice of." Hans isn't allowed to have a cold. Illnesses: part of the ardent, vital *process* of life ≠ Illness, the slow, contemplative approach of Death.

d. Sanatorium, analogon of eternity. Initially, powerful desire to escape, estimations, calculations, fantasies of leaving; a kind of military service, but where the "demob" date hasn't been set, and then: settling into perpetuity. Hans is wrenched from his fascination with Death by actual death (the war of 1914).

e. Function of the group (of Living-Together): statistical representation of the risk of death; the chances of your neighbor dying, bearing in mind that your neighbor could be you. This is no longer the indirect, it's the implicit.

2. A different *Telos* (banal paradigm): Eros. Text: Sade: Sainte-Marie-des-Bois,[15] and the chateau[16] in *120 Days of Sodom*. Eccentric example, because there's a foreclosure of idiorrhythmy. There's no *rhuthmos*, whether for the victims (that goes without saying) or for the libertines: meticulously timed schedules, obsessively observed rites, implacable rhythm = the *coenobium*, the convent, not an idiorrhythmic space. Nevertheless, an example that needs to be included in our dossier because it allows us to identify a kind of law:

strong Causes, maniacal investments (= monotropy) → coenobitic forms. For there to be idiorrhythmy—or a dream of idiorrhythmy—there has to be: a diffuse, vague, uncertain Cause, a floating *Telos*, more a fantasy than a belief. Now, Sade's libertines (this is their paradox) turn fantasy into Law, a Faith. From that point on, there's no longer any *rhuthmos*: freedom isn't a matter of sex, but of the indirect ways we invest in it. → Secular idiorrhythmy: squaring the circle, because the group mustn't prohibit Eros; rather, it must be sure to assign it an indirect position, where's not illegal but a-legal. → A great many "communes" fail because they put sex in the wrong position = the problem underlying the investigation undertaken in this lecture course. Or indeed: the *Telos* of all forms of coenobitism: faith (in Sade, there's a faith in Eros). → Discourse of *It goes without saying*, that is to say of arrogance. Saint Basil of Caesarea: "Faith is a definite, unhesitating consent to God's teachings, with the full conviction of the truth of what is proclaimed and taught by the grace of God."[17] ≠ The idiorrhythmic project: a matter of non-discourse, of suspending the discourse of *It goes without saying* (it's not a question of doubt, but of *epoché*, of the suspension of discourse: Death in the sanatorial space).

Amand, p. 290

BION

Bion, p. 59 and p. 66

The problem of the group's *Telos*, its objectives: dealt with in a parapsychoanalytical manner by the English doctor Wilfred Ruprecht Bion: *Experiences in Groups and Other Papers* (1961).[18] Small groups of patients (parapsychiatric hospital, psychotherapy), who meet regularly: sort of group therapy. What we're calling Cause (*Telos*): related to the "basic assumption": the common goal that brings the group together in the first place. For Bion: there are three basic assumptions; but it's not that they each correspond to a distinctive type of group, rather that all three can sometimes be successively mobilized within the space of an hour → a shimmering of three objectives:

1. *The dependency assumption*: the group meets to obtain security from a leader upon whom they depend for material and spiritual nourishment and protection (the leader can be mediated by an idea—a Cause: some Causes provide subsistence and protection: monasteries).

2. *The pairing assumption* (the most original, the most interesting): as soon as two subjects in a group become involved with each

other—even if it's only temporary—you have the figure of the couple, the figure of marriage.→ the group starts anticipating an event to come. But all that's dependent on the leader having not yet emerged: the individual or idea destined to save the group, the messianic hope.→ *Telos* of awaiting[19] (the couple ≠ the true leader).

3. *The fight-flight assumption*: the group meets to fight an outside threat or to escape it. Leader = someone whose exigencies provide the group with opportunities for fight or flight: otherwise, he isn't followed.

Again, the group can switch between "basic assumptions" (its *Telos*) two or three times within the space of an hour—or the same assumption can be maintained over several months.

Bion's categories aren't directly applicable to Living-Together because they pertain to provisional groups such as meetings, classes, and seem to require verbalization. But:

1. They can be partially, *fleetingly* relevant to certain episodes of everyday communal living (a group of friends sharing a house for the holidays). Something to be studied (we could all do this the next time we spend an evening with friends): it would be very interesting to note the changes in leader (individual, idea, thing), the effects of pairings, the movements of fight or flight.

2. There's one space we're all familiar with that corresponds fairly closely to Bion's small group: the weekly seminar. Issues to do with intellectual fights, with complicity (pairings), with subjects asserting themselves through their dependence on the leader—who isn't necessarily or isn't always, continuously, the person teaching (the doctor, in the case of Bion's small groups). Bion's contribution: to point up the extreme mutability and subtlety of leadership. Something to be studied; any one of us could do it.

HOMEOSTASIS[20]

In fact, all that: to ask the following question: Is it possible to conceive of a (small) group with no *Telos*? Would such a group be viable? Insofar as the small group fantasized here is idiorrhythmic, asking that amounts to asking this decisive question: Is there not an affinity between idiorrhythmy and the absence of a *Telos*? And yet, isn't a group with no *Telos* unviable? In other words: Is an idiorrhythmic group possible?

We shan't—we're not yet in a position to answer that; for now, we shall limit ourselves to defining the problem in the following way:

1. The vaguest (non-militant) Cause or *Telos*: for the sake of "happiness," for the sake of "pleasure" = sociability as an end in itself. Someone (AB)[21] provided me with the following quotation from Victor du Bled (*Société française du XVᵉ au XXᵉ siècle*, Didier, 1900, p. xx): "The chief concern of people living in the world is sociality. But the world is not interested in love or family, or friendship, or doing good works . . . it brings men together, it wants them to take pleasure in joining together, everything is set out with that in view—the rest is not its concern." An excellent quotation—uncompromising in that it explicitly dismisses the possibility of any Cause, any *Telos*. The group is defined as a pure homeostatic machine that runs by itself: a closed circuit of charge and expenditure. An idyllic view of worldliness: a machine with no goal, where there's no transformation, that generates pleasure in its purest form (cf. Sade's machines). Worldly pleasure: without origin, unsubstituable, untransformable. Being together = a sort of primitive of pleasure.[22]

2. *Homeostasis* of the group: would be possible in a utopian world that has no class structure and no language. Because the fact is, as soon as you have language (enunciation), you have the staging—or the setting up of a competition between—a system of positions (the position you speak from, the position you want to assign, that you presume to allocate someone else, etc.), or in other words a system of strategies of enunciation (cf. Flahaut).[23] → Second aspect of worldliness, which the French moralists, from La Bruyère and La Rochefoucauld to Proust, were very good at describing: we join together (we live together) in order to be recognized. Our existence is dependent upon being recognized as occupying a certain position. From our corpus: the bourgeois apartment building in *Pot Luck*. A grouping determined by contingencies, motivations relating to money, social class (as with the rental of any apartment building, any group of tenants), but what's immediately established is a shared *Telos* (a Cause). From top to bottom of the building, they all: want to be seen as figures of Respectability. Living-Together: *stairwell* of false mirrors (not forgetting that a mirror conceals what's behind it).

3. Fantasy of the idiorrhythmic group: takes up the idea of Living-Together as *homeostasis*, as the everlasting preservation of the pure pleasure of sociability. However, in a more philosophical manner, it sheds its worldliness (which can't be dissociated from competing for position) and fantasizes the following paradox: the idiorrhythmic project involves the impossible (superhuman) establishing of a group whose *Telos* would be perpetually to destroy itself as a

group, that is to say, in Nietzschean terms: to enable the group (the Living-Together) to leap beyond ressentiment.

CHAMBRE / ROOM

Enclosed personal space: *kellion, cella*: foundation of idiorrhythmy. But to understand the Room, we need to take a wider view—or start on a bigger scale.

1. THE TOTAL SPACE

(Joseph) Rykwert's thesis: *On Adam's House in Paradise* (1972): paradise implies the "house."[24]

Eden: initially, in the sense of domain (country house). God creating Adam and Eve so that they might keep each other company and talk with one another: but also with Him when He "walked in the garden in the cool of the day." House: countersolitude, from God's point of view; idiorrhythmic proposition: coming together for the evening walk. → Eden: ideal circumscription of the idiorrhythmic community (of three). Adam was to cultivate and maintain Eden: terraces, flowerbeds, places to walk, to sit and talk + cuttings, jars, provisions, storerooms. The country dwellers' domain = the total space.

Hut: then, house in the strict sense: the hut → Adam's hut. Rykwert's thesis: that primitive, fantasized hut—for architects, an ancient model—has always played a central role. Every architect tries to remake Adam's hut—at least within a certain tradition of architecture, the kind modeled on timber constructions (notably the Bauhaus).

Why the thesis is interesting: hut (house): not a functional determination (providing shelter in bad weather), but a symbolic operation. To create a space that the subject can interpret through his own body. Hut: at once body and world; the world as a projection of the body. Cf. esoteric interpretation of the Egyptian temples: diagram of the body.[25]

House can't be understood without reference to the sacred (dwelling = language?).[26] In the Scriptures, three forms are revealed → ideal models for architects (= expanded variations on Adam's hut, if you will):

1. *Noah's Ark*: total autarky: compendium of the world, encyclopedia of all species, the guarantee of reproduction. → the family

Rykwert, p. 9

44

120

in the patriarchal sense → model for all rural domains → its novelistic realization (*The Mysterious Island* = salvaging + autarky). Nevertheless: destined for catastrophe, because no reproduction takes place → a real colony set up in Iowa. As a form, it's the direct descendent of Adam's hut—what's more, it's made of timber: God rebuilds the hut, in a more compact version.

No lecture on February 23.

Next lecture: March 2.

Another novel of Living-Together: Gorky: Summerfolk *(intellectuals spending the summer in a dacha).*[1]

CHAMBRE / ROOM
(continued)

2. *The Desert Tabernacle.* Greek: *skene:*[2] tent, pavilion, dwelling, Tabernacle (the tent in which the Ark of the Covenant would be placed)—and also *skene:*[3] a meal shared among friends, shelter for actors. Thematic idea (the model, the productive configuration): the twelve tribes around the Tabernacle. Different groups spread around an uninhabited centre = the very principle of idiorrhythmic organizations (I'd like a less voluntarist term: constellations?). Cf. Nitria, Athos, beguinages, Port-Royal (empty center: the church, place where people eat; cf. *skene.*

3. *Temple of Jerusalem.* Solomon's temple + Ezekiel's two visions[4] = fantasy of the "total building." Solomon's temple: where priests lived and the palace of Jerusalem.→ Early model of the monastic structure: an exclusive, total, multifunctional space. The Temple of Jerusalem inspired → the palace (the King and his court: Charlemagne). Notably: Escorial. As a result of a vow Philip II made shortly after the Battle of Saint-Quentin. The vow: August 10, 1557. The palace was to be orientated on the axis of the sunset on August 10, Saint Lawrence's Day: in the shape of a gridiron. Herrera,[5] the second architect; theorized by J. B. Villalpanda, his disciple[6] (a follower of R. Lulle).[7] Sacred calculations: the Temple and the tribes around the Tabernacle.→ Monastery, palace and church.

120–21

144

2. THE ROOM BECOMES ISOLATED WITHIN THE HOUSE

The room becomes detached from the total space. The room and the house are no longer interchangeable. Room = an autonomous symbolic space: the conjugal bedroom.

Conjugality and property, archetypically: Husband + Wife = Father + Mother = Master and Mistress. → A protected space: as secret (the secret of the primal scene) and as treasure (the room as a storehouse for the most valuable things). → It would be interesting to propose a relation between the scene, secrecy and property. The economy of rural domains: Xenophon, *OEconomicus*, the landowning gentry. *Ho thalamus*,[8] Homer: a shop, then a room to sleep in. In the most private part of the house, the women's quarters: where the most precious possessions were stored (coverings and furniture). Even today, a survey to be carried out: the conjugal chest. A depository for money, jewels, passports (cf. grandmother:[9] anything that might get "stolen," little silver spoons, sugar, jam.) → Treasure mixed up with sex (sexual rights), secrecy with property. See all the myths of the hidden room, starting with Bluebeard.

Xenophon, p. 72. and endnote

3. THE ROOM LOSES ITS ASSOCIATION WITH THE COUPLE → *CELLA*

Origins of the *cella* (and thus: of the single room as a symbolic space): the hermit's hut (in the desert). In Pachomian convents: cells, not dormitories.

Clearly, *cella* = representation of interiority. Whence its ambivalence: (a) space to do battle with the devil: *anachoretale certamen*,[10] hand-to-hand combat: *solus cum solo*; (b) a calming interiority: *cella continuata dulcescit*.[11] Rilke: "He carried the obscurity, the refuge and the tranquility of a house deep within himself."[12] The room's secular, modern ambivalence: a symbol of what one wants to escape (Pascal: all unhappiness springs from not knowing how to stay in one's room),[13] symbol of Flaubert's "marinade"[14] + symbol of shelter, of discovering and consolidating a sense of self (not having "a room of one's own" → a teenage rite of passage: being given your own room).

Secular version of the interiority of the room, as value: the *quant-à-soi* (= reserve, a distant attitude). Room: a space for fantasizing in that it's protected; it's not subjected to surveillance. → Fight for a room = the fight for freedom. Room: anti-gregarious element, space of a "will to power"? ≠ Transparency, an instrument of

Le Millénaire du mont Athos, p. 175

power? Beaubourg: the great hall–vast open-plan offices (Richard Rogers).[15] American principle: transparency does away with surveillance (everyone keeps a watch over everyone else) + the most profitable use of space.[16]

Does the room, the cell (= the space of *quant-à-soi*) have to be luxurious? The question is beside the point. (a) Monastic cells: asceticism, poverty. Cf. Abbé Faugas's bedroom in *The Conquest of Plassans*, the object of Mouret's burning curiosity. It's absolutely plain, without a single decoration, but more pertinently without a single personal effect: nothing is left lying around (leaving things lying around = sensuousness). The room (the cell): submits to the metaphor: bare. "There was not a single paper on the table, not an article of any kind on the chest of drawers, not a garment hanging against the walls: the wood was bare, the marble was bare, the walls were bare."[17] (b) By contrast, Buddhist monasteries in Ceylon. Cells: little comforts, even a degree of luxury: cushions; a few small blankets; clean, white, good-quality linen; a few books on the bookshelves; a radio; a couple of photographs (cf. Charlie Chaplin's cell in *Modern Times*). A kind of Epicureanism: not having much, but what you do have is good quality.[18]

The problem of the room's "social standing": not relevant here (monastic poverty relates to a different set of concerns). What matters is the complete, total autonomy of the room's (the *cella*'s) structure. The room is its own structure, distinct from any of its contiguous structures. The room: always structured to a greater or lesser degree. My sense of the room's structure is a loose, local constellation (a diagram) of functional spaces: bed, desk, places to store personal effects.[19] → Proof that such a structure exists: it can be transported (rediscovered, recreated) anywhere, irrespective of the objects themselves. This is because structure: a network of relations (or functions) uninterested in contents. We can therefore say: the room in *The Confined Woman of Poitiers* = a structure, albeit one reduced to a bed she never leaves (bed: its own self-contained structure; hospitals, sanatorium, Aunt Léonie's bedroom, reduced to her bed and bedside table). Objects:[20] debris (a commode with no drawers, four empty bottles, three cans of food, a lotto set, two small cabinets, a couch-frame piled with rags and tatters crawling with vermin, a doll's head, a rosary, five pencil stubs). From her bed, mad, prostrate (but eating well), Mélanie revels in her room's utter lack of structure. She exercises every kind of power over her room, even that of destructuring it, and that structure (or non-structure): independent of the house-structure.

The Conquest of Plassans,
p. 28

Bareau, p. 23

Proust, I, p. 47

The Confined Woman of
Poitiers, pp. 135–36

Indeed, the luxury of the bedroom derives from its freedom: a structure protected from all norms, all powers; as a structure—an exorbitant paradox: it's unique.

THE *MAGNIFICENZA*

Is there such a thing as a model of the anti-hut? An architecture that rejects the *quant-à-soi*, the room, the *cella* as an epicurean value of interiority? In art and architecture, a historical opposition and debate between the Greeks, who derived their temples from the hut, and those who followed the example of Rome.[21] Piranesi: *Prisons* are supposed to be the anti-hut (note that they're vast, anti-cellular structures, demonic capsizing of levels) → Space of crisis, of drama, of the sublime (Burke = "a sort of delight full of horror, a sort of tranquility tinged with terror.") → Piranesi: "Out of fear, springs pleasure."[22] That dramatic, criticized breaching of the *quant-à-soi*, that foreclosure of the interiority of the room as a refuge and as a *pleasure* (cf. the quotation from Rilke), that space of emotional agitation, that ornamental and hysterical transparency: the *magnificenza*.[23]

Rykwert, p. 56 p. 55

CHEF / CHIEF[24]

Historically: the passage from eremitism to coenobitism (Pachomius, Egypt, 314) → Living-Together: immediately marked the introduction of a hierarchy: the invention of the chief.

Let's be clear on the following:

Amand, p. 47

—anachoritism: not especially characterized by solitude: groups of anachorites. Characterized by the absence of a chief. Opposition idiorrhythmy / coenobitism = group with no chief / group with a chief.
— Pachomius → monasteries: the first rule: obedience. One chief for every house of monks: the *praepositus*.[25] Whence, in the West, the two fundamentals (defining features) of the monk: under an Abbot's command + stability (lives his whole life in an unchanging environment).

Schmitz, I, p. 25

Naturally, that defining feature → then comes in for ideological— or symbolic—elaboration, especially following Saint Benedict. The Abbot = the pivot of the monastery, but one who appears to occupy the position of Christ. *Pater et Magister*:[26] the Vicar of Christ. The broader aim (the *Telos* of the abbatial institution): not the observation of rules but the salvation of souls. Line of descent that follows the ecclesiastic model: bishop and diocese—not the Roman image of the family, the *Paterfamilias*.[27]

The point of that post-Pachomian development was to activate—or to render plausible—a key opposition between two types of charisma. *Anax*:[28] someone who wields power. *Basileus*:[29] virtually a God, someone with a magico-religious function. Scepter: the messenger's staff, the transmitter of authorized speech.[30]

1. The militant type of charisma, of Roman (military) origin: the chief.

2. The oriental type of charisma: the elder, the model, the *guru*, the type compatible with idiorrhythmic constellations: colonies of anachorites, athonite *skites*, gathered around an "elder": a role model rather than a leader.[31] Originally, unelected: the group acknowledges whoever occupies the position of someone they can emulate: someone with a certain charisma, rather than an authority. A type of charisma with a degree of self-evidence about it (self-evidence of the model, of the *guru*). Which is why, when circumstances demand that a form of community be established, to respect or to mimic the self-evidence of the model (≠ chief): election has to be unanimous (a sign that a chief is in the process of becoming a *guru*: when he or she is elected by an overwhelming 99 percent majority; that 1 percent is a concession to the sacred: it might be sacred, religious, but it's still secular, rational!).[32] Example: Ceylon monasteries. Voting is very rare, because it splits the community. After polite discussion, a unanimous verdict is reached. Cf. Monastery, Middle Ages and Rousseau, *The Social Contract*.[33]

The dividing line between the chief and the *guru* can be given a modern definition (Bion). As we saw:[34] Bion: the third "basic assumption," the third objective of the group, the third *Telos* (after dependency and pairing): the hypothesis of fight / flight. The group meets to confront an outside threat or to run away from it → Leader = someone whose exigencies provide the group with opportunities for flight or fight. Bion makes this clear: "Leaders who neither fight nor run away are not easily understood." This would be the second charismatic type (the *guru*): someone who neither fights nor flees: isn't a leader (≠ "chief").

The "chief" = someone who takes decisions:

Bareau, p. 72

Bion, p. 65

Golding, p. 21

The Magic Mountain,
p. 184

1. Golding, *The Lord of the Flies*:[35] Ralph: "'Seems to me we ought to have a chief to decide things.' 'A chief! A chief!' 'I ought to be chief,' said Jack with simple arrogance. 'Because I'm chapter chorister and head boy. I can sing C sharp.'"

2. *The Magic Mountain*: the Chief = the doctor, because he's the one who makes the decisions (and gives no explanation for them): "Hans Castorp, then, went to bed on the Saturday afternoon, as had been ordained by Hofrat Behrens, the highest authority in our little world." At the opposite extreme, there's the *guru* who neither fights nor flees, who makes no decisions. Tao: "The wise man does not fight," and "Tao offers no difficulty, except that it avoids choosing."[36]

(23rd = vacation)

Idiorrhythmic novel: brought to my attention: Giono: Joy of Man's Desiring—*and the community Giono tried to set up in 1935.*[1]

CLÔTURE / ENCLOSURE

The closing off—enclosure—of living space: a vast dossier, with elements from various scientific disciplines. A truly multidisciplinary theme. Here, I shall simply list the anthropological functions of enclosure.

FUNCTIONS

Anthropology: enclosure needs to be considered in relation to an ethological fact: territorial animals (territory: we'll probably come across this word again). A safe space (food, reproduction); any encroachment on the part of neighboring animals is immediately resisted. The subject rules over his or her own territory. Especially: rodents, carnivores, hoofed animals, primates—and some birds (the robin, for example). Leroi-Gourhan: man = a territorial animal, like the stag and the robin.[2] The idea of territory incorporates the opposition public / private.[3] There are some historical, ideological aspects to that opposition (legislation, the legal right to "privacy"), but its basis is anthropological. Private space is the same thing as territory. It's possible to have concentric (concentrated) spheres of private space, or in other words a territory within a territory: estate[4] → house (servants, land workers aren't allowed inside) → room (not all the inhabitants of the house are admitted) → bed. Aunt Léonie's territory: her bed, a table next to the window = her absolutely private space ≠ repression (prisons, hospitals, barracks, boarding schools: where privacy, territory is prohibited).

Ethology: not only is territory defended, it's marked out (the hippopotamus marks out his territory with his excrement).[5] Whence

Ekambi, p. 11
Moles, p. 11

two functions of enclosure (with respect to its original relation to the idea of territory): that of protection, that of definition.

A. Protection

The protective function of enclosure. Just for the record, because it's a banal point and our dossier is huge: ethology, architecture, ideology (the transformation of territory into property, protection into prohibition). From our corpus, let's simply note:

1. Monasteries. Physically enclosed: boundary walls + the "cloister" in the monastic sense. Area where non-believers aren't permitted to enter; closed off from the world, negating the worldly as liable to corrupt the monk's identity; a prohibition linked to a sacred, that is to say a consecrated space (the monk is consecrated by his vows; cf. Benveniste's studies on the sacred[6]). ≠ Idiorrhythmic spaces (with the exception of beguinages). No enclosure, or only partially, not very rigorously enclosed. The function of idiorrhythmy is not to protect a "purity," that is to say an identity. Its arrangement in spatial terms: not concentration, but dispersion, spacing.

Robinson Crusoe, p. 160

2. Description of the protective-enclosure: *Robinson Crusoe*.

Robinson Crusoe, p. 159

Robinson: meticulous, almost excessive (quasi-obsessive) set of defenses against others. As soon there's the suggestion of the presence of another man on the island (footprints): mad defensive measures; a house that's completely *buried from view*, invisible, a whole system of fortifications, of hiding places. → Enclosure as craziness, as an extreme-experience (cf. *infra*).

B. Definition

The very meaning of "to define": to mark out borders, frontiers. Enclosure = defines a territory, and by extension the identity of its occupant(s). For example:

Bareau

1. Buddhist monasteries (of Ceylon). Buildings scattered around a courtyard-garden: there's enclosure (≠ catholic monasteries and, as we've seen: beguinages) but no protection or prohibition, only a fairly loose marking out of the confines of the space: wire fences, double doors that are always left open, and after that: the countryside:[7] a wide open doorway, with no doors. → The community defines itself, it doesn't close itself off, it doesn't prohibit, it doesn't exclude.

2. The bourgeois apartment building (*Pot Luck*) is certainly protected (closed, locked doors, the concierge and these days a peep-

hole), but it also disposes of a complex mechanism of delimitation: its surfaces. The surfaces are charged with the function of announcing the retreat indoors, withdrawal into the "private" sphere. Zola describes them in a great deal of detail: façades, doors, rows of windows, all the same, without even a birdcage (in the courtyard), the shutters that are eternally closed. What's more (symbolism): moldings, gilt, velvet carpet on the stairs, paint "only done twelve years ago and already it's peeling." The shared territory (the apartment building) defines the community's mode of being: bourgeois respectability. Within that shared territory, smaller territories (that are just as exactingly circumscribed): the apartments, which define the mode of being of each family. The (bourgeois) staircase, with all its closed doors, comes to function as a no-man's land. When Berthe, who's having an adulterous affair with Octave, is caught with her lover, she finds all the doors are closed, she's forced to flee down the main staircase—pursued, so to speak, by an implacable exterior: every one of the families excludes her from their *familial existence*. So enclosure = a sign-system.

Pot Luck, p. 7

EXTREME-EXPERIENCE

The most important question that anthropology raises: is not, in actual fact: How long has mankind existed?[8] But: When, how, and why did symbolism begin? Did it emerge all of a sudden (Lévi-Strauss),[9] since it's impossible for things to start signifying gradually? Or in a manifold way, on several different fronts at once, all at the same time? It's been proposed and there seems to be some truth in the suggestion that the three main prehistoric manifestations of the symbolic emerged concurrently: tools, language, incest[10]—then, on those three points, transition to "double articulation"[11] (Jakobson, Lévi-Strauss)—parietal, regular incisions (prior to figuration), the burial of the dead, habitation.

We therefore need to be careful when talking about basic needs being satisfied in purely functional terms: enclosure = protection? Yes, probably, but defenses and sign-systems (which exist among animals) are activated by symbolism. Enclosure is bound up with a neurosis of a predominantly obsessive kind: there are rituals of enclosure—extreme-experiences of enclosure; or, if you'll allow me the expression: crazy-enclosures (this is a term of affection).

Already in *Robinson Crusoe*, a "healthy," "rational," "empirical" subject if ever there was one, panics at the prospect of danger (the

Robinson Crusoe, p. 62

footprints in the sand) → endlessly reinforces his defenses (absolute protection is never achieved: mirage, asymptotic): stockade-enclosure camouflaged by a thicket, no door (unmistakably the theme of absolute enclosure, cf. *infra*), just a little ladder that Robinson pulls up behind him. Cf. the colonists' apartment in the granite wall in *The Mysterious Island*: a ladder that can be pulled up, then an elevator. The symbolism of burying oneself below ground and walling oneself up is based on the empirical fact of protecting oneself (symbolically speaking, the only absolutely protected space is the mother's womb). To go outside is to be exposed, to be defenseless: it's life itself.

Festugière, I, p. 46

Making it impossible for an enemy to get in gets converted, through excess, through neurotic exaggeration, into the self-imposed impossibility of getting out. A great many anachorites, having shut themselves away in their huts, would only talk to visitors through a little window, *dia thuridos*.[12] *The Lausiac History*: Dorotheus, Elias's successor, oversees a women's monastery from afar. He shuts

The Lausiac History, p. 90

himself away in the upper story of a barn with no ladder. There is, however, a window overlooking the monastery, where he'd sit, exhorting the women not to quarrel.

Now we come to the grand forms of the "madness" of the enclosure, or self-sequestration. Two examples:

1. *Symeon the Stylite* (the son of a shepherd, Syria and Cilicia: southeast Anatolia: 390–459). A passion for asceticism through self-sequestration: he buries himself up to his head in a garden ditch for a whole summer; forty days in a cave with no light (→ the monastery tries to get rid of him). Walls himself up, has the door cemented

Festugière, I, p. 62

over: forty days without food.[13] In 423, near Antioch: sets up home on top of a pillar,[14] initially a low one, but that gets gradually raised in height; by 430: forty cubits = twenty meters. Now, once up top: erects a balustrade (and incites the Emperor against the Jews).[15] A kind of athletic performance of asceticism: Who can wall themselves up themselves the most effectively, the longest? A kind of ascetic Olympics, but with reclusion in place of pole-vaulting. Establishment of coenobitism: to limit such excesses, through the ultimate Benedictine virtue: *discretio*.[16] Cf. Dostoevsky: in *The Possessed*,

Le Millénaire du mont Athos, p. 366

speaks of Lizaveta, who's Fool-for-Christ: she's been living in a sort of cage for seventeen years, without speaking to anyone, without washing or combing her hair.[17]

2. Which brings us to secular confinement (according to our normative criteria, amounts to pure psychosis): *The Confined Woman*

The Confined Woman, p.
153

168

134

134

143

of Poitiers. Voluntary sequestration or one imposed by the family? The norm would say: imposed by the family (police inquiry, trial); but in fact, if you read the documents: they were all partially responsible. A family caught up in the collective madness of confinement:

a. Monsieur de Chartreux, the grandfather on the mother's side: a voluntary recluse in his bedroom. Total reclusion: he doesn't come out when his son-in-law dies in the next room.

b. Bourgeois house: grand front door that's always locked (to get in, you have to go through the courtyard; just the maids, incidentally).

c. What triggers the process of sequestration: Mélanie, young, neurotic, exhibitionist, was in the habit of standing naked at the window. → Boarding up the window.

d. Absolute enclosure (for 25 years → 1901): shutters closed, the second-floor casement window padlocked. Shutters chained shut, window kept closed by a padlocked iron bar. (police: to open the window, they remove it from its hinges). Evidently, the stench was unbearable (filth, excrement, rodents). Nevertheless, a maid used to sleep in the room on a little iron bed. Stench bearable if the door was left ajar; but the mother would forbid it: "She would have said that we wanted to make her daughter catch cold."

Could the madness of enclosure get any more extreme than this? Yes, and it's Mélanie herself who provides the secret thematic key. Her deepest and most singular compulsion, at the center of the sequestration: her blanket. The mother's statement: "She didn't want to sleep with sheets; she refused to wear a nightdress. . . . She was only happy when she was entirely covered by a blanket." And: "She has a passion for covering herself up." The subtle theme of the blanket over a naked body (cf. monks are forbidden to sleep naked):[18] distances the body from the protocols of the family, from the domesticity of bedtime. The blanket is the veil that envelops and blocks out the light (the child burying him or herself under the covers), providing total isolation: to be enclosed within a second skin; to regress back to the amniotic fluid. (Making love in bed: shutting yourself away, eliminating the world = to become androgynous).

For Mélanie, burying herself so deeply was a source of happiness: she gave this absolute hole a name: her "dear little grotto." When she's taken to hospital: "Anything you like, but don't take me away from my dear little grotto"; or indeed: "the dear good-great-Back"; or, in her own peculiar made-up language, her "dear-good-back-mill-in-plaster"; "my dear great Back Malampia."

*The Confined Woman of
Poitiers,* p. 147
138, 171

147

Note: because it has a name and what's more a new name, an invented name—*Malampia*—the thing we're describing here, absolute enclosure, is a concept. Mélanie is a logothete[19] (hence a God). Let's call *Malampianism* any movement of affect, however fleeting, that compels the subject to bury themselves, to cover themselves up, to obliterate the world, not in order to follow the path of asceticism (monastic reclusion), but the path of pleasure. You don't need me to remind you that society suppresses Malampianism: the Law wrenches Mélanie from her "dear little grotto," she's made to live in daylight, in a hospital bed, cleanly and religiously.

It's not for me to give a pseudo-psychiatric or pseudo-psychoanalytic explanation—or description—of the types of "madness" associated with reclusion; I note merely that the clinic has a great deal to say about claustro-phobia, but nothing about claustro-philia or claustro-mania. Yet it might be that it's a common experience. Personally, at any rate, I observe traces of it in myself: I like to create enclosed spaces (to work in, to live in, to sleep in), protected by winding paths, by fortifications.

To bring this to a close, I'd like to point up two archetypal forms of the enclosed space—I mention them only because they're paradoxical, in that they appear to be open:

1. *The Labyrinth*: symbolizes the paradoxical labor whereby the subject sets about creating difficulties for himself—walling himself up within the impasses of a system. It is the archetypal space of the obsessive. The labyrinth is the space of active enclosure (≠ the locked cell: you may as well curl up in a corner, unless your name is Edmund Dantès that is!).[20] Endless, futile efforts expended on finding the way out. In the subject's efforts to find the exit, he only exacerbates his own imprisonment. He walks, constantly changes direction, etc., yet remains in the same place. Labyrinth: a system that's hermetically sealed by its autonomy. Example: the system of a love affair; once inside, there's no way out, and yet the labor it requires is immense. Finding a way out: an almost magical act; the glimpse of a different system, through which you then have to pass: Ariadne's thread. The labyrinth is a very effective symbol of that state;[21] an inextricable system of walls, but one that's out in the open air: there's no roof (the episode in Fellini's *Satyricon*).[22] To someone looking on from the outside (looking down from above), the solution is obvious, in contrast to the person inside it: a situation typical of a love affair.

2. A second form, the antithesis of the labyrinth but still an archetypal space of enclosure: one that's even more archetypal be-

Guillaumont, *Philon*

*Le Millénaire du mont
Athos*, p. 163

cause it has no walls: the Desert (*eremos*,[23] eremus → hermit). The anachoritic desert points up the fundamental ambivalence of enclosure: (a) a joyous space of solitude, of calm; the influence of Hellenism (Philo):[24] *hesuchia*[25]; (b) demonic, sterile region: its Egyptian and Semitic representation. What's more, for Christians in the patristic era: *eremus* = a Biblical reality, part of the culture of the time: Exodus, Sinai, Moses, Elias, Eli, John the Baptist, fast and temptation of Christ.[26]

The point I want to make is: the desert = existential theme: *vita eremitica*.[27] Which means it can be experienced with varying degrees of intensity. There's an ultimate degree of intensity, which is what identifies the desert with total reclusion: the "absolute-desert" (*paneremos*)[28] as Anthony experienced it. It's the superlative form of Malampianism: *paneremos* is very much like Mélanie's blanket.

COLONIE D'ANACHORÈTES / COLONY OF ANACHORITES[29]

Let's go back over some of the facts—already referred to—so it's quite clear in our minds that the anachorite (= someone who's animated by a desire for retreat, for withdrawal) is not necessarily someone who lives alone—and that it's groups-constellations of anachorites who best represent the field of idiorrhythmy (which is our field of interest). (*Drop-outs*:[30] those who want to drop everything, who desert the ranks ≠ *drop-ins*, those who fall in somewhere.)[31] Already dealt with in some detail, two types of idiorrhythmic colony: the *skites* on Mount Athos + (very sketchily) beguinages. Here are four more:

1. QUMRAN SECT

Needs to be mentioned because it's Jewish, pre-Christian. The Dead Sea Scrolls (spring 1947). The Manual of Discipline, Hebrew text = small group of men living in retreat in the Juda Desert, at Qumran: holy and austere life. Fled to the desert around 140 B.C. Contemporaries of Jesus Christ. First group: twelve laymen and three priests = twelve tribes and three levitical clans: Israel in miniature. Then an influx of volunteers, new buildings. Why this flight to the desert? Let's say: they were an assimilative group. Opposed to the political and religious authorities in Jerusalem on the question of the calendar;

the decision [taken by Jerusalem] to do away with the traditional liturgical calendar and replace it with the official Hellenistic moon-sun calendar. → Community attached to traditions, sectarian, predominantly sacerdotal. → Ritual purity: no contact with impious men, not even Jews. Organization: authoritarian structure, communal living, the sharing of possessions, a three-year novitiate period, punishments = virtually a coenobitism.

I mention this sect because: a right-wing, assimilative marginality.

2. THE MONKS OF NITRIA

Guillaumont, *Philon*

The desert mountains of Nitria, south of Alexandria, to the west of the Nile (fourth century).[32] A vast colony of five thousand anachorites—six hundred of whom lived out in the desert. Organizing principle: each subject lives in his own hut, situated at some distance from the others, meaning that they live in solitude but can still visit one another. Nitria: a very flexible model:

The Lausiac History, pp. 40–41

— Space: "the central services": a large church, seven bread ovens, a guesthouse (that would receive guests for unlimited periods of time; they allow a guest to remain at leisure for one week; from then on, manual labor—in the garden, in the bakery, in the kitchen; if the guest is educated, he's given a book to read), several doctors. Food: bread and salt; an evening meal.
— Lifestyle: six days in the *cella*; weaving baskets while: meditatively reciting the Scriptures (*melete*,[33] looking after oneself, study, declamation, meditation). Saturday: everyone goes to church + communal meal (*agape*)[34] + prayers throughout the night from Saturday to Sunday = the idiorrhythmic model exactly: a balance between solitude and contact with other people.

Massebieau, pp. 170–289

NB: In the fourth century, the Monks of Nitria were repeating the Therapeuts' experiment, as described by Filon (≠ Essenes, Jews, practical life).[35] Contemplative life, healers of souls and servants of Being. Egypt, on the outskirts of Alexandria: would have received their instruction from Mark.

3. CARTHUSIANS

Encyclopaedia Universalis

Successors of the solitaires of Egypt, of Filon's Therapeuts. #[36] 1084, Bruno, born in Cologne, founds a colony of solitaires in the valley of the Grande Chartreuse.[37] = A vast domain with very definite boundaries (cf. Enclosure) = the "desert"[38] (the bottom of the valley); a narrow pass: easily blocked:

a. The "Low House": brothers: farmers and craftsmen.

b. The "High House": the Fathers' monastery: important liturgical service (based on the Benedictine model, because they would also copy books). Each Father: his own individual *cella* = a small house. On the ground floor: woodshed and workshop. First floor: two rooms: (a) The *Ave Maria*: private kitchen (abolished in 1276), (b)[39] for prayer, reading, eating, sleeping + small garden + veranda (in case of bad weather).

Organizing principle: solitude; prayers carried out in the *cella*. Church (collective): at night (matins and laudes), morning (mass) and afternoon (vespers). Meal taken together: on Sundays. Every week: a communal walk. Note: (a) social division (brothers, fathers)—cf. Infra "Servants": originally, the monk is on the side of *otium*;[40] (b) the individuation of the living space—cf. *The Brothers Karamazov*: Father Zossima doesn't live in the monastery, but in a *skite* (a little house, set apart). More interestingly, to begin with: the individuation of food, of mealtimes.[41] Symbolically, this is very important: a rejection of conviviality[42] (taste ≠ dislike of the communal meal; even today: two different types of subject).

Le Millénaire du mont Athos, p. 361

4. THE SOLITAIRES OF PORT-ROYAL

Formless community: no profession, no vows, no dress code; not even a stable place of abode. Le Maître: "The solitaires are men who live together in accordance with ordinary and general freedom."[43] → No institutional basis. The person who came up with the idea: Saint Cyran. The Carthusian rule: life lived as one + the freedom of solitude.

An empirical grouping from the summer of 1637. Then, a project, the Duc de Luynes's vision: around the abbey = twelve identical hermitages, reserved for twelve specially selected Gentlemen (once again, the twelve tribes, the Tabernacle). In the event of their death, replaced by a preapproved successor = ideal image of Zion.

Noteworthy: despite its Christian, Jansenist aspects, remarkable that the professed, much-repeated founding ethos of the group should be friendship. Determination: the perfection of life ≠ *Telos*: friendship.

Through those four examples, we see what's at stake in these idiorrhythmic experiments. As always: the relation to the institution:[44]

— two assimilative or assimulationist examples: Qumran and the Carthusians;

— two flexible forms: the Nitriotes and Port-Royal.

What emerges: the vulnerability of marginality; the authorities, whether external (coenobitism) or internal (Qumran), are always ready to intervene. Beguinages, Carthusians—a very centralized order. Institutionalization: means of survival. Nitriotes, stamped out by Pachmonian coenobitism. The solitaires: engulfed by the very marginality of Port-Royal, destroyed by power.

COUPLAGE / PAIRING

I'm saying: pairing, not couple, because this trait of Living-Together doesn't deal with the conjugal or pseudo-conjugal couple (even though that kind of couple presents a real problem for communities); it relates only to the pairing of two partners linked—cemented—by a form of mutual alienation ("*folie-à-deux*").

Merely as an introduction to the dossier, I'll indicate: an insubstantial, fleeting, pairing and two examples of strong, structured pairing.

1. THE PRINCIPLE OF PAIRING

Bion, p. 61

Provided by Bion (cf. Supra, "Cause," the second "basic assumption,"[1] one possible *Telos* of the group): " . . . two members of the group would become involved in a discussion; sometimes the exchange between the two could hardly be described but it would be evident that they were involved with each other, and that the group of the whole thought so too." → The group would sit in attentive silence: "Whenever two people begin to have this kind of relationship in a group <a session>—whether these two are man and woman, man and man, or woman and woman—it seems to be a "basic assumption," held by both the group and the pair concerned, that their relationship is a sexual one. It is as if there could be no reason for two people's coming together except sex."

What's being described is the configuring—the provisional arrangement—of the elements in a group: fleeting, transitory, yet generalized and recurrent. Whatever the party, the group: a pair of individuals, animated by a warm relation of mutual interpellation, mutual seduction will isolate themselves, stand slightly apart. Regardless of the motive, the setting, the excuse: it's clear that the pair find each other unsettling, a form of mutual agitation of an erotic (rather than a sexual) sort. In such situations, there can be no doubt that the group becomes a spectator. For a short while, the pair structures the group (it's rare for the pairing to outlast the evening): the fleeting passage of a *folie-à-deux*. It's worth playing on *affolement / folie* {agitation / madness}. The notion of feeling agitated (by something, someone): isn't relevant in psychoanalysis; would belong to a detailed description of relationships. We spend our lives getting agitated by something, by someone.

2. TWO EXAMPLES OF STRONG PAIRING

(1) *The Lausiac History*, chapter 11 in Draguet, *Les Pères du désert*: Story of Eulogius and the cripple.[2] (2) Aunt Léonie and Françoise, *Swann's Way* I, 113–15.[3]

LAUSIAC HISTORY, 71–75

This Eulogius who was, moreover, well educated in the humanities and inspired with a love of immortality, had parted with the excitement of the world and disposed of everything, keeping a little money out for himself, as he was not able to work. Bored, and not wishing to enter a community, he had found someone lying in the marketplace, a cripple who had neither feet nor hands—only his tongue was still functioning and served as contact with passersby. Well, Eulogius stood and looked intently at him and he prayed to God and made a compact with Him: "Lord, in your name I will take this crippled man and look after him until death, so that I may be saved through him. Graciously grant me to endure this undertaking." And he approached the cripple and said to him: "Would you like me, sir, to take you into my house and take care of you?" He replied: "Certainly I would." "Well, I will fetch my mule and take you." It was agreed, he brought the mule, took him to his cell, and looked after him.

The cripple lived then for fifteen years under his care. Eulogius with his own hands washed and looked after him as his needs required. Now after fifteen years a demon assailed the cripple and he turned against Eulogius. He proceeded to abuse the man with foul talk and blasphemy, adding insult to injury: "Assassin, deserter, you steal what belongs to others and wish to be saved through caring for me. Throw me into the marketplace—it is meat I crave." Eulogius bought him meat. Again he called out: "I am not satisfied. Crowds are what I need—I want to go back to the marketplace! What violence! Take me back where you found me!" Had he had hands to do so, he would quickly have choked Eulogius, so much the demon exasperated him.

Eulogius then went off to the ascetics nearby and said: "What should I do? The cripple has led me to despair. Shall I throw him out? I made an oath to God and I fear for myself. But should I not cast him out? I am at a loss to know what to do." Then they said: "As the Great One (for so they called Anthony) still lives, go to him. Take the cripple on a boat and bring him to the monastery. Wait until the Great One comes out of his cave and put the case to him. Whatever he tells you, follow his decision, for God speaks to you through him." Now he agreed with them, put the cripple on a rustic bark, and took him to the monastery of Anthony's disciples. . . .

"I found this cripple in the market place, and I made an oath to God that I would care for him and be saved through him and him through me. Then after all these years he troubles me so that I am of a mind to cast him out. Therefore, I come to your Holiness so you may tell me what I should do, and so that you may pray on my behalf, for I am sorely grieved."

Anthony addressed him in a dignified and austere manner: "You would cast him out? But He who made him would not cast him out. You cast him out? God will raise up a finer man than you and He will gather him up."

Eulogius kept his peace and cowered. Anthony left him and began to lash the cripple verbally and to rail against him; "You cripple, maimed, unworthy of either earth or heaven, why do you not stop fighting against God himself? Do you not realise it is Christ who is your servant? How dare you utter such things against Christ? Did this man not make himself your servant because of Christ?" He was harsh to him, and then he left off. When he had conversed with the rest of them in regard to their wants, he resumed conversation with Eulogius and the cripple in this way: "Do not tarry here, but go. Do not separate from each other, except in the cell which you have shared for so long a time. God is even now calling for you. This temptation has come your way as you are both near death and will be judged worthy to be crowned. Therefore, do nothing else, so that the angel may not find you here when he comes." Quickly they made the journey back to their cell. And in forty days Euogius died, and in three days more the cripple also died.

She would beguile herself with a sudden pretense that Françoise had been robbing her, that she had set a trap to make certain, and had caught her betrayer red-handed; and being in the habit, when she made up a game of cards by herself, of playing her own and her adversary's hands at once, she would first stammer out Françoise's awkward excuses, and then reply to them with such a fiery indignation that any one of us who happened to intrude upon her at one of these moments would find her bathed in perspiration, her eyes blazing, her false hair askew and exposing the baldness of her brows. Françoise must often, from the next room, have heard these mordant sarcasms leveled at herself, the mere framing of which in words would not have relieved my aunt's feelings sufficiently, had they been allowed to remain in a purely immaterial form, without the degree of substance and reality which she added to them by muttering them half-aloud. Sometimes, however, even these counterpane dramas would not satisfy my aunt; she must see her work staged. And so, on a Sunday, with all the doors mysteriously closed, she would confide to Eulalie her doubts of Françoise's integrity and her determination to be rid of her, and another time she would confide to Françoise her suspicions of the disloyalty of Eulalie, to whom the front-door would very soon be closed for good. A few days later she would be sick of her latest confidante and once more "as thick as thieves" with the traitor, but before the next performance, the two would yet again have changed roles. But the suspicions which Eulalie might occasionally arouse in her were no more than a flash in the pan that soon subsided for lack of fuel, since Eulalie was not living with her in the house. It was a very different matter in the case of Françoise, of whose presence under the same roof as herself my aunt was perpetually conscious, though for fear of catching cold were she to leave her bed, she never dared go down into the kitchen to establish whether or not there were any grounds for her suspicions. Gradually her mind came to be exclusively occupied with trying to guess what Françoise might at any given moment be doing behind her back. She would detect a furtive look on Françoise's face, something contradictory in what she said, some desire which she appeared to be concealing. And she would show her that she was unmasked, with a single word, which made Françoise turn pale and which my aunt seemed to find a cruel satisfaction in driving deep into her poor servant's heart.... And so by degrees Françoise and my aunt, the quarry and the hunter, had reached the point of constantly trying to forestall each other's ruses. My mother was afraid lest Françoise should develop a genuine hatred of my aunt, who did everything in her power to hurt her. However that might be, Françoise had come, more and more, to pay an infinitely scrupulous attention to my aunt's least word and gesture. When she had to ask her anything she would hesitate for a long time over how best to go about it. And when she had uttered her request, she would watch my aunt covertly, trying to guess from the expression on her face what she thought of it and how she would reply. And so it was that—whereas an artist who, reading the memoirs of the seventeenth century and, wishing to bring himself nearer to the great Louis, considers that he is making progress in that direction by constructing a pedigree that traces his own descent from some historic family, or by engaging in correspondence with one of the reigning sovereigns in Europe, is actually turning his back on what he mistakenly seeks under identical and therefore moribund forms—an elderly provincial lady, by doing no more than yielding wholeheartedly to her own irresistible eccentricities and a cruelty born of idleness, could see; without ever having given a thought to Louis XIV, the most trivial occupations of her daily life, her morning toilet, her lunch, her afternoon nap, assume, by virtue of their despotic singularity, something of the interest that was to be found in what Saint-Simon called the 'mechanics' of life at Versailles; and was able, too, to persuade herself that her silences, a suggestion of good humour or of haughtiness on her features, would provide Françoise with matter for a mental commentary as intense with passion and terror as did the silence, the good humour or the haughtiness of the King when a courtier, or even his greatest nobles, had presented a petition to him in an avenue at Versailles.[4]

Structure common to both of these instances of *folie-à-deux*:

1. Idleness of one of the pair. Aunt Léonie: total inaction, absence of events, claustration. Eulogius: sells his possessions, gives them away, but retains a small income because he doesn't want to work.

2. Léonie's anxious, difficult, capricious personality. Eulogius complains wherever he is: alone, in a group (the cripple: never happy: wants meat, people around him, etc. = troublesome, spoilt children: "*chaouchoun*").[5]

3. Physical inertia of one of the pair. Léonie in bed (she can't even get to the kitchen); the cripple: no hands, no legs, a sort of object that gets carried around like a parcel (on a mule, a bark).

4. A nurse-patient, anaclitic relation.[6] One of the pair entirely dependent on the other, they've relinquished their body, daily contact on the basic bodily level: caring for, washing, feeding.

5. Intense linguistic relation. The cripple is extremely talkative. Léonie: in a continuous spurt of interior language (sometimes the pressure mounts to such a degree that she speaks out loud).

6. A binding cohabitation contract. Françoise will be a servant for life, a kind of feudal devotion (Françoise represents Old France). Eulogius: solemn contract made before God (that's precisely his problem): symbolic and quasi-juridical, like the contract of marriage.

7. Verbal attacks, scenes (or the fantasy of them), angry outbursts, allegations. Trying to come up with the accusation that will hurt the most: that Françoise is a thief, that Eulogius just wants to save his soul on the back of a cripple.

8. The only possible dénouement: death.

Folie-à-deux: In how many households, families (mother / daughter), couples? Inextricable mixture of hate and love (Françoise's wild grief at Léonie's death). Such strong pairing points to an archetypal relation: quarry / hunter (the comparison is Proust's), victim / executioner, with the possibility of the roles being reversed → a situation (or structural fact): Sadeian, Dostoevskian.

DISTANCE / DISTANCE

Living-Together, especially idiorrhythmic Living-Together, implies an ethics (or a physics) of distance between cohabiting subjects. The problem is a formidable one—without doubt the fundamental problem of Living-Together and consequently of this lecture course. We will approach the problem through fragments, partial, indirect themes. Here, I'll briefly set out one of the forms that the problem can take (but by no means propose a solution): the distance between bodies (in Living-Together).

The problem can be formulated as an aporia, and that aporia is a chain:

1. I find other people's bodies—someone else's body—unsettling, disconcerting. I desire, I experience the energy and the absence of desire, I engage in the exhausting strategies of desire.

2. From my confusion, I infer, I fantasize a state that ought to make it go away: *hesuchia*:[7] respite from desire, a vacancy without distress, equanimity.

3. I then set out the rules that would enable me to achieve *hesuchia*. Generally speaking, they're rules of distance with respect to other bodies—which are what give rise to desire.

4. But by extinguishing my desire for the other, for others, I extinguish the desire to live. If I'm never unsettled by someone else's body, if I can never touch anyone else, what's the point in living? The aporia is closed.

In the Christian monastic system, the subject stops at number three (rules of distance). He breaks the chain at the right moment, appealing to the properly religious *Telos*: the desire for perfection. He changes desire, he switches to a different desire. If he doesn't redirect his desire, he falls into acedy: or, more specifically, he falls between two desires. Whence the meticulous rigor of the monastic rules with respect to distances between bodies:

Amand, p. 191

1. It's worth making a finer distinction than is usually proposed between: (a) the depreciative ideology of the body: to kill the body, dematerialize it, disdain it, punish it, etc. and (b) the rules of distance = rules of distance, rules propedeutic to redirecting desire. Not mistreating it, but suspending it: *epoché*:[8] suspension of judgment and suspension of desire? Suspend ≠ abolish.

2. Those rules of distance: so specific that they're formulated in purely spatial, metrical terms:

Ladeuze, p. 264

a. Sleep: detailed prescriptions. Pachomius: prohibits two monks from sleeping together in the same cell. Saint Benedict: all monks are to sleep in their own separate beds. St Benedict, chap. 22: "The youngest brothers are not to sleep in beds next to each other, but between the elders." ≠ *The Banquet*: the exchange of positions (of beds) is wholly eroticized.

Ladeuze, p. 282

b. The body is completely isolated, meticulously enveloped by distance. Pachomius's rules:

Totum corpus nemo unguet nisi causa infirmitatis
nec lavabitur aqua nudo corpore.
Nullus lavare alterum poterit aut unguere.
Nemo alteri loquatur in tenebris.
Manum alterius ne teneat, sed, sive steterit, sive ambulaverit,
  uno cubito distet ab altero.[9]

What's remarkable about that series of interdictions: subtle, keen sense of the paths of desire = auto-eroticism (washing naked, spending hours in the shower), a functional excuse for touching someone else's body (washing someone else: the threshold between anaclitism[10] and erotic pleasure: the mother caring for her newborn baby), talking without being able to see the person you're talking to (intense eroticism of language, of nighttime), the strategic play of distances (always keeping the other at an arm's length) ≠ all the strategies of furtive contact (cf. *Werther*).[11] → A veritable manual of the pleasures of contact, of brushing up against. (The meaning of brushing up against: not genital satisfaction, but—herein lies the perversion—seeking to relieve a frustration. The other's body isn't prohibited. I prove it to myself by touching it—even if I do so under the cover of an innocent pretext.)[12]

The best of distances, because there's investment in an activity, a labor of distanciation: alert; keeping your body on alert, in control:

St. Benedict, chap. 22

Ladeuze, p. 301

Amand, p. 220

— Lights on in the dormitory until morning (Saint Benedict): the theme of surveillance.
— Likewise: Pachomius; sleeping upright on low seats—rather than lying flat.
— Symbolism of the belt. Saint Basil: monks: a tunic with a belt; sign of virility:[13] a will poised to act. Job 38:3: "Gird up now thy loins like a man." (Even today: belt = virility: big leather belts, dressing like a cowboy, leather outfits, SM;[14] braces are no longer in fashion,[15] etc.)

In sum, a set of rules elaborated according to a very subtle understanding of the workings of desire. Opposition between: (1) a thematics of sensuousness: skin and language; the child's polymorphous perversion:[16] the caresses of babble ≠ (2) a thematics of the muscles, of tension, of the loins as the origin of genital movement.

To bring things to a close (but not to conclude), two corrective notes:

1. The body's "armor" (Reich),[17] or the body as armor. Not just in the case of monks; in the majority of modern subjects: the body protects itself from its desire for the other. A protection that's often distressing for the subject, who finds himself unable to "let go." In such cases, certain drugs can have the desired effect (*yellow pills*):[18] not aphrodisiacs, but ones that help you come out of your shell. Very occasionally, that relaxing of the rules, could occur among the

monks themselves: during prayer, seeing his "neighbor fall asleep during psalmody" Poemen the monk "gently moved his head, and let him finish his nap on his lap."

2. Control over the body's eroticism: in our Christian culture: the solution is to mutilate, castrate, the fantasy of castration.[19] The story of Elias, who takes a great interest in the welfare of virgins. Elias teaches at a monastery of three hundred women in the town of Athribé; the women quarrel, so he's obliged to go and live among them. → Tormented → he dreams he's being castrated → he awakes, cured of all passion.

But in the Orient, Tao: a non-mutilating form of control; *coitus reservatus*: a completely different philosophy of the orgasm to that of the very Occidental Reich.[20] The orgasm isn't the Sovereign Good: a deeply considered theory of perverse sexuality, one approaching this utopia: that of non-repression (the child is the absolutely utopian figure of humanity in the grips of repression).

DOMESTIQUES / SERVANTS

Let's refer to a classical distinction: man lives off his needs and his desires. Now, Living-Together is a field of desire, and idiorrhythmy is the subtle (non-scientific, notionally or only ineffectually institutionalized) form of that desire. But alongside that desire, what happens to needs? How do needs get satisfied? Who takes care of the domestic tasks? Thorny issue for modern "communes": Who does the washing up? → The problem of servants. Note: in cultures of slavery, needs are automatically distinguished from desires. On this, see the description of an instance of Living-Together in Ancient Greek society: the community (*oikia*),[21] the "house" as described by Xenophon in his *OEconomicus*: an absolutely hierarchical and functionalist community. The problem servants / no servants presents itself in cultures where there's no slavery. It only becomes active, pertinent (yes / no) in the Christian world.

1. NEED = DESIRE

Individuals or communities where, for a given subject, the satisfaction of domestic needs and the satisfaction of desires are deemed to amount to the same thing (let's say, to simplify: the sublimated, contemplative life of a subject devoted to a religious *Telos*). → Exemption from all domesticity: the contemplative subject is responsible for meeting his own needs, which he duly reduces to a bare minimum:

Draguet, p. xxi

1. Anachorites in the patristic era: Oriental monks (Egypt, Palestine, Syria, Constantinople). Overwhelmingly from the peasant classes: either lacking in culture or they reject it (Anthony refuses to study so as to avoid being corrupted by culture); anti-intellectualist marginality. Each anachorite is solely responsible for the totality of his needs.

Festugière, I, p. 48

— Sometimes, it's simply a matter of a young disciple, a *famulus*[22] whose role, incidentally, is less that of a servant than a courier, enabling an elder to remain in reclusion. In such cases, the exchange (sublimated domesticity) is a matter of spiritual goods: the wisdom, the perfection of the "elder" in exchange for small services performed by the "youth."

Robinson Crusoe, pp. 202–209

— *Robinson Crusoe*: world of slavery. Robinson: traffics slaves to Brazil. Living-Together with Friday is a matter of living with a slave. Signs → (a) Friday places Robinson's foot on his head himself (as if it were the essential nature of a black man to be instantly enslaved); (b) The first word Robinson Crusoe teaches Friday to say is "master"; (c) While Robinson Crusoe teaches Friday to speak English (to ensure his needs will be met), Friday doesn't teach Robinson Crusoe to speak his language; (d) Friday is almost as well-dressed as his master. Yet, prior to the shipwreck, when Robinson Crusoe himself was a slave (the property of one of the Salé pirates, from whom he escapes on a small boat), he strikes up a friendship with Xury, a young boy. Their arrangement has all the appearances of a *famulus*: experience in exchange for services. But in fact, when it comes to it, Robinson sells him: so Xury is indeed a slave.

38

2. *Athos*: we've seen two sorts of idiorrhythmy: one old, on the "pure" (and "strict") eremitic model and another, more recent, which incorporates social divisions: wealthy monks (with a source of income) and monks who act as their servants, monks who're assigned domestic tasks. Originally, Athos: idiorrhythmy with no servants, even with a rule prohibiting servants. This needs to be set alongside a much misunderstood particularity of Athos: the rule prohibiting access to female animals; possibly introduced by Saint Athanasius. Apparently it has nothing to do sexual morality. Relates to the rule prohibiting servants: to prevent monasteries from living off any in-

J. Leroy, *Le Millénaire du mont Athos*, p. 114

come earned from herds tended by waged servants. (Once you have herds you have to have slaves or servants.) The five colonizers in *The Mysterious Island* assign the task of tending the herd (in the corral) to the condemned Ayrton, whom they found on another island—so "crime" ([*The Children of Captain Grant*] converts him, through atonement, into a pseudoslave).[23]

2. NEED ≠ DESIRE

To dedicate itself to spiritual occupations (to spiritual desire), the community delegates the task of meeting its needs to a functional group of servant-monks:

Bareau, p. 75

Bareau

— In the coenobitic monasteries: the convers; *convertiti*:[24] the converted. It's the price of conversion, the price paid for integration + lack of education, peasants, the reinstating of social divisions. As we saw, Carthusians: brothers (Low House) ≠ fathers (idiorrhythmy as luxury).[25]
— The Buddhist monasteries of Ceylon (moderate Buddhism): monks are relieved of their daily tasks by a team of domestic staff: (a) old people with no profession and no family who choose to end their days doing small domestic tasks = the *upasaka*; (b) teenagers who see the work as a way of financing their studies; (c) waged servants, paid for by laymen. This brings us back to the social specificity of the Singhalese monasteries: living conditions modeled on those of the petite and moyenne bourgeoisie.

Clearly, this communitary problem repeats the major structural problems of all societies: the division of labor, exchange, class divisions, the reconstruction of a social microcosm at the margins of society, the circumscription of an idle, privileged group. But what I find more interesting is the internal structuring within the two groups: masters / servants. It's a structure of reproduction, imitation, anamorphosis, duplication: the masters are reflected in their servants, but the image reflected back is a distorted one, a farcical image.

The *famuli*,[26] the convers: conscious of being lesser, uneducated versions of the grand solitaires, the incomparable fathers. *Convertiti*: only recently converted: it's as if they're forcing themselves to mimic the status of the group they wish to join.

Zola gives a very precise description of this game of farcical duplication in the communal space that is the apartment building in

Pot Luck. Two types of human being: the bourgeoisie, the masters (grand apartments, off the main staircase) ≠ the servants (the servants' entrance, opening onto the courtyard), a category that includes the adulterers: the kept mistresses. Now, between those two types of humanity, their replicated representations:

Pot Luck I, p. 134 and elsewhere

— The domestic staff: the farcical reproduction of the masters' speech. In the little courtyard (the kitchens), the repressed language of the masters is unpacked and reflected back in vulgar language.

I, p. 3

— The concierges, Monsieur and Madame Gourd, mimic the respectability of apartment-owners. Monsieur Gourd, with his long, clean-shaven face like a diplomat's, reads *Le Moniteur*.[27] The lodge: like a dining room, with its shining mirrors, red-flowered carpet, rosewood furniture and a bed hung with garnet rep: the concierges dress themselves up as the sorts of people who require concierges.

I, p. 170, 143

— Clarisse, Duveyrier's mistress: the decor in her rooms reproduces that of a respectable woman. Ultrarespectability: she owns a piano, an instrument that exasperates the husband.

I'm merely opening a dossier (a vast dossier) whose question would be: every division implies—or necessitates—a mirror. Whence: the mirroring effects of the divisions in the social field.

ÉCOUTE / HEARING

Hierarchy of the five senses: not only is it different for animals and for man (dogs: smell → hearing → sight), it's changed over the history of humankind. Febvre:[1] medieval man: the prevalence of hearing over sight; then, since the Renaissance, a reversal. A culture of sight: hearing is now of secondary importance. Perhaps it's simply been repressed? → Space of Living-Together: active traces of hearing. Here, hearing is constitutive of something. Once again, we're opening a dossier.

TERRITORY AND HEARING

Animal territory: often marked out by smell. Human territory, its boundaries (a) can be defined by sight: everything the eye can see belongs to me[2] (there must be legends about this); (b) can be defined by touch: everything within touching range, everything within my gestural range, within an arm's reach belongs to me: it's the nest, the microterritory (cf. infra "Proxemics"). But also:

— Territory: a polyphonic network of familiar sounds: the ones I'm able to identify and thereafter function as signs of my space.
— Kafka and the apartment (*Diaries*, p. 104):[3]

I sit in my room in the very headquarters of the uproar of the entire apartment. I hear all the doors slam, because of their noise only the footsteps of those running between them are spared me, I hear even the slamming of the oven door in the kitchen. My father bursts through the doors of my room and passes through in his dragging dressing-gown, the ashes are scraped out of the stove in the next room, Valli asks, shouting into the indefinite through the ante-room as though through a Paris street, whether Father's hat has been brushed yet, a hushing that claims to be friendly to me raises the shout of an answering voice. The house door is unlatched and screeches as though from a catarrhal throat, then opens wider with the brief singing of a woman's voice and closes with a dull manly jerk that sounds most inconsiderate. My father is gone, now begins the more delicate, more distracted, more hopeless noise led by the voices of the two canaries.

= A veritable sonorous, familial landscape: reassuring. Interesting, because the landscape is discontinuous, erratic and yet at the same time very coded—whence the force of the unfamiliar sound: an unexpected silence or unidentifiable noise that calls for an inner labor of interpretation. The difference between the apartment and the house in this respect. Apartment: a very limited, masterable range of sounds. House: heightened risk of there being an unfamiliar noise. House: fantastical object; a whole folklore of the fear produced by an unidentifiable noise. Apartment: safety, because you can be sure that the distant sound of a tap or the radiator behind the wall comes from a neighbor. House: integrates all noises. All its noises belong to me, concern me: I'm targeted by the unfamiliar noise.

REPRESSION AND HEARING

Relations between hearing and sexuality; identified and proposed by Freud: notably, the theory of the Primal Scene[4] (scene of hearing) and the case study that appears to contradict the theory of paranoia (the clicking of the camera and the clicking of the clitoris):[5]

The Magic Mountain, p. 40

— Within a community, a form of erotic hearing, listening in on the pleasure that calls out to me and from which I'm excluded. Hans Castorp overhearing his Russian neighbors making love in the room next door.

The Conquest of Plassans, p. 18

— Then, the insuperable mechanics of covert listening: listening in, eavesdropping on someone else, on other people. In *Pot Luck,* the entire apartment building is a space of eavesdropping and espionage. The wall, that boundary line of respectability, a mask pulled over the eyes, can be penetrated by the ear. A good example: Mouret, the idle owner, eagerly listening in on his tenant, the priest. A sexual interest in the priest in the nineteenth century: Zola, Michelet, Goncourt (the Noah complex?):[6] "Henceforth he would have an occupation, an amusement which would relieve the monotony of his everyday life."

— Idyllic, utopian community: a space where there's no repression, that is to say no listening, where there would be hearing but no listening. Absolutely transparent sonority = the very definition of music. With music, we're not listening in on anything or anyone else—nor, in a sense, are we listening.

Alternative to this lifting of repression: a space where all the noises are wholly coded: a monastery. The bell, at once the instrument of rules and the fullest expression of a noise without anxiety, without paranoia; whence its metonymy with the heavens.

ÉPONGE / SPONGE

I'll justify my use of this word in a moment.

It's possible for individual subjects (any one of us) to have fantasies of Living-Together. We set about elaborating a fantasmatic form of Living-Together, selecting our would-be companions from our network of acquaintances. Now, what's interesting about that fantasmatic elaboration is not who we choose, but who we exclude: the criteria for exclusion don't necessarily overlap with the imperatives of affect. The criteria are often subtle, and merit study.

In many communities: this paradox (the object of this figure): what's excluded is included, but retains its status as excluded. It's the contradictory status of the pariah: rejected and integrated, integrated as a reject.[7] Perhaps there's no such thing as a community without an integrated reject. Take the world of today: very different types of societies, but probably not one without its integrated reject. All societies jealously guard their rejects, prevent them from leaving. So what would be needed as part of a globalized sociology is a theory of the incorporated reject, of the retained reject (simply: the different forms of hypocrisy, of ideological justification with regard to the pariah, who no longer tends to be recognized as such).

The Lausiac History, p. 96

From our corpus: "The Nun who Feigned Madness":

[Women's monastery, p. 96]: *In this monastery there was another maiden who feigned madness and demon-possession. The others felt such contempt for her that they never ate with her, which pleased her entirely. Taking herself to the kitchen she used to perform every menial service and she was, as the saying goes, "the sponge of the kitchen", putting these words of Scripture into practice:* If any man among you may seem wise in this world, let him become a fool that he may be wise.[8]

Cf. Tao, Grenier, 125: "*Even if wise, pretend to be mad (persist in living as a recluse), that's the essential truth.*"

[That sponge]⁹ *wore a rag round her head—all the others had their hair closely cropped and wore cowls. In this way she used to serve. Not one of the four hundred ever saw her eating all the years of her life. She never sat down at table or partook of a particle of bread, but she wiped up with a sponge the crumbs from the tables and was satisfied with scouring pots. She was never angry at anyone, nor did she grumble or talk, either too little or too much, although she was maltreated, insulted, cursed and loathed.*

Then there's the evangelical reversal: an angel appears to Saint Piteroum, and tells him that there is someone more pious than himself. Piteroum goes to the convent (p. 97).

[Upon his arrival at the convent]: *he insisted upon seeing all of them. She did not appear. Finally he said to them: "Bring them all to me, for she is missing." They told him: "We have one inside the kitchen who is touched"—that is what they call the afflicted ones. He told them: "Bring her to me. Let me see her." They went to call her; but she did not answer, either because she knew of the incident or because it was revealed to her. They seized her forcibly and told her: "The holy Piteroum wishes to see you"—for he was renowned. When she came he saw the rag on her head and, falling down at her feet, he said: "Bless me!" In a similar manner she too fell down at his feet and said: "Bless me, lord." All the women were amazed at this and said: "Father, take no insults. She is touched." Piteroum then addressed all the women: "You are the ones who are touched! This woman is your spiritual mother"—so they called them spiritually—"to both you and me and I pray that I may be deemed as worthy as she on the Day of Judgment." Hearing this, they fell at his feet, confessing various things— one how she had poured the leavings of her plate over her; another had beaten her with her fists; another had blistered her nose. So they confessed various and sundry outrages. After praying for them, he left. And after a few days she was unable to bear the praise and honor of the sisters, and all their apologizing was so burdensome to her that she left the monastery. Where she went and where she disappeared to, and how she died, nobody knows.*¹⁰

We're reminded of Greimas's actantial model.¹¹ Subject → Object + Sender / Receiver + Opposer / Helper. The model is too rational, too replete and harmonious: what's missing is the Reject-Actant, the Sponge. Depending on the role played by the Reject-Actant, it might even be possible to imagine—merely as a working hypothesis— a typology of narratives and communities, of fictional communities:

1. Community where the actant is present: integrated reject (*The Lausiac History*). *The Lord of the Flies*: one of the kids in the gang is assigned the role of sponge: Piggy. *Pot Luck*: Adèle, the serving girl; bourgeois apartment building: circles of social standing. The masters' social standing (and that of the different floors of the building) is mirrored by analogy in that of the servants (cf. "Servants"). The lowest-ranking family (on the top floor), the Pichons: no maid. The poorest family used to be the Josserands (the mother who's desperately trying to marry her daughters): they have a serving girl, Adèle. Zola sees it all very clearly: Adèle is the sponge, not only the masters' sponge, but also that of the servants, who dispose of their own communal space, the kitchen courtyard, where she's routinely mocked and abused. Doubly a sponge: her solitude as the absolute pariah is illustrated by the horrific childbirth scene. Adèle secretly gives birth alone in her tiny attic room, with no one to help or to look out for her; the infant is thrown in the rubbish, and life goes on as normal. Pariah = a blank (cf. The madwoman's departure, her fainting fit in the *Lausiac History*).

2. Narratives where there's no Reject-Actant: (1) *Robinson Crusoe*: space (a) of shared solitude (with Friday), (b) of a group of slaves (a different problem = more straightforwardly economic: slaves ≠ pariahs. (2) *The Magic Mountain*: no rejects. In a sense, this is bizarre, a "failing" of the narrative: but, on a human level, it's actually an idyllic narrative. Its "darkness" comes from death, not from affects. The reject = death. In its account of the community: a very civilized, humane narrative.

3. A wholly paradoxical structure: when the Reject-Actant gets confused with the Subject-Actant; when the two actants get mixed up within the same agent. The Sponge is the Subject of the narrative: the confined woman of Poitiers as "actor." In terms of her novelistic attributes, on the authority of the descriptions: she's the absolute reject (the waste-bin-grotto, filth, excrement, rodents); yet at the same time it's Mélanie who's the enigma-Subject of the narrative. (A paradoxical Subject, because there's no Object, no quest: it's society, the police that turn it into a narrative).

All of these can be linked: either to a theory of the Scapegoat (cf. René Girard, *Violence and the Sacred*) or to the theory of the sorcerer as per Lévi-Strauss (*Introduction to Structural Anthropology*). A community fixates on someone or something as the source of all its ills (a target for its grievances) and it's this that then enables it to exorcise it, to get rid of it. I integrate the anomic by coding its position as anomic. I allow it back in, but in a position where it poses no threat = if they're shrewd enough, it's what authorities do to marginalities. They set up reservations (like for Indians). They turn intellectuals, for example, into a distinctive, recognized caste.[12] For, to bring things to a close, the final twist in the handling of the reject problem involves glorifying, honoring, consecrating the reject. It's what the monastery would like to do. So, if he or she reflects for a moment, all the reject need do is go further away: which is precisely what our "Sponge" does.

ÉVÉNEMENT / EVENT

Why does *Robinson Crusoe,* a novel about solitude, figure in our corpus? Because Living-Together, especially idiorrhythmic Living-Together, must incorporate the values of Living-Alone as its paradigmatic opposite. Now, reading *Robinson Crusoe,* and making an attempt to analyze my reading pleasure, I note—for me personally, at any rate—the following:

In my reading, I (presumably) do the opposite to what so-called normal readers do, and contravene the author's intention. With the exception of the episode with Friday, which involves the intrusion of an affect, all the other events impinging on Robinson Crusoe's solitary existence on the island (to do with the savages, cannibals) interfere with my pleasure as a reader, I find them irritating. A charm—the powerful charm of the book—is broken. Its charm is precisely that of a day-to-day existence with no events. I find I'm no longer able to fantasize about the way Robinson Crusoe organizes his life, his domestic set-up, the hut, the vines, the bucolic. The event turns me into a different kind of subject. I become a subject of suspense, of the murder of the Father—I'm no longer a subject of the nest, of the Mother: the event as Father (Oedipus and the protocol of the event; all events are Oedipal).[13] The charm of *Robinson Crusoe* = the non-event.

To fantasize Living-Together as an everyday reality: to refuse, repel, violently reject the event. The event is the enemy of Living-Together: (a) Pachomius's prescriptions: no news is to be admitted into the community; (b) within a small community, the ambiva-

Robinson Crusoe, # p. 226

lence of subjects who "take the initiative" (a character type that, in my view, the various branches of psychology have not yet fully recognized). The initiative, the invention of what's more or less unexpected has to be a communal affair: a welcome distraction + the danger of introducing something new into the affective network, generating what's most harmful to Living-Together: the repercussion. → Durable-interminable systems: ones with no "initiatives." That of the Confined Woman, for example, can be defined—necessarily and adequately—as a total absence of events over a twenty-five year period. The sanatorium in *The Magic Mountain* only consolidates its status as a community once it ceases to respond to outside events (the last pages).

The "suspension of events, of initiatives": a fairly apt definition of Tao; relates to the principle of Taoism: *Wou-wei*, non-action:

Jean Grenier, *L'Esprit du Tao* (Flammarion, 1973), p. 108 *sq*.

— Lao-Tzu (p. 127): "Act without action; do without doing; taste without tasting; view the big, the small, the many, the few with the same eye; set the same store by reproaches as by thanks; *that is the way of the Wise Man*." (for our purposes, let's not say the Saint, or the Wise Man, the words have too many connotations—let's simply say the Tao subject.)

— *Wou-wei* involves much more than the rejection of the event. It's a method that entails a whole way of living. It's not just a matter of avoiding the event, but of not inviting it: "do nothing evil, for fear of being punished; do nothing good, for fear, having acquired a good reputation, of being charged with time-consuming and dangerous functions." (p. 108). Abstain from exercising authority, from fulfilling a role. If you have no choice, treat both the "good" and the "bad" as you would children (kindness, not charity, "transcendent" goodness.) (p. 110) Don't judge, speak little, cease to acknowledge logical and moral oppositions, and all distinctions generally speaking (p. 111). Whence the two key images of *Wou-wei*, the Mirror: "The <Tao subject> uses his mind as a mirror: he does not respond to things, nor does he anticipate them; he reflects them without retaining them . . ." etc. (p. 112)—and still Water, calm Water. Let's note, even if it's not directly related to our topic:

1. *Wou-wei* has some perfectly scandalous political effects. For us, it's in the political realm that *Wou-wei* seems wholly inconceivable: our entire civilization is in the Will-to-Act; but that's a different dossier to be opened (Grenier, *L'Esprit du Tao*).

2. The *Wou-wei*, particularly with its inflections of quietism and negative mysticism, seems to have some affinity with the Christian monastic ideal. But a hair separates them, and that hair is not nothing: God, Revelation, the Bible (likewise for Muslims). Similarly for Zen Buddhism: the Zen subject, whatever form his *Wou-wei* takes, is absent from the world, he considers the world to be nothing, he's elsewhere, even if that elsewhere is nothing. The Tao subject is always present. Proof = anecdotes, parables, examples: sharp sense of humour, keen sense of "life," of "reality." Yes, he thinks that the world is an illusion, but one with the sharply defined contours of a vision: I'll say that [the Taoist sage] accepts the Imaginary, he doesn't divert it toward schism.

FLEURS / FLOWERS

Ceylon Monastery: courtyards and gardens: trees, lawns, flowering shrubs, like a private garden. And Mélanie, who'd spent twenty-five years living among rodents, in filth and in darkness, no doubt willingly and gratuitously (no religious gain), once she's taken to hospital: asks for flowers, adores them.

Accordingly, I'd like to propose a "dossier on flowers" that, to my knowledge, no one has ever opened. Flowers (in gardens, on tables) go without saying. Now, it's when something "goes without saying" that it needs to be looked at closely—and it then emerges that what "goes without saying" is in fact comprised of a number of unanswered questions. Those questions would be the following: Why flowers? Put simply: some lines of inquiry the dossier could pursue:

1. Flowers: associated with the myth of Paradise. Xenophon: gardens = paradises. *Hoi paradeisoi*,[14] avestic (Iranian): *pairidaeza*: the King of Persia's vast oriental gardens. In all likelihood, representation of a climatic optimum: "paradise"; its origins in hot countries = the opposite of too hot. Garden = a luxury that's anti-nature, privilege of the Lord: top-end product and pleasure.

2. Flowers as an offering to the gods: especially in Buddhism. On the way to the temple, the layman stops to buy flowers. The flower-seller presents them on a little tray that the layman will return on his way out. Inside the temple, he offers them to Buddha, arranging them on a table, the table of offerings: the flowers are always cut at the sepal (≠ bouquet; stems = unaesthetic). Note: thematically, the

p. 115

Bareau, p. 11

The Confined Woman of Poitiers, p. 147

Bareau, p. 11

exact opposite of the carnal offering: blood, fat, victim. Religion with no victim; so not strictly [speaking] a religion: a ritual that originates elsewhere, but where? Indeed, ancient religions, Judaism, and even Christianity: offering the flesh incarnate ("This is my blood, this is my body . . ." etc.). A question that's been quite extensively studied by anthropology. But flowers? Probably the essence of luxury, of the supplement: what exceeds or falls short of being a useful fruit. Can only be understood within an economy of luxury, albeit a modest one:[15] in country churches, the meager (and unaesthetic) bouquets that get set down at the feet of plaster Sulpician virgins ≠ ostentatious bouquets in bourgeois churches.

3. Flowers, arrangements of flowers: as an object incorporated into symbolic practices. Relates to a classic paradigm: scarcity / profusion: (a) the profuse, abundant, overflowing bouquet; the spray: Expense, Celebration, Potlatch, Mme Verdurin's bouquets at the Raspelière or Odette Swann's;[16] (b) the small, elliptical bouquet: a whole mythology; the child's gift (theme of wildflowers), the tiny bouquet of violets (symbolic gesture + coding of the violet: humility, discretion) and above all the Zen bouquet: *ikebana*,[17] scarcity animated by a complex symbolic system (in Japan: you can take classes in *ikebana*). Bouquet (from *bosquet*):[18] etymologically, suggests the composite and the few (cf. a wine's *bouquet*). Actually, two contradictory themes of essence: an essence represented by plenitude, the infinite, the inexhaustible ≠ an essence represented by the scarce, the insubstantial, the reduced (Valéry: the essential thinness of things).[19]

4. Finally: flowers = colors. Now, color = would be of the order of a drive. The flower would be the culturally coded offering or figuration of a drive: the drive as delicate (fragile, perishable).

There are many other ways in which the dossier could be expanded, notably around: the *aesthetic* (paintings of flowers); the *metonymic* (flowers, metonymy of the seasons); the *hermeneutic* (the language of flowers); the *sociological* (How are flowers used today, in our society? It's a whole industry). But it's likely that the flower's meaning springs from: the fact of it being of no use (≠ fruit), scarce (climate-dependent), of color (to do with the drives).

To bring this dossier to a close, I'll provide two anecdotes; what you make of them will depend on what sort of person you are:[20]

1. Marcel Liebman: *Leninism under Lenin*: "In the memoirs on Lenin that Valentinov, one of Lenin's first companions in combat—

cf. A. Bois

though he would not be for long—left us, it is related that one day a question of doctrine was debated among the entourage of the future founder of the Soviet regime: Could a professional revolutionary legitimately like flowers? One of Lenin's comrades, animated by a zeal that even his leader judged excessive, claimed it was forbidden: you start by liking flowers and before you know it you are seized by the desire to live like a landowner lazily stretched out in a hammock who reads French novels and is waited on by obsequious valets in the midst of his magnificent garden."[21]

Bois, p. 19

2. At the time of his *Compositions in the Square* (# 1924), Mondrian was still drawing flowers, solely as a means to make ends meet. Consequently, in that period (that of full-blown "abstraction") Mondrian would still paint the odd flower, which he had no trouble selling to his friends in Holland. Whence Brassaï's comment as he left Mondrian's studio: "There's a man who paints flowers to live. And why does he want to live? So he can paint straight lines."

IDYLLIQUE / IDYLL[22]

Let's call "idyllic" any space of human relations defined by an absence of conflict. (Note: idyllic, in the modern sense—"How idyllic!"—is recent. *Littré*: a short lyrical poem on a rural theme).

Idyll is not exactly the description of a utopia. Fourier's utopia doesn't eliminate conflicts, it acknowledges them (therein lies its great originality): it stages conflicts, and as a result succeeds in neutralizing them. "Idyllic," in contrast, as its etymology suggests, refers to a literary representation (or fantasmatization) of its relational space.

Example of an idyllic network (an idyllic Living-Together): the five colonists from *The Mysterious Island*: Cyrus Smith, the scholar, the engineer, the chief + Harbert, the very young man, the very gifted pupil + Gideon Spilett, the reporter + Pencroff, the sailor, the laborer + Nab, negro and cook. Note: it's a social microcosm. Upper classes: the scientist, the reporter, the pupil = the "managers" + a proletarian + a sub-proletarian, almost a slave, an animal even (the affectivity of a dog).

Here's how the relations between the five characters who live together are described:

<pre>
                   Attachment
                      →
     1. Cyrus   ←→   Harbert
                      ←→   Keenly felt, respectful friendship

         Pencroff   ←→   Nab
         Very fond of each other, speak to one another familiarly

     2. Nab   ←→   Cyrus
                   Devotion
</pre>

Pencroff sees Cyrus + Harbert but isn't jealous.

3. Spilett: the reporter, the intellectual: not one affective marker.

Note:

1. Reciprocity only exists within the same class. So: affective equilibrium: differentiation of feeling (attachment / respectful friendship) → complementary nuances. Between social classes, no reciprocity, and no contamination (Pencroff sees, but isn't jealous).

2. In reality, feelings are structured by social divisions. Cf. Eighteenth-century theater, from Marivaux to Beaumarchais: *pathos* of the masters ≠ *pathos* of the valets; but precisely as a result of (what sets everything off): disturbance, interferences, contamination, genetic recombinations. Order is only (artificially) reestablished when those acting on feeling return to or are made to return to their social rank. The (literary) idyll = the form that erases social or parasocial reality, on the one hand, by leaving it in place, not subverting it, allowing it the differences between its homogeneities and, on the other, by scotomizing the abrasion, the friction, the chafing between those distinct homogeneities = the world, the creation of Noah's Ark. Man and animal are kept apart, but they get along.

3. Lastly, note the atopical position of the intellectual. He's neither a manager nor a laborer, he's assigned no responsibility in terms of tasks, roles: he therefore has no affective existence.

MARGINALITÉS / MARGINALITIES

Encyclopaedia Universalis

In the Occident, from the tenth century on:[1] inclination toward idiorrhythmy (notably: Athos). Particular individuals (or individuals in very small groups) permitted to live at a distance from the community center: the *skites* on Mount Athos, still very close to the main monasteries, the Carthusians, Father Zosima in *The Brothers Karamazov*.[2] We're therefore dealing with an experience of marginality. But—in the Occident at least—that marginality: secondary, isolated with regard to a first marginality, that of coenobitism itself, which is a first marginality → two marginalities: of the community / idiorrhythmic.

FIRST MARGIN: COENOBITISM

Festugière, I, # 18

Christianity persecuted → Christians are excluded from power: painful marginality → the Martyrs ≠ Constantine's conversion. The year 313, the Edict of Milan → Christians come into power: recognition, responsibilities, material advantages associated with being a Christian. Emergence, within Christianity itself, of marginal zones, now separated from the world: monasteries. The monk is the successor—the hypostasis—of the Martyr. The monk is therefore—quite literally—an exceptional individual, even when he lives in a community:

— In a spiritual sense: a dense concentration of the sacred among the elite;
— In a worldly sense, in the fourth century (explosion of coenobitism in the Orient). The monastic condition is associated with an aristocratic conception of *otium*:[3] a way of life that's not productive in economic terms—but extremely productive spiritually and/or intellectually (Benedictine erudition). It's the luxury of symbolic systems, something no society can do without, because without the symbolic, mankind dies (psychosomatic: absence of symbolization → somatic illness). In order

Encyclopaedia Universalis

90

to meet the essential needs of the species (symbolic requirement),[4] a society will marginalize a small portion of its members (cf. The Sorcerer, Lévi-Strauss).[5]

SECOND MARGIN: IDIORRHYTHMY

Décarreaux, p. 21

Historically, diachronically: idiorrhythmy is the first known marginality. Anachorites, hermits marginalized themselves with respect to the State. Egypt: for the most part and above all, individuals avoiding taxation or military service.[6] Structurally, a secondary marginality: a marginality contained within the marginality of coenobitism. How did that happen?

From the moment you have coenobitism (Pachomius: let's remind ourselves once again of the temporal, historical, political concomitance between the founding of the first monasteries and Christianity's accession to power, fourth century)[7] → the risks, the dangers of eremitism get denounced. Risks that are interpreted on different consecutive levels:

Amand, p. 47

1. Psychic risk: terrible spleen, nocturnal phantasies = the risk of depression (= acedy).

Ladeuze, p. 169

2. Pecanimous risk:[8] infatuation, self-love, egoism, pride, laziness, solitude considered as a weakness. The hermit shuts himself away because he lacks the strength to face the daily clash with other people's wills: he can't cope with the burden of mixing with his fellow men, etc. (≠ communal life: its difficulties are precisely what make it a means for self-improvement)

Then there are the risks that follow from the requirement of social integration, which society imposes on the individual as a natural law, risks that no longer impact directly on the psyche, but on society as a whole:

1. Not communicating. Christianity: a space where sins are heard (auricular confession was actually instated much later; previously, all confessions were public). The hermit is unable to communicate his victories and his defeats.

Décarreaux, p. 31

2. Eccentricity. In other words, an individual's subversion of the norms of social life: physical appearance (strictly regulated for coenobites), abode, relationships, lifestyle. To recall a few of those "eccentricities" (notably those pertaining to mortification). Syria, fourth century: a sharp rise in the number of ascetics driven to new extremes in terms of intransigence and idiosyncrasy:

— Grazers: herbs, roots;
— Dendrites:[9] nest in trees to be closer to the heavens (and whose idea of nature is also perhaps the most archaic: the hominoid's habitat);
— Recluses: shut themselves away: their sole access to the outside world is through an underground tunnel;
— Stationaries: live in society; but don't communicate with it, they don't speak or move, like statues, they don't eat or drink, but remain out in the open (→ catatonia). A different version: the Stylites.

The latent (at times explicit) condemnation of eremitism in the name of coenobitism = society's condemnation of individualism. Secular tension between:

1. The voice of society as a community, establishing the need for "social stimulants": voice of the species as a whole (cf. "boy-scout-ism,"[10] for example).

Encyclopaedia Universalis

2. The voice of asocial, solipsistic mysticism. → Society: imposes a law of integration that's actively undermined by eremitism and its more moderate version: idiorrhythmy.[11]

We can now see what's at stake:

— What society condemns in the marginal (a person belonging to the second marginality) is in fact: the madman. The norm is what is communal, the community. The madman is abnormal. Perhaps there's no other definition of the madman (the paranoiac excepted) than this: someone who's devoid of all power. Whence his excessive position, excessive because it's neutral: being neither for nor against power (neither master nor slave), he strives to remain outside of it. A position that's untenable, which is why the madman, the marginal is the source of such intense social anxiety.
— Pachomius and the first monastery: key, decisive moment. The law, the community, the fact of being made to obey a superior serves to recuperate Christian "madness" as a form of individual madness; in short, in Nietzsche's terms: as gregariousness.
— The margin is tolerated nevertheless—it serves as the focal point for all that a society perceives as dangerous (the sorcerer in Lévi-Strauss)[12]—but only so long as it's controlled, that is to say coded, by society. Example: the progressive coding of eremitism in the Occident:[13] (1) → end of the tenth century: patristic conception of the *eremus* (Egypt). Hermitages in proximity

Le Millénaire du mont Athos, p. 177

to monasteries, but separate from them. (2) Eleventh–twelfth century: eremitism becomes coenobitic and clerical: lauriote solitude (type: Carthusian). (3) Thirteenth century: Saint Augustine's order of hermits, a sort of communal eremitism, which if necessary did not have to involve any solitude at all ("desert"[14] = taking a vow of silence in the *coenobium*). As a general rule, Occidental eremitism: very integrated: sociable and social → "works of eremitic forgiveness and friendship" (*humanitas hospitalitatis*).[15]

Le Millénaire du mont Athos, p. 166

Society keeps a close eye on the margin: hermitages get built within the precincts of abbeys, with the hermits now dependent on the abbey, a negation of the basic idiorrhythmic premise, which is to operate outside the remit of any given authority. But society exercises its control through the two values it imposes on the monk: obedience and stability: values that are essential to integration.[16]

Gallien, p. 11

Here we'd have to append a whole dossier on the social repression of marginalities; the lawful repression of certain anormalities (drugs, mental disorders) and, when not explicitly authorized by law, repression by the police: "communes," France, after 1968: Police chiefs refusing to supply lists of abandoned villages, police raids.

MONÔSIS / MONOSIS

Monk < *monicus*   (→*Münch*[17]
                     →in old provençal: *monge*)
     a modified form of *monachus, monachos* (→ Italian: *monaco*) = solitary, someone who lives alone, with no family (*singularis*)[18]

Guillaumont, "Monachism"

     → *monosis*: state, system of unmarried living, girded loins (vow of chastity) → *Monachos*: type of ascetic who renounces conjugal living.[19]

ONE / TWO

I don't want to get into the vast dossier on the One and the Two (from Lacan to Mao).[20] I'll simply remind you of the ideology implicit in the way languages are structured (theme of the power inherent in language, of its mandatory categories). For us, in French: one / several (singular / plural). But in many other languages: one / two / several → the dual. Bodily proof: pairs: eyes, ears, arms, legs, hands, testicles. → Image of the natural unity of the two, dramatized in the myth of Androgyne,[21] which provides a minute description of the organs splitting into pairs. What this means: the One (the single body) is already virtually divided. The most basic theme is the pair. Whence the incessant dialectic between (1) the virtual division of the One, (2) the pair reconstituted as a whole (the fusion of love: to bond, to mate). That dialectic is comprised of the following two movements, visible in language: the One is made up of two (the One is divided) / the Two is a whole (the pair, duality).

THE DESIRE FOR TWO

The dossier I'm opening here is not that of loving desire, the desire for union, for loving fusion. I'm merely noting that (the ambivalence of the dialectic I referred to) the One is construed as a punishment. Condemned to being just One is to be punished for something. Robinson Crusoe repeatedly articulates this belief: in being condemned to live alone on a desert island he's being made pay for the sins of his youth and, above all, his defiance of his father, who'd forbidden him to set sail. When, after the shipwreck, he takes stock of his situation, Robinson gives vent to the desire for Two: "O that there had been but one or two, nay, or but one soul, saved out of this ship!" And later, following the sight of human footprints in the sand: everything is structured by the anticipation of discovering another man. Something that can be applied to all of us, that we'll phrase in the following way: Two is the anticipation of One (and One is pregnant with Two).

Robinson Crusoe, p. 185

152

Guillaumont, "Monachism"

That dialectic is subtly expressed by the myth of Adam. To begin with, Adam is created alone: he is One, *heis*.[22] But the creation of Eve is nothing less than the actualization, the materialization of the latent duality inscribed within Adam from the beginning. It's exactly the same schema as for Androgyne. But according to Aristophanes in *The Banquet*,[23] the division of the One into two is distressing (it's Zeus's punishment for[24] the "arrogance" of androgynous happiness). Happiness is the One as a composite. In Genesis, the fall comes after the division—although it also derives from that division, since it derives from Eve.

IN PRAISE OF ONE

It's therefore not so much the One and the Two that need to be mythically opposed. It's the composite One and the divided One. Whence Patrology's systematic praise of the One[25] *(monachos)*:

Guillaumont

1. *Monosis*: movement whereby the subject mimics Adam's condition prior to being divided into two: Adam's solitude.
2. *Monachos*: not just an unmarried man, but one with a sole purpose in life. The monk is *monotropos*:[26] he invests in a single goal (cf. *mania*, loving madness).[27] Perhaps this relates to Plato's theory of the unification of the soul: compression through the focus on a single goal.
3. Society = space of sharing, of mixing, of the divided Two. Marriage: someone who's married = divided, torn. ≠ Monk: world of the unshared, of the pure, of the unmixed. The monk is someone with no ties.
4. Opposition between the monk who has no ties and the husband who's torn: found in two paradigmatic notions:[28]

   — *haplotes*:[29] simplicity, no conflict, rectitude, experience of the composite One, of integration.
   — *dipsuchia*:[30] the state of someone with a double, divided, conflicted soul, who's experienced hesitation, doubt *(psuchè)*.[31] In the Bible: the heart = the affective soul.

Guillaumont, *Philon*

5. Same paradigm in another important opposition of the period:

   — *Bios praktikos*:[32] practical life = political and social activity, political and social duties. This is not pejorative. For the Stoics, the *bios praktikos* meant correct moral conduct *(askesis)*: the exercise of virtues, the struggle to control the passions.
   — *Bios theoretikos*:[33] contemplative life, unified life, one with no conflicts, no struggles, someone who has achieved *haplotes*; especially good in old age, after a period of *bios praktikos*.
   — It's the opposition between the mixed and the *pure*. *Bios praktikos*: a way of life comparable to someone dressed in a coat of many colors,[34] cut from a composite, complex cloth = *poikilos*[35] ≠ someone who lives in the desert, a place of calm, of unvaried activity, of peaceful solitude: of *hesuchia*.

Droit-Gallien, p. 8

   — This dream of *hesuchia* can be very modern. In an interview, a "communard" (a member of some community or other in the Ardèche) was asked to justify Living-Together. He replied: "I don't want a life that grates all day long. What I need is a quiet life, a life with no noise." = Precise definition of *hesuchia*, of *haplotes*, of Adam's dream, of a composite One rather than a divided One.

6. For the One of *monachos* (of the anachorite I've been dealing with here: not the coenobite) is a composite One, who (like Adam) is inhabited by the virtuality of Two. The anachorite in a situation of total retreat: it's actually a matter of a loving retreat, of a dual retreat. Cassien apropos of Paphnucius:[36] Paphnucius wanting to live alone, "in order to unite more completely with the Master, to whom he longed to be inseparably attached."[37] As if, through his substitutes for sublimation, man had set himself the task of reestablishing duality, the pair within the One since, as both our bodies and our grammars tell us, the true Unity is dual. For me, this figure suggests an investigation, a question, a hypothesis: something I have a vague notion of but am not yet able to fully grasp. That something is this: what's opposed—what produces meaning—isn't so much the One and the Two but rather: the integrated (which is perhaps better than composite) One and the disintegrated (disassociated, divided, conflicted) One. Whence the two following remarks:

1. The notion of being torn (*dipsuchia*) is fundamental: existential feeling of panic when confronted with a situation (or a lifestyle) where the subject is required to submit to contradictory rules. It's typically a prepsychological situation (*double-bind*): "Heads, I win, tails, you lose." (Bruno Bettelheim).[38] Now, generally speaking, this is also what it's like out in the world: the subject is tumultuously, with arrogance, torn between conflicting responsibilities ≠ *Haplotes*, *hesuchia* = integrated state, degree zero of responsibility, of unconflicted readiness: it's what characterizes *monosis*.

2. Methodologically: we mustn't think of the One and the Two as endowed with attributes: peace / conflict; but rather as metaphors for elementary states. One would refer to a subject outside of any jurisdiction, who has wholly integrated the law (mystical state), and Two to a subject who's both submissive and rebellious, in the grips of the long, hard history of repression.

NOMS / NAMES

The aim of this figure is to introduce the dossier of proper names as they operate within the space of Living-Together. Three points of reference (or departure), no more than indicated:

NICKNAMES

Vast problem for historical ethnology, as to begin with our surnames were either the names of places[39] or nicknames (professions, physical characteristics). In the Christian world, the mechanism of onomatogenesis appears to work in the following way:

1. Within a very small community (for example: a family), it's unlikely that a first name will be used twice, ensuring that each member is distinctive, important. Within a family, among those who are closely related, the same first name is never used: the family = an onomastic paradigm;

2. Should the community grow, become a tribe, a village, it's important to be able to distinguish between bearers of the same first name: Dark John, Fair John, Henry the Blacksmith / Henry the Peasant, etc. Note how the procedure *separates out*: in the case of a surname common to a "tribe," additional differentiating nicknames are spontaneously produced: Goupi Red-Hands / Goupi Tonkin;[40] Guermantes: the Duc / the Prince, etc. In this process, fundamental linguistic problem: the *shifter*:[41] a unit that's only meaningful in the context in which it's used ("I," "here," "now"). When I say "Jean" within the space of the family, it's a shifter: it doesn't refer to a lexical essence, to a semanteme,[42] but to a distinctive entity that's entirely dependent on the context. Outside of that context, I'm lost. Postcard[43] signed "Jean-François" (I know of five or six people called Jean-François). Which is why, within a group, a nickname will be generated: "Jean-François. Which one? You know, the doctor (the medical student)" → Jean-François Doctor. When we start moving toward the nickname-as-surname, we "de-shift" language, we draw closer to the dictionary (the Bottin,[44] the phone book). We "de-program" language (semantic / pragmatic). We repress the circumstance, the mode of being (mythic relation, today, between lists of surnames and the theme of oppressive bureaucracy: it's slightly insulting to say Barthes, Roland).[45]

In our corpus: trace of this problem in *The Magic Mountain*. Closed community of people in frequent contact, but who don't

The Magic Mountain, p. 125

actually know one another, who don't know one another's actual surnames. So what happens is a distinguishing feature (the vocation of all that's identifiable is to become a sign) gradually attains the status of a surname: "Frau Magnus, the one with an albumin deficiency." Before long it'll be hyphenated and, were it not such a mouthful, eventually become her nickname ("Frau Albumin") = procedure used in the epic, typical of narrative: Athena (the goddess with blue-green eyes). Indian names (Eye-of-the-Lynx). Names of the multitude of Gods in the Taoist religion: the God of Horses = Flower of mysterious Signs: the God of Eyes = Inspector of the Void → One possible avenue to explore: the relation between the nickname and narrative. Again, in *The Magic Mountain*, the birth of a real nickname: the Mexican lady, *Tous-les-deux*. One of her sons is dying and the other, who'd come to visit his brother, has since fallen ill too. All she's capable of saying is: "*Tous-les-deux*" "the tragic formula that had become her nickname."

The Magic Mountain, p. 41, 108

NOMS / NAMES
(continued)

CARITATISM

Linguistic term for the affectionate forms that are sometimes given to nouns referring to everyday objects. In fashion magazines: "The snug little coat." Let's indicate (in our corpus) two forms of caritatism. Oddly enough, we find them in the most "horrific" narrative, a mix of bourgeois respectability, vermin, and madness: *The Confined Woman of Poitiers*.

1. In that reclusive family, with its seemingly inhuman relationships (mother and brother are accused of sequestering the daughter—something that, if it stopped to think, might have given the Law cause for concern): use of affectionate nicknames. The brother calls Mélanie: "my little Gertrude." The sister calls her alleged imprisoner: "Little Pierre." Both children call their mother, an elderly, austere, respectable lady: "Booneen."

The Confined Woman of Poitiers, p. 124

Interesting phenomenon (I still don't know how to fully explain it): sometimes, within a family, changing names, conferring alternative first names to a person's official name, or inventing inexplicable nicknames—(probably, a forgotten incident from childhood). Most likely, the invention of new names: a way of breaking with everyone else and creating a supremely-safe enclosure, a new integration; in short, a conversion (the point of baptism). Changing language is the first step in all renewals, all births, all strong integrations. Sometimes, in a "communal" language, the break is merely symbolic—and a new language isn't created: members of a rural commune (communes, around 1966, U.S.A., then in France). A woman called Lise finds she could no longer breathe in Paris (theme of pollution; hygiene, decency as pollution):[2] "She speaks with a Parisian accent; the majority of her sentences begin with 'fuck' and end with 'can't be arsed.' When Dadoun, her son, tears a page in a book, she shouts: 'Fuck, that guy's an idiot!' The 'guy' looks up at her startled, then wanders off to play with his puppy in the dungheap." = Reject-language? Yes, so long as it's understood that all

Droit-Gallien, p. 18
La Chasse au Bonheur, 1972, Calmann-Lévy

languages are defined by what they reject → there's no degree-zero of language (even if we're all convinced that the language we speak is "natural").[3]

2. There are two languages in Mélanie, depending on the social context:

a. An extremely foul language. In the hospital, she refuses to reply to questions, and instantly dismisses anyone who tries to speak to her. Swear words and obscenities = Mélanie's "social" language, a language for the other, what's left over from the rupture: a sign of the infraction of her grotto, of her Great-Back-Malampia.

The Confined Woman of Poitiers, p. 147

145

149

b. A "communal" language (for her, the community is her own company, her solitude, her grotto) = constantly punctuated by childish caritatisms: "her dear little pencil," "her dear little rose." Asks for her "dear little blanket" (encrusted with filth and insects; she would cover her head with it); wants to eat "a dear little chicken," "some dear little punnets" (strawberries), and "a dear little chocolate macaroon." I think the function of these caritatisms is to change the status of the common noun, turning it into a proper name for Mélanie's own personal use, or at least to sketch out that movement. The caritatism individualizes the object through an affective projection. It turns the object into a (narcissistic) expansion of the Ego and baptizes it incomparable[4] (the ideal status of the proper name, as the term itself indicates). Denotation of ultimate difference, as irreducible; now, the ultimate difference is myself. Cf. Corneille's *Medée*: #[5] "In such extreme misery (Medea takes revenge against Jason—who had left her for another woman—by slitting her children's throats), what are you left with?—Myself."[6] In total confinement, what you are left with?—My pencil, my chicken, my strawberries, my chocolate macaroon. The name is the name of what I love, it's my name: I only name what I love. I only name what's worth naming.

NO NAME

Consequently, the caritatic appellation starts looking like a form of anti-nomination: I draw names out of the generality of language. The purpose of nomination in language is to classify the whole of reality so that it's manageable, manipulable, but in my language I reject everything that isn't an object of love: I destroy language, I turn it into an immense ruin, leaving only a few loving names still standing. Caritatic nomination has to do with the space of love, which is dual (outside of generality). In communities, the caritatism is foreclosed. Communities tend to want to be spaces of manipulation, so only proper names are retained: first names, surnames. But—in the communal space—the proper name presents a danger: that of gossip.

The pronominal substitute for the proper name is he / she. It therefore absents the other: it turns the other into someone being talked about:

a. Either the proper name is a vocative, in which case it's an expletive expansion of the familiar You, a caress in sound ("Ariadne, I love you," says Nietzsche's Dionysus).[7] The name stands up, outside of any generality, irrespective of other people—irrespective of the other, in idyllic duality: the vocative is the opposite of gossip.

b. Or the proper name is a referential name, in other words: the name of something or someone who's not present, and the community is transformed into a space of gossip (he / she / so-and-so are pronouns and unkind names).[8] In an ideal (utopian) community, there would be no names, making it impossible for people to gossip about one another: there would be only direct addresses, presences, not images, absences. There would be no manipulations effected by the name, whether good or bad.

NOURRITURE / FOOD

Symbolism of food

The problem of the symbolism of food merits its own encyclopedia. I had thought of producing one, in reaction to the unilateral commercialization of "modern" cookery books, which expend a great deal of effort describing a diet presented as "rational," seemingly oblivious to the fact that we still associate food with symbols and rituals. And then there's the grand ideological imposture of "hygiene," of "health." That encyclopedia: from Tao to the Bible, from the Bible to Lévi-Strauss (*The Raw and the Cooked*).

So all I'll do here is provide a preliminary sketch of the shape of dossier (taking our corpus as a starting point): (1) rhythms, (2) the foods themselves, (3) practices. Each one of those categories is encyclopedic in itself: across the planet and over time.

1. RHYTHMS

= Rhythms (schedules) of food consumption. Three problems:

Draguet, p. xlv

1. Community meal times. Important, because (a) more than in other contexts, they're what give rhythm to daily life; relation between an implacable rhythm and *otium* (the rural pensioner's meticulously planned schedule; meals: antiboredom), (b) provide an opportunity to come together, for conviviality (a modest celebration). Anachorites of Egypt: even in solitude, still abide by a regulating norm. In general, just one meal a day: taken around *none* (three P.M.), after the afternoon nap. Emergence of coenobitism: great deal of variation; at one extreme, the strict rules of Occidental coenobitism: Saint Pachomius's monasteries. In some contexts, only one meal a day, taken whenever it's wanted; in others, a communal

Ladeuze, p. 298

meal in a refectory (midday and evening) + the possibility of eating your meal alone in your cell, but being forbidden to store any food there. In the ascetic context, the problem is how to absent food: either you reduce eating times as far as possible or you regularize them to an extreme, for the aim of a well-conceived and easily observed rule is to make time transparent. The code absents (far more than spontaneity, irregularity).

2. Schedules and fasts: ascetic excesses (Oriental anachorites) deal with fasts by doing away with mealtimes altogether. In many hagiographies: veritable hunger-strikes for several days—and commonly: just one paltry meal per day. Whence the "assimilationist" reaction: true fasting doesn't mean suddenly and radically depriving yourself of food, but ensuring that you're always just a little bit hungry (today, it's the rule of weight-loss cures: eat hardly anything, but often). Saint Jerome (fourth century) to Furia, a young

Festugière, I, p. 66

widow: "Rather than fast for three days, choose plain foods so your stomach is never full: it is better to eat a little each day than gorge yourself every so often." On the subject of irregular fasting, Saint Jerome speaks of a "voracious abstinence." Note: for many centuries, the rhythm that Saint Jerome condemns derived from economic constraints. The irregularity of resources → erratic alternation between meager meals and the sudden abundance of food: very common dietary regime in the Middle Ages. Whence, for us, the unintelligible—unrealistic—character of descriptions of menus from the past: These were the only kind recorded (Feasts). Due to the endless sequence of different courses, they seem impossible to us today (even those in Brillat-Savarin). What's more, it was the table as display, as potlatch, that was so plentiful: people could take whatever they wanted.

3. A different way of absenting food: not paying for it, forcing it to operate outside an economy of exchange (working to earn a crust). This is the practice of food charity: to ask for and be given

Bareau, p. 65

food (nature's gifts / monetary gifts). Universal practice. But what's most interesting is the way food charity is symbolized in Buddhism. Food is absented on three counts: (a) by not earning it, letting it come, (b) by not asking for it, (c) by not looking at it. Charity rounds are now increasingly rare in the Ceylon monasteries (food is brought into the monastery), but they do still exist and have lost none of their symbolic plenitude. The round takes place at around 10 to 11 A.M. The monks come out one by one, one monk for every group of houses (they return to the monastery singly at around 11.30 A.M.; the meal is around noon). The monk holds the bowl against his chest, hidden under his robe. He walks with his eyes cast down, slowly, but resolutely. Every now and then, he pauses in front of a house or shop door and waits, completely still and silent, without looking at the door. Someone comes out, opens the monk's robe and puts some food in the bowl—or takes it from him to fill it up in the kitchen—and returns it to the monk. The layman bows; the monk mutters a blessing and slowly walks away. = Monk, still and silent, does not even glance at the food. You'll have noted all the operations of annulment, not only of the food, but even of the act of asking for it: either great hypocrisy or great dignity (I tend toward the latter).

In all of these, it's clear that we associate different structures (strictly speaking: ideologies) with two different sorts of rhythm: (1) a mortifactory rhythm that suppresses food (punishes the body), (2) a neutral rhythm that absents food, that wants to render it transparent, insignificant, nonaffective.

2. THE FOODS THEMSELVES

Here, again, an endless list of questions, notably around the taboo, the old hobbyhorse of anthropo-ethnology—not to speak of psychoanalysis:

A. The divisions of the forbidden: What's forbidden / what's tolerated

Interdictions everyone knows about: meat / fish (Lent); animal / vegetable substances (vegetarianism); fish with scales / without scales and other Judaic taboos (not cooking a calf in its mother's milk: no Normandy escalopes then!)[9] and the whole issue of Kosher). I'll only point up two lesser known interdictions, ones which lay bare the labyrinth of interdictions (obsessional fortifications) and the subtlety of the distinctions made:

Festugière, I, p. 59

1. Oriental anachorites. Essentially: raw salad leaves (lettuce, *lachana*),[10] green vegetables (the ones that can be eaten raw), salt, bread (per day: two six-ounce loaves per person = a roman pound #[11] 340 grams). ≠ Forbidden: cooked food, wine, oil (other than at the

Draguet, p. xlv

communal meal on Saturdays), plants with pods. Oil: Pachomius sees some oil on his crushed salt: "The Lord was crucified and I'm eating oil!"[12] (Oil: not a liquid, but a dense substance, extremely nourishing,

Amand, p. 43

cf. eating up your soup + possibly, the euphoric theme of lubrication ≠ dry, rough, what doesn't slide down). Podded vegetables (peas, broad beans): similar to grains; no doubt because they're too nourishing. In Tao, cereals are strictly forbidden, but for a completely different symbolic reason to that of luxury, mortification, sin. Cereals cause death (Tao wants to immortalize the body—not the soul), they cause worms to hatch inside the body that then eat away at its vitality (= transcendent Beings). Three worms: (1) the Old-Blue (causes blindness, deafness, baldness, makes your teeth fall out, blocks your nose), (2) the White-Lady: heart palpitations, asthma, melancholy, (3) The Bloody-Corpse: colic, rheumatism, causes your skin to age, fatigue, the early

Maspero, *Taoism and Chinese Religion*, p. 367

onset of dementia. Remedy: "Stop eating Cereals" (rice, millet, wheat, oats and beans): "The Five Cereals are scissors that cut off life, they rot the five internal organs, they shorten life. If a grain enters your mouth, do not hope for Life Eternal! If you desire to escape death, your intestines must be free of it!"[13] Cereals are evil because they're the essence of the Earth, they're entirely *yin*, while the Sky is *yang*.

I mention Tao because the interdiction is not directly related to a sin (and therefore to atonement through mortification) but rather to a metaphysical anatomy of the body (incidentally, something to be studied: our body is historical).

2. Another subtle distinction: the charity sought by Buddhist monks (cf. supra). They can accept anything (that's put in their

bowls)—with the exception of wine—as long as it's already been prepared (vegetables, fish, meat). If the food is uncooked, they're not allowed to accept meat, fish, or eggs. The servants can purchase meat and fish, but not eggs, because by breaking them = they are killing life = the same abstention from responsibility as in the request for food. The object isn't refused, but the monk isn't involved with it in any way: cf. *Wou-wei*, nonaction. The equation is: nonaction and yet life nevertheless (not an easy equation to balance!).

Bareau, p. 65

B. The connotations of food (foods with connotations)

1. From the moment it's glanced at or narrated, a menu carries a meaning in excess of its basic function. To read "ham + salad + potatoes" is not the same thing as reading "foie gras, stuffed quails, pheasant, asparagus, etc." It's not just the straightforward mechanism of transformation turning a fact into a marker and a marker into a sign: what's expensive indexes what's in small supply and that marker becomes a sign, a sign of luxury (or festivity). It's that—from the moment there's a sign—it gets caught up in a complex, self-perpetuating system of interlocutory images.[14] *Pot-au-feu* = rusticity, peasant food (in Paris at one time, salted beef in restaurants for coach drivers); through snobbery, the same meal can become a mark of luxury. A whole system of social images associated with food. For example, the eventful history of the pizza: the most ordinary meal (for the proletariat of Naples) → in Paris, snobbish Italianness → then goes back to being a sign of ordinary food, not too expensive for a cheap night out: pizzeria in Saint-Germain.[15] The system would of course have to be redescribed for each historical period. In Brillat-Savarin, standard menus indicating varying degrees of social standing—a veritable code of menus but, as with every language, one with its own diachrony (Brillat-Savarin #[16] 1825):

Brillat-Savarin, pp. 184–86

FIRST SERIES[17]
Presumed Income: 5,000 Francs (not well-off)

A large fillet of veal larded with fat bacon and cooked in its own juices;
A domestic turkey stuffed with Lyon chestnuts;
Fattened pigeons covered with bacon and well cooked;
Eggs à la neige;
A dish of sauerkraut (SAUR-KRAUT) *bristling with sausages and crowned with smoked bacon from Strasbourg.*

Comment: "Say, now! That looks damned good! Come on, let's do it justice!"

SECOND SERIES
Presumed Income: 15,000 Francs (comfortably well-off)

A fillet of beef, pink inside, larded and cooked in its own juices;
A side of venison, with sauce of chopped gherkins;
A boiled turbot;
A choice leg of mutton à la provençale;
A truffled turkey;
The first green peas of the season.
Comment: "Ah, my dear fellow! What a delightful sight! It's a veritable wedding feast!"

THIRD SERIES
Presumed Income: 30,000 Francs or More (wealthy)

A seven-pound fowl, stuffed round as a ball with Périgord truffles;
An enormous pâté de foie gras *from Strasbourg, in the shape of a bastion;*
A large carp from the Rhine, à la Chambord, *richly dressed and decorated;*
Truffled quails à la moelle, *on canapés of toast spread with butter flavored with sweet basil;*
A stuffed and basted river pike, covered with a cream of shrimps, secundum artem;
A pheasant served roasted à la sainte alliance *and dressed in its tail feathers;*
One hundred stalks of the first asparagus of the season, each the thickness of a pencil, with sauce à l'osmazone;
Two dozen ortolans à la provençale, *prepared according to the recipe given in* The Secretary and the Cook;
Comment: "Ah, Sir or My Lord, what an admirable chef you have! It is only at your banquets that we can enjoy such delicacies!"[18]

Meals are values quoted on the Stock Exchange of History. For Brillat: "eggs *à la neige*": a sign of "low income" → today, of a good restaurant. The system of food connotations = secular traces of the grand symbolism of food that the Imaginary takes from "Nature" (metaphysical, religious) and projects onto social standing ("Society" has become our "Nature").

2. A semiology of food? The codes of connotation = its chief concern. But that's not all: a different semiological problem: the profile (the "prospects") of the alimentary word. As a general rule, I'm convinced that the relation between the word and the referent cannot be reduced, once and for all, to a generalized scheme. A reading, listening subject's relation to a word will be different depending on what those words refer to. There you have a future line of inquiry for an active philology, the kind Nietzsche wanted: philology of forces, of differences, of intensities. Reading can't (won't) be able to find its theory unless it takes the relation to the word (in the singular) into account—insofar that relation is differentiated by affect, desire, disgust, etc. An image, an idea of the referent briefly glimmers, like a flash, in certain words: I can't read "omelet" without feeling briefly hungry or queasy. → Whatever the narrative, the account, reading menus is to find yourself at the point where those two semiological axes intersect: connotation and affect.

3. A few examples of menus worth reading in that they lend themselves to semiological analysis. (It goes without saying that no interpretation can account for affective reading, which is of the order of: "That sounds nice" / "That sounds horrible"). → Sorts of exercises in symbolic interpretation that I'll merely gesture toward:

Bareau, p. 67

— Buddhist monasteries of Ceylon. Breakfast: tea or coffee with sugar, bread, biscuits, butter, jam, honey. Lunch: rice with *kari*, vegetables, fresh or fermented milk, fruit. Dinner: tea or coffee with sugar but no milk, or fruit juice. → Frugality, vegetarianism, but Occidentality and comfort: nothing ascetic about it.

Droit-Gallien, p. 20

— Communards, France #[19] 1970. Midday: a mushroom omelet, a salad, some goat's cheese. Evening: potatoes cooked in garlic or brown rice, grilled chestnuts. → Rusticity, Frenchness, semivegetarianism, cult of the macro-biotic.

***The Confined Woman of Poitiers*, p. 156, p. 157**

— Mélanie's food. Lives in unbelievable filth, in confinement, but paradox: sophisticated and ultrabourgeois food, expensive (although her mother is miserly in every other respect). Breakfast: will only take a cup of Companie Coloniale[20] hot chocolate, doesn't want any bread. Lunch: a fried fillet of sole, a chop surrounded by potatoes: sometimes, from the Hotel de France (in Poitiers): chicken breast with mushrooms, chicken in tomato sauce, oysters, foie gras → best quality

Pot Luck, I, # p. 41

wine (Bordeaux, at two or three francs a bottle). Dinner: will only take a brioche or cake called a "Jesuit"(?)[21] → Frenchness, bourgeoisie, capriciousness.

— the meal in the Josserand's apartment: typical hard-up bourgeois household, struggling with the need to "keep up appearances," "to try not to arouse suspicion" {*donner le change*}, "to try to impress" {*la poudre aux yeux*} (title of a play by Labiche).[22] To butter up Uncle Bachelard and get him to stump up fifty thousand francs as a dowry for one of the girls: some dubious skate in an overly vinegary black butter + a greasy meat pie (*vol-au-vent, bouchée à la reine*)[23] + a piece of veal, green beans swimming in water + vanilla and currant ice cream. Note that, borrowing the technique from the epic, Zola provides the signifieds himself, or at least splits the signifier into: its apparently objective social standing, should we take it on face value (fish, starter, roast, ice cream = ranks highly) + an unappealing attribute (greasy, too much vinegar, swimming in water). It's the epic theme. Bourgeoisie: a façade of appearances concealing a different reality (adultery, money worries) = the social lie.[24]

— The menu of the man eating alone (theme of the singleton). Gloomy descriptions of meals eaten in bad local restaurants: Huysmans's *A Vau-l'eau* (the same epic technique as in Zola).[25] Everything he eats serves to connote the disinvestment, the disaffiliation of the urban singleton—with, between the lines, the appeal of the mystical regeneration of the monastery. ≠ The solitary philosopher's food: sober, happy food. At the end of his life, Spinoza retreats to a room in Voorburg. He lives a whole day on a milk-soup done with butter and a pot of beer. Another day he eats nothing but gruel done with raisins and butter—two half-pints of wine a month → Sobriety, frugality, naturality (cf. the monks of Ceylon).

Life of Spinosa by Jean Colerus, p. 37

It goes without saying that what we're dealing with here are connotations. Not objective attributes associated with a given social condition (a matter for sociology), but signs (semiology). A play of images, of mirrors: food as it's captured in a story, a narrative (hagiography, journalism, novel, biography): food such as it's read. But do we ever do anything other than read each other? We read each other eating: food as a private secret (the case of the École pratique des hautes études seminar, 63–64).[26] Can reality exist without any image? The image is immediate, concomitant, need collapses when it comes up against desire, marker against sign, function against symbol.

3. PRACTICES

= the problem of Eating-Together: conviviality in the strict sense. I would just like to present this heading for the record, because it's an enormous ethnographical dossier: all the rituals of feasts, banquets, or gatherings involving Eating-Together. All I'll do here is indicate some of the ways in which the dossier could be approached:

— The horror of eating alone seems to be widespread. Mark of malediction: the essence of solitude. Hence a privileged object of philosophical or mystical reversal (hermits, Spinoza) + occasionally, a narcissistic pleasure in eating alone while reading (Gide at the Lutetia).[27]

— the rituals of communion: collective ingestion of a symbolic food stuff, where the sharing itself is symbolic. ≠ No one breaks bread with their enemy. Communion: ritual of inclusion, integration, imitation (after-dinner speeches: inclusive speech acts).

— ecstatic communions: the effects of food (of drink) and the fact of bringing bodies together rids the subject of his personal protective armor. Extreme form: the orgy. But in our culture, blander substitutes of that incitement to ecstasy: banquets, family meals. Alcohol, food + excessive length of meal times → sort of intoxication effected by time: the characteristic feature of the orgy is its lack of moderation; cf. the Balkan Kiefs.[28]

— conviviality as encounter: the meal-eaten-together is a crypto-erotic scene where things happen. *The Magic Mountain*: "meal times that he found diverting and full of interesting episode." + Changing places at the table: the seating plan is erotic (cf. *The Banquet*). Conviviality produces two effects: (1) the overdetermination of pleasures (Brillat-Savarin says the pleasure only lasts for the first hour),[29] (2) With respect to the "official," gastronomic pleasure, Eros is placed in an indirect position—that is, the position of perversion (secondary pleasure).

— in coenobitic practices: communal meal (introduced by Saint Benedict). Food is absented (cf. supra). But the pleasure of conviviality is absented too, due to the monodic chanting of religious texts.

The Magic Mountain, p. 135

426

CONCLUSION or final remark, at any rate:

— Food: associated with life, with what is vital (biological). Through a metonymical reversal: all the metaphors for life, insofar as they have meaning, value, are reversed when it comes to food. There's a symbolic exchange between changing your lifestyle and changing the food you eat. To be reborn = to eat different sorts of food: the embryo's intussusception (ingestion of a substance to promote growth) / the mother's breast-milk / weaning.

— the patients in the sanatorium of *The Magic Mountain*: they're there to save their lives, because they want to be reborn outside of illness. Are served monstrously stodgy foods, are stuffed with food in the hope that it will turn them into new human beings. But on the other hand (it's perfectly logical, it all depends where you're coming from), weight-loss cures:[30] very often come with a desire to "change your life," to be born into a new life, to be reborn young, in control of your desire and thus of the world.

— Passages from one sort of food to another. To get married: to pass from your mother's food to your wife's (whose food, if it goes down well, will become that of a second mother): petit-bourgeois men calling their wives "Mother"). That passage can involve a whole inner labor: work both of mourning and of rebirth.

The Confined Woman of Poitiers. *Mélanie: hot chocolate + a cake called a "jesuit." A few clarifications, producing somewhat enigmatic results; though for a "jesuit" this is hardly surprising:*

— *a cake filled with a kind of almond paste (de facto proof: someone actually wanted to give me one);*
— *a cake that looks like a chocolate cake from the outside but inside is made up of layers of chocolate and meringue. Like a Jesuit, it's careful not to show its hand = Most likely: dark chocolate = the Black of the Jesuit* (The Red and the Black).

PROXÉMIE / PROXEMICS

Nighttime: I get into bed, I turn off the light, I lie back under the covers to go to sleep. But I need to blow my nose. I reach out in the dark and successfully locate the top drawer of my bedside table; I open the drawer and with the same assurance find the handkerchief on the right-hand side. I put it back and close the drawer again just as infallibly.

This is the kind of episode that enables us to formulate a notion of proxemics.

THE NOTION

Dictionnaire de sciences sociales

Neologism coined by Edward Twitchell Hall (*The Hidden Dimension*, 1966; French translation in 1971). *Proxemics* = "the interrelated observations and theories of man's use of space as a specialized elaboration of culture":[1] dialectics of distance. For my part, I shall restrict my use of the word to the very localized space of the subject's immediate surroundings: the familiar space, the space of objects that can be easily reached (blindly, almost; cf. our first example), without having to get up; privileged space of sleep, of rest, of the kind of work you can do sitting at home: the sphere of the "direct gesture" (Moles),[2] the cubic meter of space within reach of the immobile body: microspace. Examples provided by Moles: the child

La Perception de l'habitat, p. 16

in his cot, the business man in his office, the intellectual at his desk, the pensioner in his armchair (TV, pipe, spectacles, newspapers).

Proxemics: belongs to a typology of subjective spaces in that the subject inhabits them affectively: >[3] (1) Territory (domain) → (2) Hideout (room, Robinson Crusoe's hut, the colonists' apartment in the granite cliff in *The Mysterious Island*). (Chombart: family = "a group of people living under the shelter of a single key.")[4] Proxemical space: niche, nest. Which means, in a certain sense: (a) the space of your field of vision (or smell, or hearing),[5] (b) where things get taken, where things get hidden,[6] (c) where things are reached for, where things are touched.[7]

Ekambi, p. 10

Two objects that are natural generators of proxemics (of proxemical space): the lamp, the bed = central objects that the subject tends to gravitate toward.

THE LAMP

Cited here as an object-center, a crystallizer of proxemics:

— Yet those objects have varied over History. For centuries: the hearth, the fireplace, the source of heat; visible source (symbolism of the fireplace). A stove = less proxemical than a wood fire (the odor, the soft, flickering light + the flickering fire as an ever-changing spectacle of incidents). Today: the television tends to serve the same purpose. Straddling those two regimes, an important object, a generator of sedentary microspace: the lamp.

— Lamp, as proxemical center. Bound up with a style of civilization: (1) light bulb: communal rooms in farmhouses, (2) suspended from the ceiling: petit-bourgeois dining rooms, (3) lamp (often coincides with the suppression of the central ceiling light). A whole history of lighting, a diachrony that can still be actualized over the course of a train journey, the fact of being plunged into different interior spaces, each corresponding to a different phase of civilization.

— Note that the proxemics differ with each phase: (1) light bulb at ceiling height: no proxemics whatsoever, no interiority to the "interior"; (2) light bulb suspended from the ceiling: the beginnings of proxemics. Familial proxemics: around the dinner table (it retains its proxemical function even once the plates have been cleared: reading the paper, doing homework, playing games); (3) lamp: strong proxemics; isolates the writing desk, the armchair, produces a lit being and a dark nothing-ness → Through a paradoxical but logical reversal, it's in complete darkness that the habitual gesture is exposed: dark-ness can create the very essence of proxemics (cf. the example we began with). The essence of myself, it's what I don't even need to see to take pleasure in.

— There are ways of testing proxemics.[8] In a hotel: inadequate bedside light, no lamp on the desk, darkness without familiar-ity ≠ the reconstruction of an artificial and elaborate proxemi-cal space; the sleeping berth on an overnight train: your own light, a rack for your things, a nail to hang your watch on.

THE BED

The sick bed: the strongest form of proxemics, the one we have the most concrete experience of, usually the best organized (Matisse at the end of his life, the long bedside table he'd use to draw on).

Proust, I, pp. 47, 49

Typical example: Aunt Léonie's bed.

		→ Yellow dresser
Street ←	Bed	→ Table serving at once as dispensary and high altar

Aunt Léonie has gone through all the different stages of proxe-mics: "she declined to leave, first Combray . . . " (= territory), " . . . then her house" (hideout), then her bed (niche, nest).

The bed, the very essence of proxemics; in some ways, a part of the body; a prosthesis of the body, like a fifth limb: the limb, the body itself like an organ at rest:

Le Millénaire du mont Athos, p. 108

1. Athonite monks (before monasteries were established): no possessions whatsoever, nowhere to live and no belongings, but would travel by foot, carrying their sole item of furniture on their backs: the mat they slept on at night.[9]

2. Spinoza's curious attachment to his bed. Upon the father's death, his objects were shared out among the children: "However, when the partition came to be effected, he left them <his brothers and sisters > everything but one bed, in truth a very good one, and the items around it." Spinoza, a philosopher of proxemics?

Bed = site of the subject's fantasmatic expansion: (1) through reading; (2) if possible, through a window; bed: a comfortable look-out post; Léonie watches the street from her bed, sees people going into the grocer's; (3) through fantasmatic fabulation; Léonie invents

Proust, I, p. 113

imaginary plots to entertain herself that she then follows, enthralled (for instance: that Françoise is stealing from her) = the "sick-bed theater."[10]

(Accordingly, perhaps it would be possible to elaborate a typology: subjects who enjoy a good relationship with their beds[11]—a rich, multifunctional relationship— ≠ subjects who have no relationship whatsoever: an indifferent, impersonal, purely functional object. Cf. Subjects who need to establish a form of proxemics in order to be able to work ≠ subjects who can work anywhere.)[12]

RECTANGLE / RECTANGLE

CIVILIZATION OF THE RECTANGLE

Look at the spaces we live in: the majority of angles are at 90 and 180 degrees = houses, apartment buildings, doors, windows, roofs, lifts. It's all rectangular ≠ "nature": no rectangles (with the exception of certain rock formations). → Since we now associate city, living space, humanity, and pollution, there's a pollution effected by the rectangle. Agents of that pollution: architects. Importance (tyranny) of "regulatory lines": "every architect should use them" (Le Corbusier). Evidently, "reason" would agree ("geometric," "Greek" ideology: the hut, the opposite of the tent, circular and radial (cf. "Bedroom") + perhaps—who knows?—an ancestral reminder of the royal and religious function: *Rex* = someone who draws straight lines (*Regula*, *Orego*,[13] cf. infra) → Rectangle: as the basic shape of power.

Ekambi, p. 55

Rykwert, p. 12

THE FRAME

Two facts—or two question-facts—two themes to investigate that together expose the wholly artificial nature of the rectangle. Artificial = historical, cultural, ideological, perhaps even: neurotic. Both themes have to do with the relation between the rectangle and the image, with the creation of the image, of imagery.

1. Rectangle: archetypal shape of the pictorial frame. The image is put into a frame. Frame = square.[14] But the square is ultimately no more than an abstract (and often esoteric) version of the rectangle. (See Yve-Alain Bois' thesis[15] and Meyer Schapiro's "Champ et véhicule dans les signes iconiques," *Critique*, August, 1973).

Frame: a late invention. Prehistoric art: cave paintings in the Paleolithic period: on an unprepared surface, painting directly onto the cave wall. Homogeneous delimiting of the image (like the walls around a city): around two thousand B.C. A dossier has been opened. Something to be studied: the Italian-style scene, the cinema screen. This raises the question of mental activity:

2. Meyer Schapiro writes: " . . . such a field <the rectangle> corresponds to nothing in nature, or *in mental imagery*, where the phantoms of visual memory appear one after another in one unending wave."[16] That's not quite right. We do have recourse to the rectangular framed image in "mental imagery." Specifically, in certain episodes of imaginary activity: the kind that engages the subject in coalescent images, to which he adheres. The frame = the superlative of the image, as it were, what completes it. It's as if imaginary perversion actually called imperiously for the frame, the rectangular outline, the border. Cf. Loving enchantment, love at first sight, to be suddenly enamored = to be kidnapped by the image. Now, as a general rule, that image is framed.[17] The object of love (the object to be loved) abruptly appears (a) as a cut-out silhouette—or as a particular, fetishizable part of the body, (b) in a frame, (c) in a setting, in the process of doing something.[18] Example: Charlotte and the bread and butter, framed by the doorway.[19] The Wolfman's maid: Grusha.[20] Gradiva walking, one foot raised, in the bas-relief.

SUBVERSIONS?

Subversions of the rectangle? Here, again, an immense dossier: theatrical arts, plastic arts (painting / sculpture), architecture. It would entail a reexamination of the function of the round (of the rounded). It would entail (it's already been done, in bits and pieces, but there's a dossier to be compiled): a study of rounded forms to the extent that they supplant—or are supplanted by—the rectangle:

1. Theater of antiquity: circular (Greek), semicircular (Latin) orchestra. Stage = to begin with, a tent for the actors. They would come out and perform in front of it: *the proscenium*: conflict between the rectangle and the circus.

2. The circle as something that's difficult to make: myth of the wheel as a triumph, secret of supreme-nature (Androgyne has curves; Aristophanes is quite clear on this).[21] Robinson Crusoe makes all he needs in terms of furniture. He has no trouble making rectangles (tables, chairs, cupboards), but can't make a wheelbarrow, a barrel.

Robinson Crusoe, p. 78

In pictorial art, numerous attempts to get rid of the frame or break it. It's the whole history of pictorial space since Cézanne and, more broadly, of Oriental painting. What's less well known: in the history of comic strips, some clever subversions of the square (the rectangle). Pinchon (Bécassine)[22] draws outlines around his pictures: all sorts of different shapes (not necessarily rectangles). Even Fred the cartoonist gets his characters talking to or fighting each other across two different frames.[23] (Interesting, in metaphorical terms: the subversion of a shape, of an archetype, is not necessarily effected by its opposite but by more subtle means, by retaining the shape and inventing a distinctive play of superimposition for it, or one of effacement, of overstepping its limits.)

RÈGLE / RULE

REGULA

Benveniste (*Vocabulaire des institutions indo-européenes*, 2, the beginning) demonstrates: *Rex*: not a chief, but the person who decides which spaces are consecrated (cities, territories), someone who marks out. *Rego* > the Greek *orego* = to extend in a straight line (≠ expand outward, *petannumi*). Starting from where you are, mark a straight line out ahead—move forward in a straight line. Horses (Homer): stretching out their full length as they bound ahead.[24] → *Regio*: the point reached by following a straight line. *Regula*: the instrument used to draw a straight line. That etymological process authorizes what I consider to be an enlightening link between rule[25] and territory (we can—as I did—associate territory with "Enclosure," but it may have an even closer relation to "Rule").

Robinson Crusoe, pp. 61, 62, 69

Robinson: the moment he decides to get organized, when, since he has no way of knowing how long he will remain alone on the island, he decides to take charge of his solitary life: at precisely that juncture: he marks out the plot for his house and fixes upon a way of organizing his time, a life-rule (*timing*). It's therefore worth reminding ourselves—once again—of the ethological notion of territory.

TERRITORY

1. Territory; as we've seen: an appropriated space, protected from intruders (man, robins, deer),[26] where each individual rules

Encyclopaedia Universalis

over his own domain. But also: a space associated with certain recurrent functions or—in human terms—habits. Several different types of territory:

— Breeding, preening, mating, nesting, seeking food: warblers, robins.
— Only used for reproduction and nesting. Rivals confront each other at the boundary (peewits).
— Nest and the few square decimeters surrounding it (breeding pairs almost touching): gulls.
— Territoriality: all year round (robins) ≠ temporary (only during the breeding season). Cf. infra on superimposed *timings*.

Robinson Crusoe, pp. 61–72

2. Link between space / function (habitual behaviors) → on the human (anthropological) level = notion of the domain. *Robinson Crusoe*: Robinson creates a domain. Functions: home-fortress + two rooms for grain (subsistence) + country house + field for the cattle + mooring for the canoe. (cf. Defoe himself: house in Stoke Newington, which he extended: stables, orchard, a large garden designed by Defoe himself.) *The Magic Mountain*: two spaces: the flatland / the people up high (subjected to rules). *Pot Luck*: two overlapping spatial divisions: (a) Masters / servants (interior kitchen courtyard, sewer-courtyard), from the beginning, the maids use it as a sewer: the rabbit guts.[27] (b) Masters: the space is divided vertically, the higher up you are in the building, the less respectable (money-respectability). All these domains: associated with specific life-rules.

The Magic Mountain, # p. 237

Pot Luck, I, p. 9

3. The territory's generic function (it's worth reminding ourselves of this). Isn't just a matter of security, it also has to do with a constraint of distance: the spacing of subjects between one territory and another + a certain regulated distance between one subject and another within the territory itself. Intra-territorial spacing is reduced whenever the territory is under threat (schools of fish, flocks of starlings) but, once the danger has passed, the subjects reestablish their distance from one another. Notion of critical distance governing the relations between individuals. → One function of the rule will be simply to instate (to stage) that critical distance.

Encyclopaedia Universalis

Indeed, it would be possible to think of every system of rules as, metonymically, a territory: either temporal (*timing*), or gestural (behaviors).

RULE AND CUSTOM

Rule = a system of habitual behaviors (with an emphasis on the active: the systemizing of habitual behaviors). The rule's origins in custom: important, because it allows us to make a distinction between and even to oppose law and rule at their origin.

Encyclopaedia Universalis

1. To begin with, the principal originators of monastic rules would give the rule the allure of a simple custom: Saint Basil, Saint Augustine, Saint Benedict, and Saint Anthony (for the hermits): "no rules whatsoever, only customs."[28]

2. The rule: function and instrument of control. Associated with asceticism, but let's not forget: *askesis*: methodical effort, exercise (not limited to mortification). Idea of regulating = idea of directing: time, desires, space, objects. In that implication of mastery we rediscover the etymological root in *orego*. Rule = a way of stretching time out in a straight line, of delimiting zones (of time, of actions)—and even the metaphor for Homer's horses fits in with the paradoxical, idiosyncratic rule of idiorrhythmy. Stretching out your full length in a single bound—such is idiorrhythmical time: it's regular, but it bounds (light)—it rebounds.[29]

3. The custom-rule will start moving in the direction of the law-rule (the added element in a repressive system) via the intermediary

Encyclopaedia Universalis

notion of contract. Saint Benedict[30] (sixth century): after a one-year noviciate period, the taking of vows = bilateral contract between the community and the monk who has just professed: security (precious at that time; cf. job security today) in exchange for obedience

Ladeuze, p. 208

to the rule (along with the notion of infraction, punishment). Under Pachomius's successor monks were already being asked to sign a declaration of obedience to the rules.

RULE AND LAW

From the moment the rule is set down in a contract → infraction → disobedience → punishment = the unhappy cycle is established.

Ladeuze, p. 215

1. Pachomius's successor, Schenoudi: group of monasteries; draws up a list of infractions: leaving the monastery in contravention of the rules, escaping at night to converse with banished monks, taking excessive care over one's toilette, stealing sweets from the infirmary, keeping a portion of objects made for parents and friends for oneself. So we can say: the boarding school, the army barracks, the factory were all in there.

2. Under rule, law returns with an irresistible force. It's as if there were a drive for law within the human subject: paradoxical drive, because it would be an ideological drive, in the sense that the law is the ideological counter-side of power, in which it's clothed:

— *The Lord of the Flies*, (Golding), p. 49: from the moment the children realize they're their own masters on the island there's an immediate shift from a state of nature to a state of rule, and so of law. Jack: "We'll have rules . . . lot's of rules! Then, when anyone breaks 'em . . . "

Olievenstein, p. 300

— A community in California: *Synanon.* Two hundred girls and boys suffering from drug addiction → phalanstery with precise rules. For example: for a time, they're forbidden to make love. Then they can, but only in the bedrooms reserved for the purpose; then, couples.

— From those two sketches, it's clear where rule and regulation intersect:

a. *The rule*: an ethical act (it can even be said, in certain cases, a mystical one), whose aim, I repeat, is to give a transparency to life, to everyday life. It's an individual act, but one that can become a shared one (in very small communities), when its stipulations are not overly strict—which are of the order of: the establishing of shared habits that gradually become the norm. These belong to custom, that is to say, to what's not written (≠ regulation, law: always written). The privileged space of the rule: idiorrhythmy. Imagining an idiorrhythmic utopia (a small community of friends, for example) means at some point having to deal with the fundamental problem: how to imagine a rule (as distinct from a regulation).

b. *Regulation*: imposition of the social as power. Mediated by writing: writing (note the significant ambivalence of the term: Writing-Law ≠ Writing-Pleasure) gives rise to infraction, that is to say, sin.

— Dividing line between the rule and the regulation (the law) → observation of two extreme (and contradictory) practices:

a. Sade's universe: is based on the actualized (perpetually actualized) opposition between rule and regulation. Gentlemen = rule (mutual consent, notably based on the possibility of repayment: you consent to do for someone what they consent to do for you). ≠ Victims = regulation, merciless, written (*The 120 Days of Sodom*), a source of pleasure when it serves the Masters—and pleasure when considered from the perspective of the rule. → Aristocracy and paradise of the pleasure of the rule ≠ hell of regulation. Exemplary manifestation of the very wide gap between rule and regulation.

b. At the opposite extreme, a form of critical thinking that sees the seed of a regulation in every rule, that sees every custom as a disguised form of law (through a sort of ideological pirouette). Brecht's thinking: "Under the Rule, discover the abuse." Here, rule = the whole network of ready-made opinions, stereotyped behaviors (I had thought of putting that sentence as an exergue to *Mythologies*) = what Brecht calls "The Grand Custom."[31] Perhaps, after a certain period of time (historical, personal), every rule, even an inner one, becomes abuse? Perhaps, at certain points in one's life, it's necessary to shake up one's own rule? In every community, in every group, a "Grand Custom" always gets insidiously established. Shaking up the "Grand Custom" thus becomes an incomprehensible (unreadable) act. *The Brothers Karamazov*: Father Zosima and Aliocha. Logically, Aliocha's qualities—health, purity, modesty, isn't judgmental, isn't seduced by material goods—predestine him for the monastic state. But on his deathbed Zosima urges him to live in the world. → The metropolitan Anthony, representing young Russian monks at the beginning of the nineteenth century, protests: "Here, under the pretext of pedagogy, Dostoevsky commits a veritable sin against truth; because on no account would a Father of a monastery have sent a novice as ardent as Aliocha Karamazov out into the world."[32] Oppressive voice of the *Grand Custom* (creatures of "That's how we do things / That's not how we do things.") ≠ Zosima, the solitary voice of mystical rule.

Le Millénaire du mont Athos

SALETÉ / DIRTINESS

The question of excrement and dirtiness is raised in two of the works from our corpus: the Oriental monks (the Stylites) and the Confined Woman.

NOTEWORTHY

Of course, since Freud, we've become accustomed to assigning—we find it natural to assign—a meaning to excrement, to making it take its place within a symbolic system. And in that regard, let's not forget that, even before Freud, literature (which is always ahead of everything else) already knew a fair amount about excrement: the language of scatology irrigates a number of great works. See Norman Brown's *Eros and Thantos*, the second half of the book.[1]

Yet before we start postulating meanings (on the level of our corpus) and since excrement (dirtiness) is one of repression's privileged objects it is, so to speak, necessary to note that these objects are noteworthy. Before being assigned a meaning, excrement is noted as an event (in structural terms: it's marked; to talk about something is already to give it a meaning, prior to any content).

Some of the ways—among others, on the level of our corpus—in which excrement becomes an event:

1. Intensive marker: it's the excess of dirtiness that makes us notice it and want to describe it. With respect to what norm? At what point is a space considered dirty? On what basis would it be possible to write an "historical" account of filth? Cf. History of tears.[2] We lack a history of bodies. *The Confined Woman of Poitiers*: the insistent descriptions in the police reports. The bedroom: polluted air, making it impossible to remain in the room + revolting filth = insects, rodents feeding off the excrement on the bed + rotten straw mattress + all around: encrusted with excrement, bits of meat, vegetables, fish, rotting bread, oyster shells. Mass of hair: thick matting of hair, excrement and food waste. → Such a foul odor that (when the bedroom was discovered) the doctors gave those present permission

The Confined Woman of Poitiers, p. 134

to smoke. Note: here's a definition of excess, a notion that structural methodology finds very difficult to define, to get a handle on.[3] There's excess when accretion determines a new behavior (behavior: of the order of the gesture, the discontinuous; like the ritual, it's therefore something that structural analysis can grasp). Here, the structural function is very clear, but almost comical: police, judges, the world of "No Smoking" → the law authorizes the infraction, it's really marking the excess of dirtiness.

2. The sudden and, as a consequence, intensely meaningful lifting of the generalized repression of excrement. Daniel the Stylite: context of ardent faith, of intense spirituality, of sublimation and purity. Link between the Saint and the glorious Body (= "a body that doesn't shit": purified of the excremental function: our eternal body, in Heaven. Countless anecdotes about saints' bodies still being intact when their coffins are reopened). Daniel, in contrast, humbly recognizes that his body is human: *common* version of the "saint who plays at being a man" who's "just like everyone else": "Believe me, brother, I eat and drink as much as I need to. For I am not a pure spirit, nor I am disincarnate; I am a man and clothed in flesh. As for that other necessity, that of excreting, my turds are like a goat's due to my extreme dehydration."

Festugière, II, p. 136

MEANING

Event → hence: meaning. The "meaning" of excrement (of dirtiness); the corpus sketches out several possibilities:

Dictionnaire de sciences sociales

1. First of all (*The Confined Woman of Poitiers*), to go back once again to the ethological notion of *Territory*. Territorial animals (deer, hippopotamus, man).[4] Now, a territory can be intentionally (meaningfully) marked out with excrement (hippopotamuses). Notion (in comparative biology) of an odorous space: filling the three dimensions in which a smell is active. Smell: linked to a process of individuation, the identification of neighboring territories, of appropriation. Dogs in the street: investigating territories. Against an already well-watered tire, every dog will overmark his territory. Smells: signs competing with one another; victory to whoever manages to cancel out the other's sign with his own. Smell as sexual attraction: an invitation to enter another's territory (mating territories). Excrement is truly the (symbolic) origin of odor. In *The Confined Woman of Poitiers*, an accumulation of powerful smells; serve to reinforce her territory: the grotto, the Great Back Malampia.

Le Millénaire du mont Athos

2. *Secession*: Studite monks (the Studios monastery, near Constantinople). Don't wash, not as a form of mortification, but because they've renounced the world's habits. Already noted: dirtiness functions as anti-norm, anti-pollution. It sets you apart from society (a theme taken up by certain sorts of hippies).

3. *Intimacy*. To be taken here in the strong sense: the profound essence of the family (*intimus* is a superlative: the innermost). The Bastian family, as a genotype, is characterized by two traits: a taste for reclusion and a taste for dirt:

a. The Grandfather living as a recluse in his bedroom, refusing to leave it even when his son-in-law dies in the room next door.[5] The house: closed to all visitors. The mother receives her two visitors on Saturday afternoons—so she can spend the rest of the week in her dressing gown.

The Confined Woman of Poitiers, pp. 163–64

b. A fondness for filth: even more "singular" (noteworthy → excess, cf. supra). The brother displays all the classic traits of a perversion (scatophilia), a veritable case in the Krafft-Ebing vein.[6] Doesn't want his sheets to be changed. In the bedroom, several half-full slop pails; in the middle of the room, an overbrimming chamber pot. Would take the pot into the kitchen while the cook was eating. Puts his chamber pot next to his wife's bed "so she [might] get a good whiff of the odor." The brother visits his sister every day, staying for quite a while; sits at the window reading the *Journal de Vienne*: is never bothered by the stench. It's clear: dirtiness shared as a superlative sign of collective *intimum* (yet again, the idea of territory).

139

4. Last, predictably, excrement takes on the precise meaning of its counterpart: toilet training = Education. Function that Freud explores in depth, and which he endows with a whole parade of symbolic transformations. In our corpus: society's ruling over excrement: represented by the hospital (the nuns) where Mélanie is taken after having been wrenched from her grotto. In her grotto, Mélanie soils herself. In the hospital, to begin with, she continues to relieve herself in her bed. But slowly "she learns": the nuns are well pleased, society has saved Mélanie.

The Confined Woman of Poitiers, p. 148

TACT

"Nature" isn't clean (it's neither clean nor dirty). Behaviors relating to cleanliness: invested with a whole complex array of symbolic and cultural values, of ideological alibis. → "Cleanliness" becomes "nature" = the "natural." Contrary to what we tell ourselves, society tends to assimilate "technological progress" to nature, to what's natural. But the subject can easily divide up that mass of the "natural": they can be clean in one way and dirty in another. They choose, on the basis of a complex economy:

The Confined Woman of Poitiers, p. 147

— Mélanie—who, as we've seen: is a paragon of dirtiness—surprises the interns at the Hôtel-Dieu. Before touching her meal: "Is it clean?" Eats with her fingers, but with "great delicacy" (says an intern), keeps orange pips in the hollow of her hand until someone comes to take them away.

— It's precisely around the question of dirtiness—on a matter of dirty linen– that Sade formulates the principle of Tact (*Sade, Fourier, Loyola*, p. 174):[7] "*Charming creature, you want my linen, my old linen? Do you know, that is complete tact? You see how I sense the value of things. Listen, my angel, I have every wish in the world to satisfy you in this matter, because you know the respect I have for tastes, for fantasies: however baroque they may be, I find them all respectable, for one is not the master of them, and because the most singular and bizarre of them, when well examined, always depends on a principle of tact.*"[8]

XÉNITEIA / XENITEIA[9]

We started with a Greek word: *akedia*, acedy. We shall bring things to a close with a Greek notion and a Greek word.

SEMANTIC NETWORK

As good Saussurians, let's recall that every system (every word in that it signifies) is invested with both a meaning and a value: whence the necessity of locating it within a network.

Guillaumont

1. *Xeniteia*: key element of the ascetic doctrine of Ancient (Oriental) Christian monachism = Changing country, expatriation, voluntary exile (*xenos*:[10] foreign) = *Peregrinatio* (> pilgrim): military origin; the period of time a mercenary spends in a foreign country. (But what if we each defined ourselves as, what if we all felt like mercenaries in the worlds we have to operate in: working dispassionately in the service of various causes that aren't our own, being perpetually dispatched by those causes into regions where we're foreigners?)[11]

Equivalents:

a. The first stage of ordination for Buddhist monks: *pabbaja*:[12] exiting, leaving the prior condition behind.[13]

b. The commune movement, in its beginnings, U.S.A.: *drop-outs*:

people who've dropped everything, who've quit the ranks (≠ *drop-ins*: those who fall in somewhere, who fit in).[14] The temptation to drop out. (A fantasy that corresponds to the religious ritual of getting rid of all your belongings, embracing poverty in order to start over again on a different basis. Imaginary protocol whereby you arrange, you organize your departure, decide what objects you'll leave behind for forever, the minimum you'll take with you, etc. Fantasy of "putting your affairs in order." For instance, leaving for good to set up home in the country, etc.).

2. *Stenochoria*:[15] the way, life as a narrow path = a form of exile, like *Xeniteia*, but one that's so internal the world barely notices it. Wisdom that's forever unrecognized, an intelligence that's never divulged, a hidden life, where no one else knows about the goal I'm pursuing, a refusal of glory, an abyss of silence. I mention *Stenochoria* because it's close to *Xeniteia*. But also because it has a degree of affinity with the "narrow space" of Tao:[16] underlying behaviors whose aim is to go unnoticed.

3. I'll now present two notions that stand in paradigmatic contrast to *Xeniteia*:

a. *Thlipsis*,[17] *thlibo*:[18] to compress, press down upon, oppress, crush, give rise to anxiety. It's a trial *Xeniteia* is forced to undergo, a rupture of *Xeniteia*, the resurgence of tender feelings with respect to the world. Allowing yourself to be transported by the charm of the memory of your parents; allowing yourself to indulge, in solitude, in feelings of compassion for your father, your mother, in affection for children, in the desire to have someone to love, etc. *Thlipsis* = the good demon who returns in *Xeniteia*: to repatriate the world through tenderness. *Thlipsis*: on the side of nostalgia; homesickness for a specific place (≠ spleen: longing for an indefinite return, with no specific place in mind, exile without a positive fantasy; spleen = closer to acedy).

b. *Parresia*.[19] *Thlipsis*: the opposite of *Xeniteia*, but *Thlipsis* involves the nobility of affect, of love. ≠ *Parresia*: an opposite without nobility, an ungenerous opposite, one that's purely social, worldly. In effect, *Xeniteia* = a condition where there's no familiarity (with other people, things, memory, the world) ≠ *Parresia* (= frankness; though that's not the religious sense): ease, familiarity, without-embarrassment, lacking discretion = someone who feels at home or among friends wherever they are. → *Parresia*: fundamentally linked to a social excess of language, an arrogance of language, a will to appropriate through language, to a will-to-grasp[20] through language (I'll say for my part: *Parresia*: the dogmatic form of language). Whence its opposite: *Xeniteia*: when a man is master of his own language (not other people's). An example of *Xeniteia* (in this sense): Spinoza: "He had the command of his Anger, and if at any time he was uneasy in his mind, it did not appear outwardly; or if he happened to express his grief by some gestures, or by some words, he never failed to retire immediately, for fear of doing an unbecoming thing." Behaving appropriately: here, not just worldly conformity; a deep-rooted disposition that consists in taking care not to upset or irritate others (≠ *Parresia*: being unapologetic). In sum, *Xeniteia* is not unrelated to good manners. Not the superficial and worldly (class-related) good manners of the Occident, but the politeness of the Orient (cf. *Empire of Signs* and *bushido*).[21]

Life of Spinosa, p. 40

Such is the network—or a portion of the network—of *Xeniteia*. Like any network, its purpose is to demonstrate that meaning is alive, that is to say open to metaphorical transformations and adaptations, that it can be adapted to our own particular interests—across and often against History—not in its depth, but in its fragmentation.

FALSE IMAGE

Once *Xeniteia* has taken hold (within a subject) an infinite dialectic is set in motion to make oneself *Xenos*. As we saw, a notion close to *Xeniteia*: *Stenochoria* = the radical effacement of what can sometimes look like, what runs the risk of looking like seeming, posturing in *Xeniteia*. To be *Xenos*, but in such a way that it goes unnoticed. → Recurring problem in the debate, the struggle with the image. In order to undo or to avoid having an image it's necessary to construct a false, counterimage. There's no degree zero of the image. If a degree zero were to exist, it would in some respects be *Xeniteia* itself. For example, in the field of early Oriental Christianity (which has furnished us with a portion of our corpus), one way of making yourself foreign to the world is not to care what other people think of you. This can even involve trying to attract disdain and dishonor:

Guillaumont

1. We saw this in the story of the Sponge, with the theme of "be a fool, so that you may be wise." The Gospels and Tao.

2. John of Ephesus: *Lives of the Eastern Saints*. Story of two people from Antioch, a man and a woman; they abandon everything, lead an itinerant life. The man dresses as a mountebank, the woman as a courtesan; they live as brother and sister "without any cares"; conceal their life of prayer and abstinence from everyone + Feigning madness; a form of *Xeniteia*: Abba Or (a monk from Nitria, fourth century): "Either flee men for good or jest with the world and mankind by regularly feigning madness."

DEREALITY

Xeniteia: probably a kind of experience of dereality and, as such, has an affinity with mystical and psychotic experiences.

Unreality / Dereality. An opposition clarified by psychoanalysis (Lacan),[22] in typological terms. Cf. *A Lover's Discourse: Fragments*, p. 90; § 6. It's not the same retreat from reality:

1. To unrealize: I refuse reality in the name of a fantasy.[23] Everything around me changes value in relation to an imaginary. Example: someone who's in love unrealizes the world (which irritates him) with respect to the image of the loved one, which is his reality. In this sense, to unrealize the world is to realize the peripeteias and utopias of love.

≠

2. To derealize:[24] here, too, I lose reality, but there's no longer any substitution to compensate me for that loss. I'm no longer even in the imaginary; I'm not dreaming (even of the beloved object). Everything is frozen, petrified, dull: in other words, unsubstitutable. To unrealize: I'm neurotic ≠ to derealize: I'm mad, crazy. Someone who's in love oscillates between the two. In all likelihood *Xeniteia* does the same: between unreality (investment in loving the divinity) and dereality, the absence of all fatherland (or motherland).

Thus *Xeniteia*: can go so far as a form of inner depatriation, but where there's no other compensatory investment. Mélanie is a good example of this radical form of *Xeniteia*, which can coexist with reclusion without contradicting it: an exile that involves staying in the same place. Monks could experience *Xeniteia* in their cells = *perigrinatio in stabilitate*.[25] Mélanie practices radical *Xeniteia*: (a) she doesn't inhabit her name (the supreme, ultimate fatherland): "Is your name not Mélanie Bastian?" "There's more than one woman with that name."[26] And: "It wasn't me who had so much hair; that was another one. There are others apart from myself who

Guillaumont

The Confined Woman of Poitiers, pp. 170–72

The Confined Woman of Poitiers, p. 150

have the same name." (b) She stands by what the world would define as "egoism" (this comes close to a Taoist theme).[27] Mélanie: apropos of everyone—all the members of her family—says: "Let him stay where he is, he's just fine," or "too bad for her, too bad for everyone."

CONCLUSION: The *Xeniteia* that's within us—when it's within us—the *Xeniteia* that—why not?—is within us today—can take the form of a double fantasy:

1. A sad, or at any rate oppressive fantasy. Feeling like a foreigner in your own country, within your social class, your caste, the institutions you've been placed in. For instance, if you'll allow this very personal example, every time I read *Le Monde*: I'm overcome with a fit of *Xeniteia*.[28] Such *Xeniteia* is quick-spreading; it can easily fill the social space around the subject. Abba Pistos defined *Xeniteia* in the following way: "What is *Xeniteia*?—Be silent, and say, whatever the situation you happen to be in: I've got no business here: that's what *Xeniteia* is." My first lecture: a moment of *Xeniteia*.

Guillaumont

2. An active fantasy: the compulsion to get away, the moment a structure takes hold. For example: years spent in a monastery, the oppression of the everyday routine, of having to consider those around you, of a comfortable life → to go away, to become a foreigner again. Similarly, when around us—even if we've contributed to it—a language, a doctrine, a movement of ideas, a set of positions starts to take hold, solidifies, crystallizes, becomes a compact mass of habits, complicities, facilities (in linguistic terms: a sociolect) we can experience the impulse of *Xeniteia*: to go elsewhere, to live thus, in a state of intellectual wandering.

And so we come back to the Utopia of the affective group, the fantasy of the idiorrhythmic community. It would allow for a certain form of *Xeniteia* with respect to a common fatherland, the great Other, while at the same time sheltering its subjects from the anxiety of affective abandonment, affective expatriation: *Xeniteia* without *Thlipsis*.[29]

Duby, *Le Temps des cathédrales*, p. 99

If I had to provide the final envoi of this figure, this debate between *Xeniteia* and *Thlipsis* (as in an ancient ballad), it would be a trait borrowed from conventual Monastic life (Saint Benedict, for instance). As we know, monastic *timing* is very strictly regulated—both over the course of the year (the annual cycle is organized around Easter: each year, it's the sacrist or cantor who decides on the calendar) and over the twenty-four hours of the day:[30]

Encyclopaedia Universalis

Lauds: first light.

Prime: as the sun rises.

End of the day: Vespers

As night falls: Compline (just before bed).

The idea of compline: beautiful. The community prepares to brave the night (imagine a countryside far away from anywhere, with no lights, so where nightfall really means the threat of darkness). Living-Together: perhaps simply a way of confronting the sadness of the night together. Being among strangers is inevitable, necessary even,[31] except when night falls.

UTOPIE / UTOPIA

Utopia

I initially thought there'd be thirteen lectures on Living-Together and planned to dedicate the thirteenth to constructing, in front of you, a utopia of idiorrhythmic Living-Together—since the lecture course started out from that particular fantasy.[1] In which case, I'd have:

a. selected all the positive traits from the dossiers we've been through: I'd have picked out—from the lifestyles of the very different subjects that feature in our corpus—all I would have liked, all that would have given me pleasure, and then linked those traits together, arranged them in such a way as to produce a (quasi-novelistic) fiction of Living-Together: the Living-Together of a group that's both contingent and anonymous:

b. But I'd also have liked to invite you to provide some of the elements, some snatches, some fragments of the figuration of an idiorrhythmic community yourselves—for it's increasingly my belief that one must accept and encourage the projective labor of a work, of a discourse, of a lecture course.

Sovereign Good

The thirteenth lecture won't be taking place—or at any rate not in the pure, that is to say, subjective, form I'd imagined it. Why not? First, for contingent reasons: I didn't have time to collect your contributions; when it came to cheerfully constructing a happy utopia, I found I lacked the necessary enthusiasm. But also for a theoretical reason that's slowly become apparent to me: a utopia of idiorrhythmic Living-Together is not a social utopia. Now, from Plato to Fourier, all written utopias have been social: an attempt to fix upon the ideal organization of power. Personally, I've often regretted the fact that there hasn't been, I've often felt the desire to write a domestic utopia: an ideal (happy) manner of figuring, of anticipating the subject's optimum relation to affect, to the symbolic. But that, strictly speaking, is not a utopia. It's merely—or over and above, excessively—the figurative search for the Sovereign Good. Here: the Sovereign Good as concerns living space. Now, the Sovereign Good—its figuration—mobilizes the whole of the subject in all of his breadth and depth, in his individuation, that is to say in his entire personal history. And only a written form would be capable of taking account of that—or, if you prefer, a novelistic act (if not a novel). Only writing is capable of picking out extreme subjectivity because only in writing is there a concord between the indirectness of the expression and the truth of the subject—concord that's impossible on the level of speech (and so impossible to achieve in a lecture course) because, whatever our intentions, speech is always both direct and theatrical. The book on the Lover's Discourse may not be as rich as the seminar, but I consider it to be more true. → Consequently, all I'll be doing here is setting out some of the ostensibly objective principles of the idiorrhythmic Good—those that the study of our corpus has convinced me of at least:

Main objectives

1. To recall one example of the necessary conditions for a group to function. Wilfred Ruprecht Bion (*Experiences in Small Groups*): (a) a common purpose (overcoming an enemy, defending, etc); (b) common recognition of the boundaries of the group; (c) capacity to absorb new members, and to lose members (flexibility); (d) absence of subgroups with rigid boundaries; (e) each individual member: valued and free; (f) minimum of three members (two = personal relationship). Generally held belief that there's a qualitative threshold between two and three: "Two's company, three's a crowd."

Bion, pp. 24–25

Bareau

2. This brings us to the problem of numbers. The optimal number of members of an idiorrhythmic group. We noted a few suggestions in relation to the idiorrhythmies on Athos. Here are two more. Ceylon monasteries: around ten resident monks. Modern communes, parahippies = U.S.A.: on average twenty or thirty; France: around fifteen. (I think those numbers are excessive—although still very small compared to coenobitic monasteries. I personally think the optimal number should be under ten—or under eight even.)

Droit-Gallien, p. 204

3. As we know, in ethology, in the most tightly knit, least individualized animal groups (schools of fish, flocks of birds), and even in what appear to be the most gregarious species, there's always an attempt to regulate interindividual distance: it's the critical distance. This would probably be the most significant problem of Living-Together: how to identify and regulate that critical distance, on either side of which a crisis occurs. (However you use the word, always remember to link critical with crisis: the aim of criticism [literary criticism in particular] is to provoke a crisis). A problem that's all the more acute today (in the industrialized world of a so-called consumer society): what's most precious, our ultimate possession is

space. In houses, apartments, trains, planes, lectures, seminars, the luxury is to have space around you, in other words, to be surrounded by "a few people," but not too many: a problem characteristic of idiorrhythmy. → Were we to imagine an up-to-date version of Thelemic rule (itself adapted from monastic rule), it would look like this: the rule of Saint Benedict: the abba provides each monk with his own personal set of belongings: a cowl, a tunic, shoes, stockings, a belt, a knife, an awl, a needle, a handkerchief, a few slates = objects allocated on the basis of basic needs; the necessary and significant minimum (at that time, what was costly, and so what was provided: manufactured objects). Well, today, Thelemite rule wouldn't provide things (too easy, too inexpensive to act as a consecrating gift), it would provide space → The gift of space: would be constitutive of (utopian) rule.

4. Distance as value. This is not to be considered from the narrowly selfish perspective of plain "reserve," "*quant-à-soi*." Nietzsche makes distance a strong value—a rare value: "< . . . > the chasm between man and man, between one class and another, the multiplicity of types, the will to be one's self, and to distinguish one's self—that, in fact, I call the *pathos of distance* is proper to all strong ages" (*The Twilight of the Idols*, p. 70). → The utopian tension—that inhabits the idiorrhythmic fantasy—stems from this: what is desired is a distance that won't destroy affect ("pathos of distance": an excellent expression) → Squaring the circle, the philosopher's stone, a grand clear vision of utopia (*hupar*);[2] a distance permeated, irrigated by tender feeling: a *pathos*[3] that would allow for something of *Eros* and *Sophia*[4] (grand clear dream). Perhaps, in its way, taking the differences in historical context and ideology into account, comparable to what Plato was getting at under the name of *Sophronistery*[5] (cf. Ascetery and Plananstery) (*sophron*:[6] moderate, wise).

Here we'd rediscover the value I've been gradually trying to define under the name of "tact" (a somewhat provocative word nowadays).[7] Tact would mean: distance and respect, a relation that's in no way oppressive but at the same time where there's a real warmth of feeling. It's principle would be: not to direct the other, other people, not to manipulate them, to actively renounce images (the images we have of each other), to avoid anything that might feed the imaginary of the relation = Utopia in the strict sense, because a form of Sovereign Good.

BUT WHAT ABOUT METHOD?

Non-method

Deleuze, pp. 101–104

I began this lecture course by recalling one of Nietzsche's oppositions; the one he makes between method and *paideia* ("Culture").[8] Method: "the good will of the thinker," a "premeditated decision," a direct means, deliberately chosen to obtain the desired result. Method: to fetishize the goal as a privileged place, to the detriment of other possible places ≠ *Paideia*: eccentric path of possibilities, stumbling among blocks of knowledge. Clearly, we've not been positioning ourselves on the side of method but on that of *paideia* or, to put it more prudently (and provisionally), on the side of non-method. What this entails is a change of mindset, opting for one mindset over another. Method = phallic mindset of attack and defense ("will," "decision," "premeditation," "going straight ahead," etc.) ≠ Non-method: mindset of the journey, of extreme mutability (flitting, gleaning). We're not following a path; we're presenting our findings as we go along. A "hysterical" structure? Certainly one conducive to stage-fright;[9] not a single one of these lectures without stage-fright → "I present {*j'expose*}" = "I make myself vulnerable" {*je m'expose*} + the hysteric's perpetual question: *What am I worth?*

Not method, then—but a protocol when it comes to presentation (of our findings). Protocol, here, it seems to me, that can be summed up in five points:

1. TRAITS. FIGURES. BOXES

Cf. *A Lover's Discourse: Fragments*.[10] Figures of discourse, not in the rhetorical but rather in the gymnastic sense: a briefly held pose {*schèma*}. Not a "design," a plan of action {"*schéma*"} (phallic approach of method) but the body's gesture as it's caught in action (athletes, orators, statues). Each "figure" = the mobile posture of someone at work (not thinking of the end result). Two consequences:

  1. Boxes are put in place = a topic (grid of the places to be discussed). It's then up to each of you to fill them in; a game with several players: puzzle. I'm the maker (the artisan) cutting out the pieces of wood. You're the players = Principle of non-exhaustiveness: the presentation of a figure is not exhaustive.[11] I'll go further (perhaps a way of exonerating myself). Perhaps the ideal lecture course would be one where the professor—the locutor—is less

interesting than his audience, where what he says is of less consequence than what his lectures provoke. Typical and recent example: excrement and *The Confined Woman of Poitiers*. I might have dealt with it more intelligently; there was scope to develop things further. But if the lecture course is a symphony of propositions then each proposition has to be incomplete—otherwise it's a position, a phallic occupying of the ideal space. The dream: a kind of non-oppressive, aerated banality (cf. "Tact").

2. Allow me an imprecise metaphor: Living-Together. Slowly adding little touches of color: a drop of this, a glimmer of that. As long as it's a work in progress, as it's not clear where it's leading; cf. in painting: Tachisme, Divisionism (Seurat), Pointillism. Colors juxtaposed directly on the canvas as opposed to being mixed on the palette. Rather than mixing them at home, at my desk, I juxtapose figures in the lecture theatre. The difference being that in our case there is no final painting: at best, it would be up to you to produce one.[12]

2. CLASSIFICATION

If we've given up on the idea of assigning a meaning to a sequence of figures, and if we choose to stand by that non-meaning, then it looks as if the most appropriate procedure will be chance: to pull the figures out of a hat. But (in the words of a mathematician) chance can produce monsters.[13] The monster would be a fragment of a logical sequence, in other words: the semblance of precisely what we wanted to avoid: an argument developed over two or three points. Whence the recourse to a creative procedure, one that Chinese painting knew all about: controlled chance; a small degree of control over chance in the operation of classification: the order of the alphabet. Indeed, the alphabetical sequence doesn't actually have a meaning, it's not been subjected to any logical fiction. But chance gets corrected on two counts: (a) there's the question of the title: I'm not free to choose just any title, but I am able choose from among two or three possibilities: for example, between "Dirtiness," "Odor," "Excrement"—whence the ellipses in the alphabetical sequencing of my figures, which some of you picked up on;[14] (b) alphabetical order is aleatory with respect to reason, but not with respect to History: a very ancient order, then: chance conquered by familiarity.

3. DIGRESSION

This new rhetoric (of non-method): unlimited right to digression. Accordingly, it might even be possible to imagine a work, a lecture course that consisted solely of digressions around a fictional title: the "theme" (the *quaestrio*) would be destroyed by the ruse of perpetually skirting around it. Cf. the *Diabelli Variations*: the theme is virtually non-existent; over the course of the thirty-two variations, only very vague reminders of it return in intermittent flashes, thus making each one wholly a digression.[15]

4. TO OPEN A DOSSIER

I have said repeatedly (in relation to virtually every figure): "I'm merely opening a dossier." Opening a dossier: encyclopedic act *par excellence*. Diderot opened all the dossiers of his age. But at that time the act was effective, since knowledge could be mastered—if not by a single man (as in the time of Aristotle or Leibniz) then at least by a team. ≠ Today: no longer possible to acquire an exhaustive knowledge; knowledge is now wholly pluralized, diffracted across discrete languages. The encyclopedic act is no longer possible (cf. the failure of today's encyclopedias)—but for me personally, as a fiction, the encyclopedic gesture still has its value, its pleasure: its scandal.

5. THE SUPPORTING TEXT

All our work has been accomplished with the help of a handful of supporting texts. Tutor-texts: what allow us to speak → the intertext, in our case made explicit, is constitutive of all enunciation. Among those texts, two—not intentionally—have emerged as especially important: (a) *The Confined Woman of Poitiers*: the text of absolute marginality, a Living-Alone of a matter so intense it collides sideways on with all the secret and problematic aspects of Living-with. (b) The monks' text; I didn't expect that → It's certainly an obscure fixation. Why?

1. First and foremost, it served as point of contrast: with respect to the all too familiar monachism of the West and the coenobitism of the barracks (anachorites, idiorrhythmics): text with (for me) the same foreignizing and projective value as the Far East.

2. Or perhaps, on a deeper level: the religious—the category of the religious—not in its relation to religion, but as the privileged exposition of the symbolic. In this case, symbolism projected onto

the big screen by the conflict between marginality and the (ecclesial, communal) institution.

3. And then there's the fact that a Utopia (particularly one of daily life) is comprised of bits and pieces of reality casually drawn from a whole variety of different sources. A melting pot of what's good in a range of very different cultures, systems of thought, customs. The Oriental monks made their contribution here.

Such are, I believe, the key features of the expository protocol that has taken the place of method. I said at the beginning: non-method. As always, the "non-" is too simple. It would be better to say: premethod. As if I were preparing my materials with a view to dealing with them methodically at some later stage; as if I actually weren't too bothered what method would take them up. Anything is possible: psychoanalysis, semiology, ideological criticism could make use of them—which, as we noted, is precisely what dispensed the presentation of those materials from being psychoanalytic, semiological, political. That said—and this is the point I'd like to end on—the preparation for method is an infinite, infinitely open process. It's a form of preparation whose final achievement is forever postponed. Method is tolerated, but only in the form of a mirage: it's of the order of *Later on*. All labor is undertaken in this spirit, in that it's animated by *Later on*. Man = between *Never again* and *Later on*. There's no such thing as the present: it's an impossible tense.

That's all.

Thank you—that's not merely a rhetorical flourish: I'm well aware of the discomfort you've experienced in this lecture course, particularly in the first sessions.

That discomfort will—I hope—be alleviated next year—for those of you who'd like to come back:

a. Mostly likely to be on Saturday mornings (two hours blocked together).

b. Room 8: a semblance of comfort.

c. A public lecture course. Now, public: a suspended reality. The fact of an audience turning up, being surrounded by audience, puts the locutor in a state of enigmatic suspense: a gracious presence, graciously bestowed (which, incidentally, is what gives it its pleasure). Tide, lunar month: the public can recede. Each year, I expect it to do so.

What theme? I don't know yet. What I've just been saying about non-method would suggest that the "theme" (*quaestio*) is ultimately irrelevant. Whatever I choose as a "theme" (even, for instance, what on the face of it might look like a very literary one), the practice of digression, the right to digress. I'll say over and again the same thing. The indirect, which is of an ethical order, will be part of it. It'll involve an *Ethics*.

WHAT IS IT TO HOLD FORTH? / *TENIR UN DISCOURS*

Research on Invested Speech
1. Holding Forth / Tenir un discours
2. Charlus-Discourse
Seminar

HOLDING FORTH[1]

"SO, I WAS SAYING…"

Someone I know invariably begins each new session with his analyst with these words.

From that story (I'd like to say from that epiphany): emergence of a signifying trait, one that (for me) is striking, impressive. I immediately want to push the idea further. We hold, we are forever holding forth on the same topic—something that requires a great deal of patience from those around us, who are obliged to listen yet again to a discourse that endlessly repeats itself, to this imperturbable discourse we spend our whole lives upholding. We sustain one and the same discourse until death and death is the only power that can interrupt that unremitting taking of the same line. That unending discourse is never bowdlerized. It begins again, is reborn. And it's the tenacity of that repeated discourse that my friend is brave enough to lay bare three times a week with the help of what is, in truth, a somewhat particular listener: his analyst.

Put differently: to begin is always, at some level of the subject: to follow on from. Follow on from what? From what we were just saying. I'm following on from what I was saying. Where? At the École pratique des hautes études. When? Last year, in the context of a small seminar whose theme, set out, if not dealt with, was: "The Intimidations of Language." "So, I was saying": here, in the spirit of that expression, I'd like to point out that to my mind there's no interruption between École and Collège (what peculiar abbreviations!).[2]

Question: In a life, are there any, what are the disruptive elements—that cause this discourse to be abruptly broken off? Conversions? You can be converted to another object but not to another discourse.

THE INTIMIDATION OF LANGUAGE

Cf. Inaugural lecture: accepting to set down a fantasy at the origin of a new research topic.[3] I'm pursuing my research into a fantasy of irritation: someone else's (others': to be seen) language in that it irritates, that is to say in that it subjugates, language in that it enters, by means of certain operators (to be identified), into a relation of force, one that I feel threatened by. It would be of the order of what Plato calls misology (Plato, *Phaedo*). For him, it's pejorative: a violent distrust of reasoning. For us, more broadly: resistance to being held by the other's discourse (reasoning evidently being one of its weapons).

Method: very free digressions (all the more free to avoid anticipating the arguments of our invited speakers) circling around one point of return: language as force. Always come back to the fantasy (don't lose sight of it). The fantasy = a scenario, a cut-out image where I see the other's discourses (certain discourses pronounced by certain others) being invested with attributes (with operators) of power, of a power that I don't want or—since we mustn't jump to conclusions—that on the contrary I do want, that I take pleasure in being subjected to.

Now, I've not yet managed to transform that existential (or fantasmatic) situation, the intimidation of language, into a semiotic situation. Is such a thing possible / impossible? To some extent, it's the task of this seminar to find out. I'm repeating the fantasy without transforming it (which is somewhat the definition of the fantasy).

That repetition is effected on the level of signifiers (if it were a matter of concepts it wouldn't be a repetition): intimidation of language → linked to holding forth.

Note: the inadequacy of the French language, where it's impossible to make a noun out of the verb, as you can in Greek, which declines it in the neutral: *to diexerchesthai*[4]—except as a purely intellectual exercise. In French, I can only handle action linguistically by attaching it to a preexisting subject, of which it's necessarily the attribute, the predicate. I can't present that action in such a way that would allow it to operate as action and at the same time to absent the subject or to generalize it: which is what *to sustain a discourse* would mean. We only have "discourse" as an object, something that's manipulated—especially in archaic language, as a talent for discoursing on a topic, that is to say as potential action preserved as a pure attribute of the subject. Diderot: "Augustus possessed the prompt and ready speech fit for a King."[5]

It was while groping for the words to describe the fantasy intuitively that the expression to hold forth / *tenir un discours* forced itself upon me. (= I'm intimidated if someone lectures me / *me tient un discours* —what's more, slight paranoia, I'm very sensitive to other people "holding forth." I'm quick to feel that I'm being lectured at. And I'm also very anxious not to "lecture at" anyone else.)

THE IDIOMATIC EXPRESSION

To hold forth / *Tenir un discours* = the region to be explored. It's an idiomatic expression (a Gallicism? I don't know about other languages). Not strongly idiomatic or marked, meaning each element of the expression retains a certain degree of semantic independence—which we shall exploit (≠ *pomme de terre*).[6] But it's a fixed expression nevertheless. The proof: it's in Littré. So, lexical consecration: part of the linguistic system (in the Saussurian sense): to hold forth / *tenir un discours*. But more often: to spout on and on / *tenir des discours*. Note: it's not the same thing. The French plural minimizes, devalues, objectifies, like a piece of theater ≠ The singular refers to a monolithic, emphatic effect; closer to the meaning we're interested in.

It's necessary to dwell on the following point for a moment: that the seminar's "theme," its title, should come from an idiomatic expression; that an idiomatic expression should introduce the *quaestio*, the subject to be discussed. I'd like it if someone, one day, were to undertake a study of the titles of seminar courses, lectures, presentations, dissertations, theses—that is, of the titles of "discourses" (the word, as we shall see, is reminiscent of the school system). For my part, I'd volunteer the following hierarchy:

1. When a sentence (to be analyzed) serves as the starting point for reflection: the essay. The torture of writing a "commentary" on a sentence, since the aesthetic function of the sentence is to comprise a syntactic form of the "definitive," of what defies commentary. It's impossible to say or resay anything other than what's said in a well-formed sentence, whence the profoundly sterile nature of the exercise. The subject suffers as a result of being forced to perform a task that can't produce anything, and that even falsifies. (I don't know if they still set sentences for commentary in schools. In my day, it was more or less standard.)

2. When a word serves as the starting point for reflection. This is better. Because the word: a pure signifier. It doesn't shatter into "commentaries," but into other signifiers—along at least two roads, which to my mind are royal:

a. Etymology, the pseudo-origin, the illusion of origin, the emergence, the diachronic trembling of the vocable, its reversals, its paradoxes. Example: "discourse" itself; to run hither and thither, separating and dividing linguistic episodes: "the lover's discourse" → an indistinct and soporific layer of long, structured speech (comprised of interdependent parts).

b. Connotation, the connotative field; in other words, the sedimentation of habitual usages, the social resonance of the word. All of which means, the word—if it's well chosen (to be excluded: city, food, clothing, etc.)—as the title of a *quaestio*, permits working at the level of the signifier: the essay recedes. Cf. Journal, the *Première Livraison* (Mathieu Bénezet and Lacoue-Labarthe. Accident. Mourning. Imitation).[7]

3. When an idiomatic expression serves as the starting point for reflection. *Idios:* what is wholly specific to a language. Not as an abstract, universal structure, but as an idiom: language at the level of the historical, social body of a nation; acceptance of language's return to metaphor, that is to say to the body. The associative (signifying) field opens up in all its extensiveness, because it was prepared by language itself.

Our idiomatic expression: to hold forth / *tenir un discours*. As I said: not an especially idiomatic expression, meaning it's relatively decomposable. But that's not to say that its meaning-effect doesn't operate at the level of the syntagm as a whole. We shall therefore provisionally, artificially break it down into its component parts → The key word, I think (like Antaeus, here I reencounter my fantasy!) = to hold / to sustain / *tenir* and not discourse / *discours*. I'll begin with discourse, to see whether it contains some seme relevant to our fantasy.

"DISCOURSE" / "DISCOURS"

I noted: the French meaning, since the emergence of modern French (sixteenth century) is a smooth continuity of language. "*Discours*": 1503 (rare in the Middle Ages). As far as etymology is concerned, a reversal: *discurro* = running around in all directions (*dis* = separation, to go in opposite directions.) Only since antiquity has this been the figurative meaning of "*discourir*" (*dielthein*).[8] We'd have to look at the medieval meaning of *discursus*, particularly in scholastics: an interesting index card I've misplaced, but I remember it meaning separation, disruption.

Latin *discursus*: running this way and that, abrupt divagations. The word points us in the direction of the modern meaning. "*Dis-*

course": a sort of excursion, of divagation. Mallarmé *Divagations* (1897), (Collection: *Richard Wagner, Scribbled at the Theatre, Crisis of Verse, On the Book*, etc.). Now, when talking about that volume, with his customary foresight, Mallarmé holds in his hand the two contradictory extremes of the word "Divagation"— "Divagation" in that for us it's the screen, the screen word of "Discourse": "a book just the way I don't like them, scattered and with no architecture . . . " (there you have the *dis-cursus*, the splitting apart). But: "the Divagations that appear here treat a single subject of thought—if I look at them with the eye of a stranger, they resemble an abbey that, even though ruined, would breathe out its doctrine to the passer-by."[9] (The singular "held" / "sustained" / "*tenu*" can be heard here).

p. 1340

The intermediary meaning, falling somewhere between etymology and modern usage: "excursion" = a portion of language that's outside (outside of something, but what? In what sense is discourse the "outside of"?) but that's of a certain duration, has a certain substance, physiognomy. An excursion, something you remember. Swann's Way, The Guermantes Way: ultimately, these are "excursions."

The general seme is provided by Littré: "Said of anything pronounced with a certain method and being of a certain length." In sum:

1. A portion of language that's "outside." Already I'll say: "fit" in the way we say fit of anger, of madness; what ruptures a "normal" expression. Or even: "marked" as opposed to "unmarked."

2. Inwardly constructed: corresponding to the "eccentricity" of the "discourse" with regard to what surrounds it, there is—the same figure in reverse—an inner unification. It "breathes out its doctrine," something it is determined in relation to, that it exploits methodically.

3. Of significant length; that is to say, a portion of language that would go unremarked if it were "short"(all of this is to be taken in structural, paradigmatic terms).

Among the different entries in Littré—and there aren't very many, they're all very much the same—there's one that interests me more than the others = particular, historical and technical entry from the world of school: "A secondary school composition exercise consisting in expanding on a short outline dictated by the teacher relating to the discourse of a literary character in a given situation." (Littré) That discourse, in Latin (meriting an award in Jesuit schools), and later in French: a forefather of the dissertation and the essay. Parodic example: Proust *(Within a Budding Grove,* pp. 464–66): "Sophocles, from the Shades, writes to Racine to console him for the failure of *Athalie.*" Gisèle's essay: puts in everything she knows, one thing after another ≠ Andrée's haughty and ironic correction: "write your plan on a separate piece of paper" (the principle of "construction"). What interests me about this: the discourse produced is a copy, a "simulation," a piece of theater: a historical presentation based on an outline provided by the teacher (and also, perhaps: something of an examination exercise, a performance).

"TO HOLD" / "TENIR"

Active/Passive

Now I come "to hold"—and implicitly, of course, to being held (by a "discourse"). "Holding forth" comes down to (we'll probably come back to this later on) to repeating, in your own fashion, a discourse that's already been set out, that's already been heard a thousand times before (taking a hackneyed line), but doing so as if it were you who were inventing it, with the conviction of the first time: Callas, with passion: "I'm a woman . . . If you take away our femininity, what will we have left, etc." In other words, she's holding because she's held (by what's already been said).

"To hold" / "*tenir*": the strong word in the phrase; can perhaps be examined briefly nevertheless.

Littré. Seventy-two entries for "*tenir,*" among which (I'm running through them quickly): To hold in your hands—To retain someone—To possess—To occupy a space (military meaning)—To have in your make up—To have authority over certain things—To maintain someone or something in a certain state—To check, to prevent from—To keep to a road, a path—To keep a promise—To persist in.

There are clearly two basic semes running through all of those meanings:

— Power, force, subjection, ascendancy.
— Duration, persistence.

This comes across clearly in the idiomatic expressions (among which: "*tenir un discours*" / to hold forth) "*tenir maison*" / to keep house (force of prestige, of ostentation); "*tenir tête*" / to hold your own, not backing down; "*tenir pied*" / to hold your ground; "*tenir l'oeil*" / to hold someone's gaze (to impose through duration, to impose duration), "*s'en tenir à*" / to keep to (a force you exert upon yourself), "*en tenir*" / to take something (to have submitted to a force, to have "taken it," "dealt with it," not being able to be free of it); "*tenir sous le charme*" / to captivate, to hold someone spellbound (to subjugate, to keep someone in your power over an extended period of time, to the point of no resistance).

But that's not all: there's another seme on the protoetymological horizon. *Teneo* actually shares the same root as *Tendo*: "*tendre*" / to extend, to stretch out = in effect, to exercise a force and to keep it up for as long as possible. The essential seme probably relates to this idea of tension: holding up, holding out (*to be*, in the emphatic sense: to be alive in a way that's manifestly obvious, where the tension is spectacular). I'll say, as a shortcut: "Are you a Marxist, or are you a Lacanian?" = "Do you sustain a Marxist or a Lacanian discourse . . . ?"

"TO HOLD FORTH" / "*TENIR DISCOURS*"

All these semes are to be found in to hold forth / *tenir un discours*. Indeed, the expression implies:

1. An intentionality of force, coercion, subjection:

— a duration, a persistence;
— a tension, a taut, systematic consistency.

In other words: the aim is totality, eternity, being.

2. An effect of theatricalization: through "discourse" as an ostentatious performance of speech. + "Holding" / "sustaining," as occupying a space of being that's not your own. Playing a role → holding forth = holding up a linguistic mask.

A semiological remark:

— "To hold forth" = locution, idiomatic expression, fixed syntagm. Now, let's go back to a time when we read and practiced the theories of Saussure. The fixed syntagm:[10] a problem for Saussure with respect to his luminous dichotomy: *Langue / Parole*. Are we dealing with the linguistic system {*langue*} or with speech {*parole*}? Here we approach the limit of Saussurianism (which, incidentally, he was well aware of). A limit that the few recent advances in current linguistic thinking (the Performative, the Delocutionary)[11] start out from. "Holding forth" is an ambiguous figure because it's an "act" of *langue*, speech made of the linguistic system {*parole de langue*}.

— It seems as if "holding forth" muddles, interferes with the rhetorical, Saussurian (and even Chomskyian) taxonomy, throwing it off course. Rhetoric:

Baldwin, I, p. 23

1. *Heuresis*[12] / *inventio, taxis*[13] / *dispositio, lexis*[14] / *elocutio*: discourse that's constructed, like the linguistic system: combination of structural elements (language, competence, "geometry," Aristotle).[15]

2. *Pronuntiatio,*[16] *hupokrisis / delivery / actio*:[17] speech, performance: what's more, the vocabulary of acting. *Actio*: it's theater; orator: rhetorical performers. Note: Cicero saw what was at stake in this assimilation of the orator to an actor. He declared that training in *actio* should be acquired "not by imitating an actor or a clown, but by studying < . . . > the manners of warriors" (virility!).[18] He quits the theater for force! Now, in "holding forth," it's the linguistic system itself that's in *actio*. The "holding" itself, which pertains to performance, is coded (and, to a point, it's this code that we need to identify). Incidentally, is not "theater" (as a general category of the subject) what threatens to undermine Saussure's grand dichotomy? Indeed, the dichotomy is at risk from the moment there's a theoretical complicating of the classical sociological opposition of Saussure's time (let's not forget Saussure's relation to the sociology of his time: Tarde, and probably Durkheim) = Individual / Society. Now, the source of that complication is a new category that's now very much in the foreground: enunciation. In a sense, there's nothing outside of enunciation. The linguistic system is a sort of artifact that's in the process of losing its operative, taxonomic power: a trace of that movement in Lacan's "*lalangue*,"[19] in work on the performative, the delocutionary (Flahault, Milner).[20]

TO INVEST

It was the seme of theatricalization that I hear in "holding forth" (coupled with the seme of force) that led me to qualify the title of our seminar with the notion of "invested speech" or "investing in speech."

"Investment": the word comes from Freud (Laplanche-Pontalis): *Besetzung*.[21] "Economic concept: the fact that a certain amount of psychical energy is attached to an idea or to a group of ideas, to a part of a body, to an object, etc."[22] Note that the German and the French differ slightly. German: to occupy, (military) occupation. French: the same meaning, say Laplanche and Pontalis + a financial meaning: to invest capital in a business. We'll see in a moment that the French addition doesn't go far enough and there's a third meaning that'll be of interest to us.

Be that as it may, remember that in Freud there's the notion of physical origin (an attempt to establish a link between dynamic psychology and neuropsychology): "sum of excitation" → distinction between "ideas" and the "quantum of affect" with which they're invested. In his second theory of the psychical apparatus, origin of investments: the *id* → investment in an idea or an object → the ideas and objects (of the subject) as invested with values. The invested value: a charge can be negative, without there being any disinvestment. In phobia, the object = invested in as that-which-must-be-avoided. So it's possible for the notion of investment to be oriented toward ideas of intentionality, of value-objects, in short, phenomenology: affective aims (All this: in Laplanche-Pontalis).

Let's go back, once again, to language {*la langue*} (for the purpose of this introduction comes down to: offering a survey of language— a way of not preempting the upcoming presentations). Littré doesn't yet recognize the financial meaning in "to invest." It does however recognize the military meaning. But it devotes most of the entry to a long account of the etymological (Latin) meaning, which isn't there in the German. "To invest = to clothe," that is to say "to bestow or invest with a power, an authority, through various ceremonies, one of which is to be dressed in a garment." To illustrate this idea of investment, the best apologue would be the scene in Brecht's *Galileo*[23] where Cardinal Barberini, who's initially well-disposed toward Galileo, becomes increasingly hostile as he's slowly dressed in papal garb. With each new garment, his hostility grows; once he's put on all the official robes, it finally turns to censure: the cardinal has been invested with the pope.

This idea of clothing pulls investment away from Freud's idea of it (without contradicting it). It turns investing into playing a role: a theatricalized energy. → A speech, a discourse that's invested in ("held") = an object that's invested in (in the Freudian sense), a language whose exits have been blocked, that's cut off and occupied, a "cordoned off" language (in the way the police cordon off an area) and whose intention is to shut the other up—and at the same time a language-garment that's theatrically and ritually donned as a piece of clothing that bears the stamp of authority.

And let's not forget the Active / Passive turnstile. To invest in a discourse = to be invested by a discourse. "To hold forth" = to take orders from a phraseology, to reproduce a preexisting book with conviction: Werther and Ossian; Bouvard and Pécuchet[24] and the succession of discourses they invest in. Flaubert's novel: transforming alienation into investment: the act of copying.

ASPECTS

As you'll have grasped, the aim of this introduction is simply to unpack the words of our title. That unpacking—that unfolding—cannot but be intuitive, subjective. I've tried to give you a sense of what I pick up on in those words. For the fact of the matter is, there are no such things as machines for reading, for hearing meanings. It's simply that my ear gets drawn along certain avenues—like the paths of the code: the etymological avenue, the lexicographic avenue: avenue of the signifier.

With that in mind, I shall bring things to a close by indicating some impressions of "holding forth" gleaned from certain readings, situations. Once again, epiphanies—in no particular order (the style as befits epiphanies).

Three examples where the "holding forth" is verbal:

1. Exhortation: the beginning of *Robinson Crusoe*: the father's discourse to Robinson.[25] The problem what happens when "holding forth" coincides with a genre.

2. The sudden eruption of "holding forth." Part work-do, part social gathering: men and their wives. The men are discussing things, conversing: about Portugal, about China, about television. The women keep quiet. Then, all of a sudden, one of them—her little dog having just woken up—delivers a grand discourse on dogs: exalting the excellence of their affection, their intelligence. We come back to the problem of the invested thing that I'll simply call: the Thing.[26]

3. I take a taxi. Immediately, the driver starts talking, taking the line that "the French live above their means." As soon as we reach our destination, his discourse abruptly breaks off. But there's no sense that this does anything to alter what it is to "hold forth" (So it's not structured, then? No peroration to warn us that it's drawing to a close?). Discourse by the meter—by the taximeter: hold forth from Saint-Germain to the Rue Dutot, please!

Three examples of complex "holding forth." I have the impression—the proof—that someone's "holding forth" whenever I find myself being subjected to a kind of generalized expansion of signs: verbal, gestural, behavioral. That is to say, wherever it seems to me that a body is asserting itself, wherever I detect a self-important affirmation of the body:

1. Methodical display of a will-to-live: X is traveling abroad in a Nordic country, I see him sitting before a copious breakfast, eating calmly, with intensity, with controlled appetite: in view of everyone, he's busy satisfying a need, staging a pleasure. When consumed in such a manner, I'm struck by the impression that breakfast is actually a discourse X is sustaining: force, vigor, continuity, tension, a certain theatricality. Investment: breakfast is a garment.

2. A different (personal) epiphany. The first one: affectionate (loving someone whom you take pleasure in seeing eating heartily). This one: more irritating, more corrosive. On the train, a "young specialist nurse" (traveling with a secondary-school teacher who's clearly in thrall to her and whom she dominates): a succession of competing signs of affirmation: (a) a big tape player in our compartment, (b) a loud, booming voice, (c) unembarrassed discussion of all sorts of subjects, (d) lolls over two seats, (e) takes her shoes off, (f) eats an orange, (g) cuts in on my conversation with my traveling companion. In short, she holds forth. The meaning of the discourse she's sustaining = I don't hold back = I exist = I don't stand on ceremony. In short, "holding forth" refers to a coded figure. The proof being that Oriental monks gave it a name: *parresia* (ease, familiarity, frankness ≠ *xeniteia*: character with no familiarity).

3. Last: brief epiphany of holding forth. In Urt:[27] a young motorcyclist with his crash helmet on, parading, backfiring on the empty Place du Port. He was truly holding forth. Because isn't to hold forth—the final seme—: "to wind other people up"?

Those examples (epiphanies) can be set against the discourse that is the opposite of "holding forth." Someone who statutorily takes no line, someone deprived of language, who doesn't own language, and so can't hold anything: the Marginal {*Paumé*}. In the Marginal {*Paumé*}: neither force, nor tension, nor theater.

CONCLUSION

This introduction: its function = to link the seminar to a fantasy, to undertake an exploration of the fantasy through a few verbal signifiers. Systematic exploration of the fantasy; a precedent: Juliette's advice to the beautiful Comtesse de Donis.[29] We're now going to leave the fantasy behind, at least as a justification, and allow the expression "holding forth" to shatter even further through the various approaches of several different people.

There'll therefore be a series of wholly undirected presentations: the sole instruction the speakers received was to explore the proposed expression in their own fashion. Here's the program:[30]

January 19	Flahaut	Discourse and Emblem
January 26	Lucette Mouline	The Proustian sentence: Stances and insistences
February 2	F. Récanati	Discourse sustained, discourse tenable, discourse untenable
February 9	Cosette Martel	Woman as object of speech
February 16	J.-A. Miller	Other people's discourse, the other's discourse
February 23	Spring break	
March 2	A. Compagnon	Enthusiasm
March 9	L. Marin	
March 16	Flahaut?	

I'll take charge of the last two seminars (taking us up to Easter), probably to propose (I've no idea: it will depend on what I've learned from the other presentations: such is the principle of this seminar) a few analyses of "holding forth."

CHARLUS-DISCOURSE
SKETCH OF AN ANALYSIS OF A DISCOURSE

CHARLUS-DISCOURSE[1]

The double difference:

Type of discourse

Method: S/Z

1. Kinetics

Chance

Syllogistic logic

Marcottage

Successive markers

2. Triggers

3. Allocutionary authority

Andromache

Charlus-Discourse. The inflexemes

4. The forces

"Psychology." Explosemes

"Psychoanalysis"

Intensities

Conclusion

CHARLUS-DISCOURSE

The discourse that Charlus delivers to the Narrator, who pays him a visit one evening on the way home from the dinner at the Guermantes': *The Guermantes Way* part 2, chap. 2, pp. 528–40[3] = discourse of reproach and rupture + as a companion piece: Andromache, act 3, scene 4.

A contradictory, paradoxical impression from the very first reading:[4]

1. On the one hand, a sustained, dense, continuous, unbroken discourse browbeats the Narrator, whose occasional interjections serve only to get it going again; would appear to enact the original meaning of "holding forth": compactness and tension.

2. Yet on the other hand and at the same time: a discourse that's extremely mobile, changeable, like a landscape lit up between passing clouds. A sort of subtle shimmering of inflections: an inflective discourse. In this sense, as a result of those two characteristics, it could be said: cf. Wagner's musical textile in that it's continuous and inflective, both compact and agile: a mobility of musical gestures; what Nietzsche called Ton-Semiotik[5] and condemned as the expression of decadence.

The Case of Wagner: "Wagner starts out from phenomena of hallucination—not of sounds but of gestures. It is initially for gestures that he seeks a musical semiology; if one would admire him, one should watch him at work on this point: how he decomposes, how he separates into small units, how he animates these, valorizes them, and makes them visible! But this exhausts his strength: the rest is no good."[6]

It's this relation between the mass (the continuity) and the gesture, the expanse of material and the inflection, that interests me. Whence an approach that will be above all methodological: provisional crude generalizations, a first attempt at an analysis that'll be neither meticulous nor exhaustive. I shan't be drawing up a full inventory of the structural elements of the discourse, I'll merely raise the questions of method—or even more prudently: questions of procedure. How (in the future) might one undertake an analysis of a discourse such as the one delivered by Charlus?

Let's begin by ridding ourselves of one methodological illusion: Charlus-Discourse isn't an example, a sample. It's not a representative of a typical class of discourse, that of "holding forth." It's caught in a difference—and, to my mind (as an erstwhile structuralist), in a double difference: (1) with respect to "holding forth" on the doxa, the stereotype, (2) with respect to an earlier analysis: *S/Z*.

1. There are likely to be (an intuitive working hypothesis) a type or several types of "holding forth." This is our intuition when we listen to political speeches, for example = a type, an endoxal code = a discourse that can be constructed along the traditional lines of structural analysis: a corpus of discourses. → From which we then infer the description of a type (of a grammar). ≠ Charlus's discourse: appears to be atypical. Snatches of it are familiar, recognizable, but not the whole. Now, from the moment there's recognition, we're dealing with a sign (the sign is what's recognized, Benveniste). So we can say that there's a semiotic dimension to Charlus-Discourse (this is the point Nietzsche is making in reference to Wagner). But at the same time the speech is unique (recognized ≠ clichéd): it's "Charlus-Discourse." Which presents us with an epistemological problem: How to structure the Unique? The Unique in that it doesn't cast itself outside of structuration, that is, out into the ineffable; the Unique = the Text. "Charlus-Discourse" = a Text, pronounced by a voice, a body, and what a body! Charlus's body is very much present, constantly figured throughout the whole of *In Search of Lost Time*. This approach to the atypical text, considered independently of any corpus: the one that was retained and affirmed in *S/Z*.

2. That said, the codes in "Charlus-Discourse" can't be considered from the same perspective (to be of the same "order") as the ones in *Sarrasine*—and this has nothing to do with the distinctiveness of *Sarrasine* as a narrative. If Balzac refers to a cultural code (allusions to art, for instance): dull units are denoted (as it were), it's the being-there, the naturality of culture that's presented: a use of the code, but with no connotations → Charlus: cultural code (style of chairs, for example) + an affective, emotive, ennunciative supplement. Charlus the subject positions himself within the cultural unit: arrogance, aggression. For Charlus, the cultural code is a means to position himself in the eyes of the other, to enter into a reciprocal play of images, of positions. There's an accumulation, a stereophony of codes. *Surrender of Breda* by Velázquez:[7] painting + code of chivalry +

theatricalization of the relation, etc. → "Charlus-Discourse": a banal interweaving of codes (cf. *Sarrasine*) + some supplements. Culture, for instance, isn't simply a reference, an origin (Balzac), it's a space of enunciation. Hence: the passage about the young Berliner; he, at least, would have heard of Wagner and the *Walküre*: (a) musical cultural code, + (b) Charlus's modernity (Wagner at that time), + (c) Charlus's fondness for Germany, + (d) the code of setting someone straight. It's this polyphonic unleashing of codes that comprises our methodological problem (a problem underestimated in *S/Z*.)[8]

To undertake that preliminary (and rudimentary) exploration of a new method (of a new problem), I will start out from the familiar in order to work my way toward the less familiar. The familiar: structuralist analysis, that is to say, identifying the units, the morphemes of discourse. The less familiar: the emergence of the notion of force in the field of inquiry.

IN THE STRUCTURALIST MANNER[9]

1. KINETICS

Structuralist analysis (of the narrative): our starting point. Not surprising, since with any new and difficult analysis = tendency to want to identify the "construction" of the text (the influence of the "*explication du texte*"),[10] the plan; to reconstruct the "units" (how the codes appear) and the manner in which they're combined, a layout. → This preliminary analysis takes the form of a table. Tabular = immobile, panoramic, planimetric overview of the text as object.

Yet, very soon: awareness of the real problem. How does the text advance? Once it's begun, how does it develop, proliferate? How does the mutation of situations, of the sites (*situs*) of discourse operate (we're already making progress if we're talking about sites rather than units)? What's the key to its development, to its unfolding, to how the discourse "comes together," "takes" (cf. Being held by discourse), the translation of its units (its sites)? → Such questions would pertain to a kinetic science of speech: a mechanics (what are the motors of discourse, of the *cursus* in *dis-cursus*?). And also to an art of travel. How does the text travel? (Here we'd recover the *hodos*[11] in *hodoiporia*,[12] in travel, and in method). *In abstracto*, there are at least four possible operations, four possible motors (a first approximation).

1. Chance: not to be discounted. Besides, modernity would often play around with the chance of verbal consequences. Words, sentences, lexemes (units in whatever form): thrown into a hat. The next line would be pulled out, one after the other = stochastic procedure. The most straightforward technique, but also the one that produces the least interesting results, because what it produces is a sequence of indifferenciable elements (there's no particular relevance to their position). Once established, all chance can produce are typical differences within itself. That said: (a) it might be interesting to conduct the experiment with sentences (those of "Charlus-Discourse"); it's possible that chance would pull out a few snatches of logical sequences: would be worth looking at; (b) remember: a great many aesthetic forms have sprung from the principle of corrected chance, the controlled accident; chance is what starts off the chain—never easy.

Three further motors (what we're left with once chance has been discounted):

2. For the record, because it's not yet been sufficiently studied (other than in Perelman's *Rhetoric*):[13] logical motor: when speech advances by means of the logical connections of reasoning. One proposition leads to or necessitates the next, in keeping with the law of logical constraint, or the constraint of a certain logic. The most common: syllogistic or enthymematic logic. (Today's discourses: probably far more enthymematic than we think. Something to look out for: interesting test, because it would take us into the discourse of the essay and new types of readability.)

3. Marcottage, or layering. A principle of Russian formalism: if a nail is hammered in at the beginning it's so that the hero can hang himself on it at the end. Presupposes a sort of endoxal, diffused, ancestral logic, a storehouse of experiences, an empirical logic: a knock at the door → open it / don't open it; question → response (or no response). There's layering—or *marcottage*—because a greater or lesser number of units from other sequences can be interposed between the first sequence and the second. → Interlacing of sequences = braid, text. For further discussion on all of this, see *S/Z*. Privileged motor of the classical text.

4. In this (with the exception of the recourse to chance), the authority claimed by the analysis: sort of logic "in itself"—a parascientific or empirical logic—that gets discourse working by itself, with only very minimal assistance from a manager, the author, or the person delivering it. Impersonal structure, the sole link between a logical language {*langue*} and a speech {*parole*} that's

performing it: analysis that excludes the subject—that is, the other.

5. Here's a fourth (classical) motor that engages the other on a structural (rather than an implicit) level: system of successive markers:

— Model provided by Plato; goes back to the opposition between Bad Rhetoric (Sophists) ≠ Good Rhetoric:[14] philosophical, dialectical, or psychagogic rhetoric (instructing souls through speech).
— Pyschagogic discourse: not a matter of writing, but of speech: the kind that actively seeks out personal interlocution, ad-homination. Typical example: the dialogue between teacher and pupil, united by the love that the other inspires. Being of the same mind, that's the motor of this kind of speech. That rhetoric = a loving dialogue.

Example of "development" or "shifting gears" {"*développement*"[15]} (always bear something of the cyclist's meaning in mind = what gear are you in?). In the search for truth, start out from a general, imprecise location and work your way down, following the natural logical connections (the staircases), working your way through each kind, like landings, until you come to one that's indivisible = the staircase. With each tread of the staircase, an alternative: in order to continue in your descent, you must choose one term over another. Example: progressive definition of a Sophist:[16]

Capture of prey
    Wild / domesticated
        With a weapon / through persuasion
        In public / in private
            To give away / for your own purposes
            To eat / to sell
              Flatterers / Sophists

— That dynamic structure resembles the paradigmatic structure of language: marked / unmarked. It's the marked that gets the descent going again. Now, the marked: effected by a concession from the person responding (the pupil). There must be two interlocutors, and one of them has to assent by nodding his head or its linguistic equivalent: all the faintly ridiculous or tedious elements of the Socratic dialogues. In actual fact, those elements = ultimately, acts of love and rhetorical operators.

Which brings us to our problem: the discourse that advances by means of affective markers, or affect as the operator of that discourse.

2. TRIGGERS

We must concede, *a minimo*, that there are certain modes of discourse (of discursivity) whose advancement depends entirely on certain events (words-events) that, at certain key moments in the allocutionary situation, (abruptly) trigger a new flow of speech. These are the starters, the instigators, the gear-shifters, sorts of interlocutory *shifters*.[17] To engage (the clutch) = "to establish a connection between the engine and the organs it wants to set in motion." The interlocutory *shifter* establishes a brusque connection between the affective motor and the rhetorical organs of discourse: the discursive car starts up. These triggers can make a speech jerky, erratic. This is obvious in the case of "Charlus-Discourse" : Charlus judders discourse ("to judder": when used with reference to certain tools, to cause to vibrate; with reference to a brake, a clutch, a machine, to jump, to jerk). The metaphor (to judder) gives quite a good sense of the peculiar dialectic I spoke of at the beginning of the session: compact mass + rapid inflections. Charlus speaks like a lawnmower, a pneumatic drill: he voraciously judders discourse.

Sample triggers:

1. Gestures. Sitting in the wrong chair → disdainful and outraged tirade. Or: gesture of denial → angry reproach.

2. The other's words. The word in itself, in its standard signifying form, unleashes a wave of speech-affect: being friends, to offend (p. 530). Aeschylus: words like the lash of a whip (*Oresteia*).[18] Sometimes it's not the word, it's the idea, the signified. Thus, via the relays of an interpretation: "I have already sworn to you that I have said nothing" "So I'm lying!" (p. 534). But the affective shimmering is so changeable, the motor so capricious that it can shift gear without warning, in ways that are completely unexpected. → Astonishing U-turns: "Someone has misinformed you" → "It's quite possible" (comes abruptly in the place of "So I'm a fool, then") = Deflations: bound to be an important element of this semiology of discursive forces whose features I'm attempting to sketch out.

3. Words pronounced by the subject himself, which come to act as clutches. A word pronounced by me splits me in two and directs me toward a different kind of discourse: cf. Marceline

Hugo, *Pierres,* p. 150
Werther, p. 125

Desbordes-Valmore "At twenty, terrible sorrows forced me to give up singing because my own voice made me cry"; and Werther: "And now I am crying like a child, telling you all this so vividly."[19] = Charlus's rising emotion, which takes him to the brink of tears when he develops the theme = you might at least have written → auto-emotion = the subject split in two, he is simultaneously speaking and hearing himself speak.

4. In the order of auto-triggers, a question to be explored in more depth: that of "syntactic turns of phrase." Bits of ready-made sentences, syntactic stereotypes: "It's not for me to say . . . " "I won't lie to you . . . " These syntactic turns or modes of construction = empty, only acquire a content later on; ready-made openers, announcing a shift in gear. Now, a dossier: because they recall the verbal hallucinations (Freud, Lacan) that proliferate in the dream (cf. seminar on *The Lover's Discourse*[20] and Safouan, *Oedipe*, 43, 110).[21] Truncated sentences that get no further than their syntactical construction: "Even though you're . . . " "If you should ever do that again . . . "

In general terms, those internal triggers or internal starters of discourse, might—possibly—authorize a preliminary classification of "discursive strategies." Narratives (possibly including intellectual narratives, arguments in narrative form: to be seen) ≠ scenes (discourses prompted by internal triggers). In the discourse-scene, what triggers the shift in gear (the progression) is the repercussion: the whole of the imaginary immediately responding to a signifier-stimulus. It's precisely the situation of the subject before the illusion— of the bull before the red cape. The discourse-scene (and Charlus's in particular): a kind of bullfighting. → The illusion (words, gesture, syntactic turn of phrase, *interpretandum*)[22] = a violent image, an image I have of the other and/or an image I believe the other has or will have of me, or the image of myself whose theatricality I choose to adopt under the gaze of, under the authority of the other. Which brings me to:

CHARLUS-DISCOURSE
(continued)

3. ALLOCUTIONARY AUTHORITY

The play of positions between myself and the other: object of psychoanalytical research. But how to come up with a semiotic version of (or dimension to) that research? How to analyze a discourse-scene? How to classify those positions, their varying degrees of proximity? How to determine the positions of enunciation—of interlocution? Such is the aim of the new linguistics (or semiology) that is trying to establish itself. Or even: since it's a matter of discursive positions (mobile positions: a shimmering effect) = strategy. To point up the "stratagems," the manifestations, the operators of those positions. Indeed, in pragmatics (≠ structural analysis in the strict sense), flagging up your position amounts to deposing the other: here, any flagging up of a position is necessarily transitive.

I won't run the risk of proposing a list or a way of classifying those "stratagems." Merely, to get things started, a very broad distinction: (a) a calculated discourse, whose strategies have been well thought-out in advance: political manipulation of the other; ancient rhetoric's field exactly (to persuade someone, to change their mind, alter their decision) (*Andromache*, act 3, scene 4); ≠ (b) wild discourse, punctuated by expressive explosions; a discourse with no strategy but that's not without its effects: Charlus-Discourse. (A provisional, questionable distinction: it could be that all discourse is strategic: cf. *infra*.)

A. Andromache

A discourse that sets out to obtain something: for Hermione to plead with Pyrrhus to save Andromache's son. The whole strategy: to avoid inflicting narcissistic wounds, to create a complicity, a solidarity (a very common situation: trying to get want you want without upsetting someone, or even: flattering without upsetting someone; a situation fraught with the risk of putting your foot in it;

incidentally, something to be studied: putting your foot in it as an analyzable accident of discourse).

Andromache's discourse:

— Wholly focused on Hermione, the addressee. A case where the addressee is the absolute target. Not a single divagation, not a single weakening of resolve: don't express anything of yourself, focus solely on what the other will hear; sort of pure, oblative allocution.

— Andromache breaks Hermione down into distinct roles and, once those roles are fixed, works in between the lines, adapting her own position depending on the role. That "in between the lines": a discourse that's very careful not to be aggressive. A truly strategic discourse: it anticipates and preemptively concedes all difficult questions; that is to say, it responds in advance to Hermione's discourses, to the positions she adopts in her discourse:

The Rival	Her victory is acknowledged
The Victor	Andromache adopts a humble position
The Enemy	A truce is proposed
The Quarry	She promises to leave forever
The Mother	Complicity

Only the second column is "discursive-ized" = put into words (but together with the first = enunciation).

A questionable (dangerous) "stratagem": to remind Hermione of her debt, to expect some kind of gratitude, exchange (never oblige the other to be grateful).

Hermione's response: to drop all the roles, and retain only one: that of the Rival in a position of power. In a sense, she's the one who's holding forth: her discourse isn't strategic, it's expressive, it's taut (held), it's the affirmation of a force.

Andromache's "stratagems" have very subtle grammatical and stylistic instruments at their disposal, which she plays in a delicate shimmering of timbres: the pronouns whose function is to refer to their counterparts. There's a rewriting of the pronouns:

— "I" → Hector's widow (cf. "my Hector"). Accentuates their conjugality, withdraws Andromache from the game {*jeu*} (from the I {*je*}).

— "Our," "us" → maternal complicity.

— "One / They {*On*}" ("want to take him away from us"; "what are they afraid of?"): serves to euphemize Pyrrhus and Agamemnon, glossing over their unpleasant role.

In contrast, Hermione, cruelly, starkly: "me" / "you."

With respect[1] to "I" / "one" {*on*}, or rather: "I" → "one" {*on*} (rewritten as "one" {*on*}).

Famous and key example, Brichot's newspaper articles during the war: *In Search of Lost Time*, part 3: p. 792.

The rewriting of "I" as "one": perhaps this offers a way in to a stylistics of *écrivance*, which would be much needed (assuming of course that the proposed distinction between *écriture* and *écrivance* were accepted).[2] *Écrivance*: scientific: the text is written under the terrorizing eye of Madame Verdurin.

In a diffuse, relayed manner, by way of substitutes: problem of "I" / the familiar "you" (since every discourse involves the anticipation, if not the strategy, of its response, cf. *infra*), rewritten in impersonal, absent forms. It's the whole problem of enunciation. The advantage, to begin with at least, of focusing on how "I" is rewritten → "one" is that it offers semiology a tiny point of entry into a vast logical, psychoanalytical, pragmatic dossier (the subject's position in the enunciation, between the Other and the other).[3] For, when it comes down to it, the rewriting of "I" as "one": a matter of style. There would be "style" (along with stylistics, a notion that has greatly depreciated in value, has entirely disappeared) whenever a discursive inflection (incidentally, inflections can be a matter of lexis as well as syntax) serves to transform "I" into "one": Andromache, strike slogans. It would then offer a glimpse of a new conception of denotation (cf. the beginning of *S/Z*).[4] Not by any means a white, neutral, abstracted diagram of what's said—which has been hypothetically stripped of its stylistic ornaments (the message as such)—but on the contrary: order and field of "I," the text rewritten in "I." "I" isn't the primitive, spontaneous, expressive state of the text (there's no such thing); rather, it's the text in its amalgamated state and in that cannot be dissociated, like an adhesive (a coalescence): force of desire + force of misunderstanding ("I": pronoun of misunderstanding ≠ "one" pronoun of lying, of doing something just for show, of the blatant strategy.)[5]

B. Charlus-Discourse

Charlus's discourse isn't straightforwardly strategic (direct calculation). There's an obscure, enigmatic strategy at work, one that even the subject is not necessarily aware of using (cf. infra on "expression," "explosion"). Nevertheless, I'm convinced: strategy = to get a hold on, to seize the Narrator. Besides, is there such a thing as an unstrategic discourse? All discourses: implicitly or unconsciously, the discourse is directed at the other (other people); it's as if the other were a target, that is, a possessable, transformable object. There'd be no discourse without hope: to speak is to hope. If there's no strategy = silence, discourse falls into the ineffectual (forms of schizophrenia? Of autism?).

Charlus's strategy: can't be analyzed in the way Andromache's could: (a) at times, unconscious, (b) takes a series of winding paths = abrupt changes of direction, denials, about-turns. Desire in the guise of aggression. It's therefore not a matter of direct, straightforward triggers but rather of inflectors of discourse. The pressure of affect produces an inflection in the discourse: "inflexemes."

1. The deflection of responsibility: "That's your affair," "That's his problem": common form of aggression. Verbal act of separation, of non-communication; you're on your own and I'm telling you so = "isoleme."

2. Propositions made with the expectation they'll be contradicted (affording the speaker some narcissistic gain). Very common: "I'm getting old" "No you're not!" etc. Here "We must part forever" → "No, let us see each other again" (the proposition may be stated with sincerity; in which case, it becomes an auto-trigger: of sadness. But it's also and at the same time used as a tactic, pronounced with an infinitesimal grain of hope).

3. Accusations: "your calumnious fabrications." Insults → "people who are ignorant of their value," "in its most effectively patronizing sense" that call for denials, explanations, that the other is forced either to counter or passively ignore.

4. The description of their relationship is caressed, handled with linguistic subtlety: "declarationism." Varied, increasingly elaborate screen words. Here Charlus proceeds in an aggressive manner, but the pleasure that linguistic caress affords is the same: "sympathy," "benevolence": masks that speak desire (*Larvatus prodeo*).[6]

5. Putting the discourse that's being sustained into metadiscourse: "the interview . . . will mark the final point in our relations":

"Metemes." Subtle—or stalled—form of declarationism: caressing the caress, consciousness of the caress as caress. The secondary pleasure afforded by consciousness of the first pleasure.

There you have no more than a sketch of an intuitive classification. Nevertheless, it allows me to propose, in general terms, on the basis of this example:

— There's a variety, a particular class of discursive aggression: pushing the other back into his responsibility, into the solitude of his responsibility. Rupture of anaclitism,[7] marking the end of childish irresponsibility: forcing the loss of the Mother. Charlus wants to force the other to take responsibility: (1) we must part forever and it's your own fault; (2) it's your problem; (3) "It seems to me only that . . . you might have . . . "

— The deflection of responsibility functions as a severance of communication. Yet it's a form of communication in itself in that each one of those "inflexemes" constitutes a demand, calls for a response. Charlus puts the other in the position of having to respond—even if he doesn't give him the time to. All allocutionary discourse would therefore involve the necessity of a response. Discourse = performance of speech that implies a response. → Methodologically (structurally) speaking, it would probably not be possible to undertake a semiotic analysis of discourse without taking those tacit units of response into account. Response = requisite component of discourse.

Note: theory of the *double bind*, the double constraint.[8] (I receive two imperative orders in direct contradiction with one another) → a situation that gives rise to psychosis ("*The effort to drive the other person crazy*," Searle). It's Charlus's position: respond / don't respond. Now, he's speaking the language of police authorities everywhere = very specifically, something a cop would say: "You're responsible for this." → "Yes, but . . . " → "No yes buts." This far down the chain, the only options available to the person being interpellated are: react (assault the police officer) or opt for passivity, cowardice. The choice he has to make is between harming himself (by the risk he's taking) or his image. Note that the Narrator—who throughout *In Search of Lost Time* is careful to keep out of things, putting himself in a situation of suspended response—is in this case driven to *acting out*[9] (for the first and only time in the whole book): he tramples on Charlus's top hat. He responds to Charlus, he engages in communication—which appeases Charlus.

4. FORCES

It should be clear by now[10] that the whole of the preceding analysis was animated by the proposition that discourse ("Charlus-Discourse") is to be conceived less as a table of units subjected to organizational rules (semiological, classical, taxonomic) than as a field, a play of forces, of mobile intensities (idea of the shimmering effect, of triggers, of "stratagems," of "inflexemes"). However, from the point of view of analysis, those forces cannot be grasped directly. They operate by way of analytical (descriptive) relays—none of which, incidentally, is false, or rather invalid. What we're dealing with are, so to speak, descriptive states of forces that are set out in relays. I detect three of them.

A. "Psychology"

Should we wish to give a "psychological" description of Charlus we could well refer to this discourse. What appears to elude the analysis of Charlus-Discourse as a (kinetic) sequence of "stratagems" (thinking out one's position in relation to the other) are those moments when something seems to explode within Charlus, expressing (in the strong sense)[11] a being which exists within Charlus "in and of itself," {en soi} independent of any strategy: "Do you imagine that the envenomed spittle of five hundred little gentlemen of your type . . . would succeed in slobbering so much as the tips of my august toes?" (p. 532) An "insult" seems to provoke an intensification of pride (a passion) which then explodes; it's as if we were witnessing the exteriorization of a sort of primitive version of the Charlus-being. Charlus's character, his soul = his truth, his sincerity = miraculous and unprecedented suspension of all strategies. Pride: the last mainstay.

However: only a "natural" psychology considers those "explosemes" to be operating outside of any kind of strategy; a psychology which concedes that, at certain moments of truth, the other is placed in parenthesis. Yet other types of psychology exist that reject any notion of "in and of itself" in relation to the psyche and, as a consequence, consider every element of a speech to be engaged in constructing the locutor—a labor orientated toward the other (play of images, and so a strategy). That labor can be intentional or unconscious.

Intentional? That doesn't necessarily mean conscious in the usual sense. Think of Sartre, *Sketch for a Theory of the Emotions*:

"fainting," "anger"[12] (all this fits Charlus very well): behaviors of flight when faced with the unendurable. In reality, fainting fits, anger are intentionalized. They serve a purpose; they take their place within an economy managed by the subject: they are profitable behaviors. All anger is strategic.

Unconscious? → It would be possible to offer a interpretation of Charlus's "explosemes" → Another level of forces reveals itself.

B. "Psychoanalysis"

(In the narrow sense of interpretative psychoanalysis: vulgate).

Naturally, there's to be no question of psychoanalyzing Charlus (no point whatsoever in psychoanalyzing someone who exists on paper: there's no such thing as literary psychoanalysis). I'm merely proposing a second relay to draw us closer to the forces at work in the discourse:

— the "explosemes," the discourse's non-strategic acts can no longer be considered "in and of themselves," as irreducible expressions; they're *interprentanda*,[13] symptoms. For example, the book with myosotis on the cover: for Charlus, the message is completely clear (forget me not) but for the Narrator, totally obscure → "Could there have been a clearer way of saying to you . . . ?" Sort of excess of interpretation that lends itself to interpretation, that is to say, to being reconverted into a typology. The previous mainstay ("pride") will be moved, pushed aside, integrated into a broader table: clinical table, a complex play of symptoms. Proust sets out the components of the Charlus-syndrome himself (pp. 532–33): pride, homosexuality and madness. → classic type: the paranoiac.

— It's certainly not my intention to reduce psychoanalysis to a system of interpretation, to a hermeneutics claiming to have pushed back the mainstays of psychological interpretation (pride → paranoia). But it's nevertheless true that according to the vulgate (which irrigates present-day conversation) analytical or "dis-analytical" discourse (devalorized discourse) functions as interpretation. Its self-assigned function is to raise curtains, screens (as they operate within a given discourse). The problem (my problem) = when a curtain is raised in the infinite theatre of language, what's revealed is a backdrop; in other words: another curtain. This, in fact, is how I think of psychoanalysis today: as itself a screen, a screen that conceals (or half-conceals, or simply veils) something—and that something can sometimes be in front of it. The idea of a screen concealing what's in front of it: opposition between *onar* (the common dream) and *hupar*: the grand clear dream, the never believed prophetic vision (Pythia). Cf. *A Lover's Discourse*, p.60.[14]

— That's not all. I think of psychoanalysis as a screen, but things can and do get painted on that screen—incredibly beautiful things that I absolutely cannot do without—this time that is my own: a fiction that I profit from, a grand painted veil: the *maya*,[15] covered with names, with forms, with types.

C. Intensities

The "grand clear vision" (*hupar*): abolition of hidden / visible.[16] Forces at work within discourse that a typology (the indexing of spaces according to their depth and movement) won't necessarily be capable of registering, but that act according to intensity:

1. The notions of excess or scarcity (rarity)—in their Zen version—(discursive states, markers) become relevant. For example, it's precisely because of his excess that the Narrator esteems Charlus. The mother is loved for her discretion (*discretio*: a certain force of distance, of discontinuity).

2. Relevance of the notion of the mottling effect, of the subtle shimmering of different intensities. There's one art that—by its very nature—mobilizes that shimmering of intensities: music. (a) Music is symbolizing, but it's not symbolizable. It can't be interpreted according to the movement of a hermeneutic space (there's no such thing as a semiology of music). (b) Music: fundamental in Proust. At issue here is not music in the sense of the Vinteuil-little-phrase (philosophy of memory), but the music of language, language as music. Proust's fascinated, sustained attentiveness to voices: the mother reading *François le Champi*.[17] Voices are described in their mobility: subtlety and acuity in respect to how a voice rises and falls. Charlus specifically: where Charlus is (his identity as a field of forces): his voice. The object of a semiotics of the forces at work in discourse, of an active philology of discourse[18] would be: delivery, *pronunciatio*. One example (among others), p.530: "He gave a disdainful smile, raised his voice to the supreme pitch of its highest register, and there, softly attacking the shrillest and most contume-

Éric Marty

lious note . . . " Here, everything seems to be transcended—or annulled—by a melodic differential of intensities.

TO TAKE MY LEAVE AND FIX A NEW APPOINTMENT

As it turns out, I haven't said very much about "Charlus-Discourse," but for me it was necessary—and significant—that I should base the seminar on a text—albeit in a cavalier fashion (no speech without a supporting text: monks, Tao). For a text—this text, this discourse in that it's been inscribed in fiction—presents the three directions that the methodological text (my own, in the past and in the future) can take.

Planimetrics

1. Structuralist analysis in the traditional manner: description, anatomy of the Discourse-Thing; what the Discourse is, described according to a cartographic procedure. Discourse (Charlus's discourse) (I didn't do this but I might have done): spread out like a table, allowing us to discern its regions, its borders, its properties. → Tabular and planimetrical analysis.[19]

2. From the moment an analysis takes enunciation into account it's no longer planimetrical, tabular. Enunciation: consideration of the positions that subjects occupy within discourse. Either fictional subjects (Charlus and his addressee) or (and at the same time) reading subjects. This: a new form of topological, or perspectivist analysis: a (complex) overview of the different perspectives as they operate in discourse. That approach was perhaps given too much emphasis in the papers presented this year: a semiology of discursive positions (within discourse).

3. It's possible to give that semiology—the one I've been announcing, that I consider necessary and have already said something about—a supplementary inflection (or: that inflection is trying to make itself known, though perhaps the attempt will be ultimately unsuccessful): a vision of the forces, the intensities, the excesses and the deflations, the flushes and pallors of the person speaking, listening, writing. The model for this approach would no longer be directly linguistic, but musical → Complex inventory of (1) the different planes, (2) the cross-sections, and (3) the elevations. A sort of axonometrics of the text—or Chinese perspective (because the first systematic applications of axonometrics occurred in China), but also in architecture and modern painting. Selecting a viewpoint that's both mobile and panoptic: an aspect with walkways and exits; appraising distances and the roles played by sections hidden

from view at will: order of reading without violence, etc. Naturally: a dossier to be dealt with at some later date.

Naturally, the epistemological break (within the last decade of semiology) occurs between: 1 and 2 + 3. The work to be done is in the dialectic between 2 + 3. That's where our next appointment will be held (not in a seminar but in a plurality of research projects: this year's seminar has collectively proposed some of the directions those projects could take). This work can be placed under the sign of the pragmatics, or linguistics, of interlocutory relations—as discussed by Récanati,[20] reclaiming the expression and the idea from the English. But perhaps also (this would be my preference) under the sign of a New Philology or an Active Philology, the kind Nietzsche wanted: philology of the *who*, not of the *what*.[21]

COURSE SUMMARY BY ROLAND BARTHES FOR THE COLLÈGE DE FRANCE YEARBOOK

LITERARY SEMIOLOGY
M. Roland Barthes, professor

Course:

HOW TO LIVE TOGETHER: NOVELISTIC SIMULATIONS OF SOME EVERYDAY SPACES

A proposition was advanced in the professorial inaugural lecture: the idea of linking research to the imaginary of the researcher. The aim for this year was to explore a specific imaginary: not all forms of "living together" (societies, phalansteries, families, couples) but primarily the "living together" of very small groups, where cohabitation does not preclude individual freedom. Inspired by certain religious models—notably Athonite—the name given to that imaginary was the fantasy of idiorrhythmy. While many of the materials used in this course were drawn from Oriental monachism, our corpus in the strict sense was literary. The corpus collected (in an evidently arbitrary manner) a number of documentary or fictional works in which the daily life of a subject or a group is linked to an archetypal space: the solitary room (A. Gide, *The Confined Woman of Poitiers*); the hideout (D. Defoe, *Robinson Crusoe*); the desert (Palladius, *The Lausiac History*); the grand hotel (T. Mann, *The Magic Mountain*); the bourgeois apartment building (Zola, *Pot Luck*).

The method adopted was at once selective and digressive. In keeping with the principles of semiological research, the aim was to pick out the pertinent—hence, discontinuous—traits from the mass of modes, customs, themes, and values of "living together." Each trait was summarized by a key word, and each word (the heading of each trait) was considered a unifying "figure" under which a certain number of digressions—into the fields of historical, ethnographical or sociological knowledge—could be classified. The research thus consisted in "opening dossiers." The responsibility for filling those dossiers was assigned to those attending the lectures, who were invited to do so in their own manner—the principal role of the professor being to suggest ways of structuring the themes. Those themes (or those traits, those figures) were presented in the alphabetical order of the key words. The mode of presentation ensured that "living-together" would not be inflected with a predetermined overall meaning and made it possible to avoid having to "interpret" the idiorrhythmic fantasy. Around thirty figures were set down and dealt with in this fashion (Animals, Autarky, Chief, Colony, Enclosure, Events, Distance, Food, Hearing, Pairing, Rule, etc.). Rather than propose a final general synthesis of those themes, it was deemed preferable to consider those inflections of idiorrhythmic "living-together" in relation to the image of a utopia, with particular emphasis of the optimal number of participants (ten at most) and the necessary "critical distance" regulating their relations. The lecture course therefore could not but open out onto an ethical problem of social life that will be taken up again in another form in next year's lecture course.

Seminar:

WHAT IS IT TO "HOLD FORTH / "TENIR UN DISCOURS"? RESEARCH ON INVESTED SPEECH

Human language, as it is actualized in "discourse," is the permanent theater of a power struggle between social and affective partners. The aim of the seminar was to explore language's *intimidating* function. The professor inaugurated the seminar by unpacking the idiomatic expression "to hold forth" / "*tenir un discours*" according to the facts of language. The expression already implies the forces, intensities, durations that contribute to the subjective operations of discourse. The invited speakers then offered their own formulations of the problem in relation to their areas of expertise: the logic of language (François Flahaut: "Discourse and Emblem" and "The Relation to Completitude"; François Récanati: "Discourse Sustained, Discourse Tenable, Discourse Untenable"), literature (Lucette Mouline: "The Proustian Sentence"), psychoanalysis (Jacques-Alain Miller: "Someone's Discourse, the Other's Discourse"), semiology of discourse (Antoine Compagnon: "Enthusiasm"; Louis Marin: "The Encounter between the Crow and the Fox"; Cosette Martel: " Woman as Object of

Speech"). By way of conclusion, the professor proposed an analysis of the forces at work in the discourse Charlus delivers to the Narrator (Proust, *The Guermantes Way*, part 2, chap. 2, pp. 528–40, and the discourse Andromache addresses to Hermione (Racine, *Andromache*, act 3, scene 4).

NOTES

Foreword

1. Roland Barthes, *Writing Degree Zero*, trans. Annette Lavers and Colin Smith (New York: Hill and Wang, 1968).

2. Barthes illustrates this distinction between the "seminar" and the "book" apropos of *A Lover's Discourse: Fragments*, which he concedes that some of those participating in the seminars may have found disappointing, when he says: "The book on the lover's discourse is perhaps not as rich as the seminar, but I consider it to be more true." See p. 131.

3. Roland Barthes, "Tables rondes," *OC* 1:803.

4. Ibid., p. 802.

5. Roland Barthes, *The Neutral: Lecture Course at the Collège de France (1977–1978)*, trans. Rosalind E. Krauss and Denis Hollier (New York: Columbia University Press, 2005), pp. 132, 140.

6. The alphabetical order was selected for *How to Live Together*, the mathematical order for *The Neutral*. Only the lecture course titled *The Preparation of the Novel* appears to follow the protocols of the speech, but then it takes the form of a "simulation" of the preparation of / for a novel.

7. For example, Blanchot, Agamben, Nancy . . .

8. Barthes, *The Neutral*, p. 13.

9. The following section of Éric Marty's preface has been shortened for the English edition.—tr.

10. 1977: Roland Barthes, *Comment vivre ensemble: Simulations romanesques de quelques espaces quotidiens*, edited by Claude Coste (Paris: Seuil/IMEC, 2002); 1977–1978: *Le Neutre: Cours et séminaires au Collège de France, 1977–1978*, edited by Thomas Clerc and Éric Marty (Paris: Seuil, 2002); 1978–1980: *La Préparation du roman I et II: Cours et séminaires au Collège de France 1978–1979 et 1979–1980*, edited by Nathalie Léger (Paris: Seuil, 2003).

11. The references to the *Oeuvre completes* have been retained here in the same format; whenever Barthes's works are quoted directly, reference is also given to the available English translation.—tr.

12. Barthes's own bibliographical references in the margins of his notes have been retained; they have been completed for the English reader by footnotes, which give references, wherever possible, to an available English translation or, if it is a matter of a text in English, the original.—tr.

Preface

1. François Flahaut: "Discourse and Emblem" and "The Relation to Completitude"; François Récanati: "Discourse Sustained, Discourse Tenable, Discourse Untenable"; Lucette Mouline: "The Proustian Sentence"; Jacques-Alain Miller: "Other People's Discourse, the Other's Discourse"; Antoine Compagnon: "Enthusiasm"; Louis Marin: "The Encounter between the Crow and the Fox"; Cosette Martel: "Woman as Object of Speech."

Translator's Preface

1. Elizabeth Bruss, *Beautiful Theories: The Spectacle of Discourse in Contemporary Criticism* (Baltimore, Md.: The Johns Hopkins University Press, 1982). See her chapter on Roland Barthes, pp. 363–461.

2. Bruss, *Beautiful Theories*, p. 364.

3. According to Bruss, the reordering and compression effected by translation collapsed the years of thinking between shifts in critical position on Barthes's part, provoking complaints of inconsistency from reviewers; writing at the start of the 1980s, Bruss also saw the rush of translations as inventing a new, three-part narrative for Barthes's output, with the structuralist writings viewed as "the core of all that came before and after them, the goal and crowning achievement of the earlier work, the point of departure for his last (and ostensibly uniform) poststructuralist phase." (p. 366) It will be fascinating to see how this narrative will be rewritten following the recent flurry of translations of Barthes's posthumous works (the three volumes of lecture and seminar notes, as well as the intimate *Mourning Diary*, translated by Richard Howard and published in 2010).

4. "Who are my contemporaries?" Barthes asks on p. 6. Following Éric Marty's lead in his introduction to this volume, we might also ask: if we are no longer turning to the calendar for an answer to such a question, then which of Barthes's works can be considered contemporaries?

5. "Inaugural Lecture, Collège de France," trans. Richard Howard, in *A Barthes Reader*, ed. Susan Sontag (London: Jonathan Cape, 1982), pp. 457–78.

6. On this, see Diana Knight, *Barthes and Utopia: Space, Travel, Writing* (Oxford: Oxford University Press, 1997), pp. 16–17.

7. Roland Barthes, *The Preparation of the Novel: Lecture Courses and Seminars at the Collège de France (1978–1979 and 1979–1980)*, ed. Nathalie Léger, trans. Kate Briggs (New York: Columbia University Press, 2010). See, for instance, the section titled "Brakings," pp. 263–68.

8. Ibid., p. 132.

9. Ibid., p. 3.

10. I have recently tried elsewhere to explore and understand the role that affect can play in determining what gets translated when, by whom, and even how. See Kate Briggs, "What We Talk About When We Talk About Translation: The Gide / Bussy Correspondence," *Translation Studies* 5, no. 1 (2012): pp. 65–78.

11. Éric Marty's invaluable introduction appears in this volume almost in full; three short paragraphs relating to sound recordings available in French have been omitted.

12. On "Arrogance" see Barthes, *The Neutral: Lecture Course at the Collège de France*, ed. Thomas Clerc, trans. Rosalind E. Krauss and Denis Hollier (New York: Columbia University Press, 2005), pp. 152–62; on "Non-Arrogance" see Barthes, *The Preparation of the Novel*, p. 15.

Session of January 12, 1977

1. This trait was skipped in the lecture course and crossed out in the manuscript.

2. "Method always presupposes the goodwill of the thinker, 'a premeditated decision.' Culture, on the contrary, is a violence undergone by thought through the action of selective forces, a training which brings the whole unconscious of the thinker into play." Gilles Deleuze, *Nietzsche and Philosophy*, trans. Hugh Tomlinson (London: Continuum, 2006), p. 101.

3. Deleuze, *Nietzsche and Philosophy*, p. 102.

4. Barthes is referring to the semiological works he produced in the 1960s, particularly *The Fashion System* [1967], whose foreword is titled "Method." [Oral: Barthes replaces "taken in" with "obsessed."]

5. See Roland Barthes, "Inaugural Lecture, Collège de France," in *A Barthes Reader*, ed. Susan Sontag (New York: Hill and Wang, 1982), p. 462; *OC* 3: p. 804. By agreeing to the sacrifice of Isaac, Abraham escapes the generality of morality and of language (Kierkegaard, *Fear and Trembling* [1843]).

6. Deleuze, *Nietzsche and Philosophy*, p. 101.

7. *Paideia* (Greek): the education of children (from *pais*: child), then training, rearing.

8. In English in the text.—tr.

9. In his "Inaugural Lecture" Barthes noted that in French knowledge (*savoir*) and flavor (*saveur*) share the same Latin root, p. 464.—tr.

10. See Stéphane Mallarmé: "All method is a fiction, and is useful for demonstration. It seemed to him that language has appeared as the instrument of fiction: it will follow the method of language (determine it). Language reflecting upon itself." *Notes sur le langage,* in *Oeuvres complètes*, vol. 1 (Paris: Gallimard, Bibliothèque de la Pléiade, 1998), p. 104. Barthes quotes this passage in his "Inaugural Lecture," p. 476.—tr.

11. [Oral: Barthes adds "an attentiveness to differences."]

12. "Consequently, the scientific mind must never cease to fight against images, against analogies, and against metaphors." See Gaston Bachelard, *The Formation of the Scientific Mind*, trans. Mary McAllester Jones (Manchester: Clinamen Press, 2002), p. 47.

13. [Oral: Barthes stipulates that utopia is achieved through "the imagining of the details."]

14. Félix Armand and René Maublanc, *Fourier*, 3 vols. (Paris: Éditions Sociales, 1937).

15. The title of a famous novel by Hector Malot [1878].

16. *Familien-roman* (German): family romance. "Term coined by Freud as a name for phantasies whereby the subject imagines that his relationship to his parents has been modified (as when he imagines, for example, that he is really a foundling." J. Laplanche and J.-B. Pontalis, *The Language of Psychoanalysis* (London: Karnac Books, 1988), p. 160.

17. [Oral: Barthes clarifies: "in Nietzsche's sense of the term."] See *Unzeitgemässe Betrachtungen*, translated as Untimely Considerations or Unfashionable Observations.

18. [Oral: Barthes refers to Max Ernst's painting *A Friend's Reunion* (*Au rendez-vous des amis*; 1922), a group portrait of the Surrealists that also features Dostoevsky and Raphael.]

19. Between 1974 and 1976 Barthes gave a seminar on the "Lover's Discourse" at the École pratique des hautes études de sciences sociales, Paris. His preparatory notes for this seminar have recently been published in French as *Le Discours amoureux: Séminaire à l'École pratique des hautes études 1974–1976 suivi de Fragments d'un discours amoureux (pages inédites)*, ed. Claude Coste and Andy Stafford (Paris: Seuil, 2007).

20. Around ten of Barthes's preparatory index cards deal with "Being in love" (chiefly apropos of *The Magic Mountain*).

21. " . . . the gulf between man and man, rank and rank; the multiplicity of types, the will to be one's self, to stand out—everything I call pathos of distance—is proper to every strong period." *The Twilight of the Idols, or How to Philosophize with a Hammer*, trans. Duncan Large (Oxford: Oxford University Press, 1998), p. 64.

22. Jacques Lacarrière, *L'Été grec: Une Grèce quotidienne de 4000 ans* (Paris: Pion, 1976).

23. "The Holy Mountain has engendered a particular way of life: what is called idiorhythmy. The monasteries of Mount Athos can be divided into two kinds. Those called coenobitic, in other words communal, where all activities—meals, prayers, and labor—are undertaken collectively. And those termed idiorhythmic, where each individual literally lives according to his own rhythm. The monks have their own individual cells, where (other than at particular times of celebration in the year) they take their meals and are permitted to keep any personal items they owned at the time of taking their vows. . . . In these peculiar communities, even prayers are optional, with the exception of compline." Carrière, *L'Été grec*, p. 40. On the spelling of idiorrhythmy, see p. 181, n.2.

24. Index Card 169: "Synaxe: everyone comes together for prayer." In the space that Barthes is fantasizing, the library—as a meeting place—has the same function as synaxe in the Athonite monasteries.

25. Emile Benveniste, "The Notion of 'Rhythm' in its Linguistic Expression," in *Problems in General Linguistics*, trans. Mary Elizabeth Meek (Coral Gables, FL: University of Miami Press, 1971), pp. 281–88.

26. *Rhein* (Greek): to flow.

27. Since Aristotle, the term "Ionian" has been used to refer to the pre-Socratic philosophers that settled in the large cities along the coast of Asia Minor (sixth century).

28. *Peplos* (Greek): tunic. A sleeveless item of women's clothing that fastens at the shoulder.

29. *Rhuthmos* refers "to the pattern of a fluid element, of a letter arbitrarily shaped, of a robe which one arranges at will, of a particular state of a character or mood." Benveniste, "The Notion of 'Rhythm,'" p. 286.

30. See ibid., p. 287. Apropos of music, Socrates evokes the intervals "inherent in the movements of the body, which are numerically regulated and which must be called rhythms and measures." Philebus (17d).

31. *Idios* (Greek): personal, particular, one's own.

32. [Oral: "Idios is opposed to rhythm, but in a certain sense it's the same thing as rhythm."]

33. [Oral: Barthes refers to the definition of architecture as the art of proportions. He goes on: "If you enlarge a detail in a picture, in a painting, you produce another painting. . . . It has been possible to say (I've said it many times) that the whole of Nicholas de Staël sprang from five centimeters squared of Cézanne."]

34. In *The Sexual Revolution*, trans. Theodore P. Wolfe (New York: Octagon Books, 1971), Wilhelm Reich describes the functioning of "youth communes" in the URSS (see part 2, chap. 12, 2d), "The insoluble conflict between family and commune."

35. In English in the text.—tr.

36. *Coenobium* (Latin): convent, monastery.

37. Saint Benedict fought the Sarabaites, monks whose lives were not regulated by any specific rules and were accused of debauchery.

38. Wilfred Bion, *Experiences in Groups* (London: Tavistock, 1961).

39. [Oral: "It's when two different rhythms are put together that profound disturbances are created."]

Session of January 19, 1977

1. Expanding on this thought a little later on in the lecture course, Barthes makes a distinction between those works where the signified can be dispensed with and those where such exemption is impossible: Bossuet's work, for example, can be easily read without the signified "God" . . .

2. Exodus 3:14.

3. [Oral: Barthes states his intention to devote the next seminar to Sartre. In fact, there was no seminar in 1978. In 1979, the seminar was on the topic of the "Labyrinth" and in 1980 on "Proust and Photography." See *The Preparation of the Novel: Lecture Courses and Seminars at the Collège de France (1978–1979 and 1979–1980)*, trans. Kate Briggs (New York: Columbia University Press, 2010).]

4. A short story by Honoré de Balzac written in 1831. The aging Frenhofer spends years trying to paint the portrait of Catherine Lescault, a courtesan nicknamed the Beautiful-Nuisance. But all he manages to produce is a mass of colors, which nevertheless contain the remarkably accurate representation of a foot.

5. In *A Lover's Discourse: Fragments*, trans. Richard Howard (New York: Farrar, Straus and Giroux, 1978). Barthes uses Goethe's *Werther* as repertory of figures of the lover's discourse.

6. *Marcottage* is a horticultural term; a method for propagating trees or bushes whereby one of the higher branches is planted into the ground and forms another root. Barthes uses the term a number of times to describe a particular method of composition in *The Preparation of the Novel*. See, for example, p. 150.—tr.

7. [Oral: Barthes remarks that the lecture course is beginning to look like "pseudoerudition."]

8. *Monosis* (Greek): solitude.

9. *Monachos* (Greek): solitary, someone who lives alone.

10. *Anachoresis* (Greek): retreat, withdrawal.

11. *Koinobiosis*: communal life; a neologism created by Barthes that combines *koinos*, common, shared, and *bios*, life.

12. *Askesis* (Greek): exercise, practice.

13. *Pathos* (Greek): affect.

14. [Oral: Barthes makes clear that his understanding of the term "imaginary" is "broadly Lacanian."]

15. "Avedon. His New Portraits Analysed by Roland Barthes, of the Collège de France," *Photo*, no. 112 (January 1977) (OC 3, published as "Tels," pp. 691–98). In the lecture, Barthes is alluding to an ironic and aggressive letter he had received from a reader.

16. "Inaugural Lecture, Collège de France," in *A Barthes Reader*, ed. Susan Sontag (New York: Hill and Wang, [1978] 1982).

17. *Parlez-vous franglais?* by René Étiemble was published in 1964.

18. [Oral: Barthes expands on this reference: "From a terminological standpoint, in order to eschew the connotations of more commonly used terms such as instinct and tendency, the French translations of Freud propose *pulsion* as an equivalent to the German *Treib* {usually translated into English as 'drive'—tr.}." See J. Laplanche and J.-B. Pontalis, *The Language of Psychoanalysis* (London: Karnac Books, 1988), p. 360. Barthes notes that Lacan translates *Treib* as *dérive* {drift—tr.}.]

19. [Oral: Barthes talks of dedicating a lecture to "the evaluation of those fantasmatic projections that, borrowing the name from Joyce, we might call: epiphanies."] In the third lecture course he gave at the Collège de France, Barthes explores the notion of epiphany in Joyce at length. See *The Preparation of the Novel*, pp. 100–103.

20. "The question 'What is it?' is a way of establishing a sense from another point of view. Essence, being, is a perspectival reality and presupposes a plurality. Fundamentally, it is always the question 'What is it *for me*?'" Cited by Gilles Deleuze, *Nietzsche and Philosophy*, trans. Hugh Tomlinson (London: Continuum, 2006), p. 72.

21. Beginning of passage crossed out in the manuscript.

22. Pierre Klossowski, *Nietzsche and the Vicious Circle*, trans. Daniel W. Smith (London: Continuum, [1969, 1975] 2005), p. 32 {translation slightly modified—tr.}.

23. End of passage crossed out in the manuscript.

24. *Quaestio* (Latin): topic, question.

25. In English in the text.—tr.

26. *Oratio* (Latin): speech; *flumen* (Latin): river; *contio* (Latin): public speech.

27. See "How this Book is Constructed," in *A Lover's Discourse: Fragments*, pp. 6–8. Barthes defends the use of the order of the alphabet as a way to avoid imposing a progression or overall direction to the book.

28. 'The paradigm I am proposing here does not follow the functional division: it is not aimed at putting scientists and researchers on one side, writers and essayists on the other. On the contrary, it suggests that writing is to be found wherever words have flavor (the French words for *flavor* and *knowledge* have the same Latin root." "Inaugural Lecture," p. 464.

29. Quoted by René Draguet, *Les Pères du désert* (Paris: Plon, 1949). The reference is to Jean Cassien's *Institutions cénobitiques*. The most widely available edition is Jean-Claude Guy's translation (Paris: Editions du Cerf, 1965).

30. *Akedia* (Greek): negligence, indifference.

31. *Kedeuo* (Greek): to take care of.

32. *Akedeo* (Greek): fail to take care of, to neglect.

33. *Akedestos* (Greek): abandoned without burial.

34. *Akedes* (Greek): negligent, neglected.

35. [Oral: Barthes clarifies: "We must pay close attention to the permutations of the active and the passive, for to abandon the object invested in—in asceticism for instance—amounts to being abandoned. When the active and the passive amount to the same thing in this way, we can be sure to find a trace of the logic of affect. It would be worth looking again at Freud's analysis of the 'A Child is Being Beaten' fantasy."] See Freud, "A Child is Being Beaten: A Contribution to the Study of Sexual Perversions," *Standard Edition* 17 (1919): pp. 175–204.

36. *Aphanisis* (Greek): act of making something disappear. "Term introduced by Ernest Jones: the disappearance of sexual desire. According to Jones, *aphanisis* is the object, in both subjects, of a fear more profound than the fear of castration." J. Laplanche and J.-B. Pontalis, *The Language of Psychoanalysis*, p. 40.

37. *Taedium* (Latin): disgust, boredom.

38. In English in the text. Barthes had appropriated this Lacanian notion once before in *A Lover's Discourse: Fragments*: "Painful ordeal in which the loved being appears to withdraw from all contact, without such enigmatic indifference even being directed against the amorous subject or pronounced to the advantage of anyone else, world, or rival." *A Lover's Discourse: Fragments*, p. 112.

39. H. T. Lowe-Porter's 1927 translation differs quite significantly from Maurice Betz's French translation here. In the English, Doctor Behrens proposes a new treatment to "tide" Hans Castorp "over the crisis he was in." *The Magic Mountain*, p. 626–27; in the French, the Doctor refers specifically to a "*point mort*," a dead point or stop, a more literal translation of the German "*den toten Punkt*." *La Montagne magique*, trans. Maurice Betz (Paris: Fayard, 1961), p. 678. See also *Der Zauberberg* (Frankfurt am Main: Fischer, 1991), p. 862.—tr.

40. The figure in *A Lover's Discourse: Fragments*, pp. 218–19.

41. Barthes's margin note refers to the 1959 Pléiade edition of Defoe, *Vie et aventures de Robinson Crusoé*, trans. Pétrus Borel, which contains a number of source documents relating to *Robinson Crusoe*. The passage cited is from an

article by Richard Steele entitled "Alexander Selkirk," first published in *The Englishman* on December 1, 1713.—tr.

42. Barthes's word is "exercise."

43. Index card 220: "*Askesis*: it would be better to say *ethos*, habit, or custom, together with dwelling place, a place to stay (see index card). Because it rhymes with *pathos*. Because of Nietzsche's opposition between *ethos* and *pathos* (a propos of Wagner. Where? Bayreuth project and the manuscript version of A Lover's Discourse.)" [Barthes's error: it's *ethos* that means "dwelling place."]

Session of January 26, 1977

1. See p. 33.

2. [Oral: "I wondered why the word *idiorrhythmy* was spelt with two *r*'s and assumed, knowing deep down that I was wrong, that the second *r* came from the assimilation with the *s* of *idios*. But it's since been pointed out to me (rightly) that this *s*, which eventually became the second *r*, is simply due to the aspiration of the initial *rho* of *rhuthmos*."] Lacarrière spells the word with just one *r*.

3. *Kedeia* (Greek): the care given to a corpse.

4. *Akedia* (Greek): neglect.

5. *Ana-* (Greek): upward movement.

6. *Chorein* (Greek): to withdraw, to move away.

7. *-sis* (Greek): suffix that serves to create abstract nouns.

8. John Colerus, *The Life of Benedict de Spinosa*, trans. unknown (1706; 1906), p. 36. Index Card 121: "Off-grid. *Pot Luck*. All the apartments are given social markers. But there's a gap, an unsaid (which serves as a point of contrast, a paradigm) the apartment on the 2nd floor: the writer's."

9. *Anachorein* (Greek): to withdraw, to retreat from.

10. Gervais: a French manufacturer of dairy products.—tr.

11. Barthes is using the Lacanian expression *point de capiton*. For Lacan, the *capiton* is the point where the incessant sliding of the signifier under the signified momentarily stops, enabling moments of stable signification. [Oral: Barthes uses the expression "point of contact."]

12. In Flaubert's short story, Félicité has her parrot Loulou stuffed. In her dying moments, she imagines it to be the incarnation of the Holy Spirit.

13. "Do not think from this remark that I am a great musician; it is only two days that I began to be one; but you know how one likes to talk about what one has just learned." "Letter on the Deaf and Dumb," in *Diderot's Early Philosophical Works*, trans. Margaret Jourdain (Chicago: Open Court Publishing Company, 1916), p. 193, translation slightly modified.

14. In English in the text.—tr.

15. [Oral: "If there were only domestic animals left in the world, which seems to be the way things are heading, then the world would be an extremely fragile place. . . . Which is why we need wild animals."]

16. *Hulobioi* (Greek): lit. "who live in the woods." Name of a tribe of Garmanes, India.

17. *Dendrites* (Greek) [from *dendron*, meaning tree]: pertaining to trees.

18. *The Swiss Family Robinson* (1812) by Johann David Wyss.

19. Barthes is referring to the work of art critic Gilbert Lascault (see *Le Monstre dans l'art occidental* [Paris: Klincksieck, 1973]).

20. Jurigis Baltrusaïtus, a Lithuanian-born historian of French art with a particular interest in comparative teratology: *Le Moyen âge fantastique* (Paris: Flammarion, 1981); *Reveils et Prodiges* (Paris: Flammarion, 1988).

21. *Impossibilia* (Latin), *adunata* (Greek): impossibilities, extraordinary phenomena. "Ancient rhetoric, especially medieval, included a special topic,

the *impossibilia* (*adunata* in Greek); the *adunaton* was a common site, a *topos*, based on the notion of *overabundance*: two naturally opposite, enemy elements (vulture and dove) were presented as peacefully living together." *Sade, Fourier, Loyola*, trans. Richard Miller (Berkley: University of California Press, 1989), p. 117.

22. Virgil, *The Eclogues*, Eclogue 8, line 53.

23. The donkey playing the lyre is a medieval *topos* that derives from a Greek proverb: "The donkey is deaf to the lyre." See E. R. Curtius, *La Littérature européenne et le Moyen Age latin* (Paris: PUF, 1956), chap. 4, "La topique," "Le monde renversé."

24. Barthes is referring to an article by Jean Leclercq "L'erémétisme en Occident jusqu'à l'an mil," in *Le Millénaire du mont Athos (963, 1963): Études et mélanges,* vol. 1 (Chevetogne: Éditions de Chevetogne, 1963). See "Saint Gregory" in *La Légende dorée* by Jacques de Voragine. A hermit who has relinquished all he owned is grieved to learn that he will be admitted into Paradise along with Pope Gregory. God reproaches him: the hermit got more pleasure from stroking his kitten than Pope Gregory did from all the possessions the hermit is so disdainful of.

25. [Oral: this is how Barthes describes the table: what we're dealing with here is "facile structuralism, the way it used to be done or how I, at any rate, used to do it ten years ago."]

26. *Coenobia* (Latin): plural of *conenobium,* meaning monastery, convent.

27. Jean Décarreaux, "Du monachisme primitif au monachisme athonite," in *Le Millénaire du mont Athos,* p. 45.

28. *Encyclopaedia Universalis*, entry on "Athos (Mount)."

29. From the Greek *hesuchazein,* meaning to be calm, to keep quiet.

30. Barthes is referring to the entry titled "Athos (Mount)" in the *Encyclopaedia Universalis*: " . . . if the Mediterranean forest still exists this is at least in part due to the law prohibiting female goats . . . " Vegetation was preserved by limiting the herds' growth.

31. "In addition to the hermitages, it is important to note the presence of *skites*, from *askitica*—spaces for ascetics—smaller buildings scattered around the main monasteries whose basic function was to serve as a place to stay in the surrounding forest." J. Lacarrière, *L'Été grec: Une Grèce quotidienne de 4000 ans* (Paris: Pion, 1976), p. 36.

32. *Asketerion* (Greek): space for exercise or meditation.

33. "I think I can now dispense with the reserve I have always observed apropos of the ascetery where Durtal lived." (Huysmans, foreword to *En Route*).

34. *Kelliotes*, literally, the inhabitant of a *kellion. Kellia* are hermit's cells, scattered throughout southern Athos.

35. Jean Leroy, "La conversion de saint Athanase l'athonite et l'idéal cénobitique et l'influence studite," in *Le Millénaire du mont Athos.*

36. See p. 8.

37. *Ordo eremiticus, ordo eremiticae vitae* (Latin): eremitic order, eremitic way of life.

38. See Sade, *The Complete Justine, Philosophy in the Bedroom and Other Writings*, trans. Richard Seaver and Austryn Wainhouse (New York: Grove Press, 1966).

39. The entry titled "Chartreux" in the *Encyclopaedia Universalis*.

40. From the Greek *kathisma*: action of establishing, setting up. See J. Décarreaux, "Du monachisme primitif au monachisme athonite," p. 53.

Session of February 2, 1977

1. [Oral: "It's an idea I've had for a long time but never dared get attached to: perhaps one day we'll consider the myths of the origins of language."]

2. *Atopia* (Greek): without a place.

3. *Diaita* (Greek): way of life, regimen, dwelling; related to *diaitasthai*, to lead one's life.

4. For the references to J. Décarreaux, see "Du monarchisme primitif au monarchism athonite," in *Le Millénaire du mont Athos (963, 1963): Études et mélanges,* vol. 1 (Chevetogne: Éditions de Chevetogne, 1963), pp. 49–51.

5. [Oral: "The Essenians and the Therapeuts were Hebrew religious communities."]

6. *Encyclopaedia Universalis,* article "Athos (Mount)."

7. See J. Décarreaux, "Du monarchisme primitif," p. 24.

8. " . . . Christians, Marxists, Freudians—for whom money continues to be an accursed matter, fetish, excrement has spoken out: who would dare defend money? There is *no* discourse with which money can be compatible." *Sade, Fourier, Loyola,* trans. Richard Miller (Berkley: University of California Press, 1989), p. 86.

9. The common feature of different forms of idiorrhythmy is their autonomy with respect to religious power.

10. [Oral: those who live in lauras.]

11. In the earliest, precoenobitic structures, an "elder" is considered a model, not a leader.

12. This collegiate mode of organization is characteristic of the idiorrhythmic structure, as opposed to the *coenobium,* which operates under the power of the abbot.

13. From the Greek *epitropos*: someone responsible for the running of something.

14. See p. 9.

15. In fact, *rhuthmos,* as Barthes makes clear orally.

16. This definition figures in *Roland Barthes by Roland Barthes,* p. 157. It does not appear to be a literal quotation (there are no quotation marks in the manuscript). Barthes is paraphrasing Casals's argument: "It is all a question of balance, that good taste should know how to control. But since *rubato* is in itself such a natural mode of expression it could be said that, in a certain sense, music is *rubato*." *Conversations avec Pablo Casals* (Paris: Albin Michel, 1955 and 1992), p. 260.

17. [Oral: "To make music is not to proceed in a metronimical manner, it's to proceed in a way that's as it were regular, cadenced but that also has a supplement or a lack, a delay if you like, or a degree of haste, which is the definition of *rhuthmos*."]

18. *Autarkeia* (Greek): state of self-sufficiency.

19. Jules Verne, *Twenty Thousand Leagues under the Sea,* part 1, chap. 11, The Nautilus.

20. Nemo means "no one" in Latin.

21. The first hermits would exchange mats for bread.

22. [Oral: Barthes alludes to his own stay in the Saint-Hilaire-du-Touvet sanatorium during the occupation. The residents lived in a "state of total autarky," in a state of "abstraction with respect to the world."

23. Barthes is quoting from the article "Territoire (ethologie)" in the *Encyclopaedia Universalis.*

24. [Oral: "It's not innate with respect to the species."]

25. [Oral: Barthes clarifies his point by imagining an apologue. Following a global catastrophe, a queen bee and a drone successfully manage to rebuild their hive. In contrast, two human babies would be obliged to work their way

through each and every phase of the history of humankind " . . . eventually attaining to the delivery of a lecture course at the Collège de France—but that would take a very, very long time."]

26. [Oral: Barthes evokes a "major issue currently being debated on a number of different levels": "how to distinguish between the subject and the individual . . . the role of politics" is "to protect the subject without necessarily defending the individual."

27. Introducing this new trait, Barthes proposes to alternate between "wild imaginings and historical fact"; see the article "Béguins, Béguines, béguinages," *Dictionnaire de spiritualité*.

28. *Curtes*: plural of *cortis*, courtyard or atrium ["in the Latin of the Middle Ages" as Barthes points out orally.]

29. *Continentes* (Latin): chaste.

30. [Oral: Barthes explains his parenthesis: chastity "was one of the key principles, one of the key characteristics of the Albigensians."]

31. *Magistra*, plural of *Magistrae* (Latin): lit. "mistress." *Martha, Marthae*: from Martha, the sister of Mary and Lazarus. According to contemporary interpretations, Martha represents active life while Mary represents the contemplative life.

32. In English in the text.—tr.

33. [Oral: Barthes explains his note: at the time of the apostles the Church promoted the vow of chastity].

Session of February 9, 1977

1. 1926.

2. [Oral: Barthes explains the meaning of the word: agents "who were supposed to change every week."]

3. [Oral: Barthes defines the term: "Place where asceticism is practiced."]

4. See p. 35.

5. Wilhelm Reich, *The Sexual Revolution: Toward a Self-Governing Character Structure*, rev. ed., trans. Theodore P. Wolfe (New York: Octagon Books, 1971), pp. 223–25.

6. *Telos* (Greek): goal, end.

7. Freud is supposed to have overheard Charcot say to Brouardel, his assistant: "Mais, dans les cas pareils, c'est toujours la chose génitale, toujours . . . toujours . . . toujours." ["But in this sort of case it's always a question of the genitals—always, always, always."] "On the History of the Psychoanalytic Movement," in *The Standard Edition of the Complete Works of Sigmund Freud*, vol. 14 (London: Hogarth Press and the Institute of Psychoanalysis, 1953–1974), p. 14.

8. [Barthes discusses the difference between monks and brothers in the trait entitled "Colony," p. 63.]

9. Index Card 158: "Saint Augustine's rules. Religious life: 1. coenobitism. *Monks*: silent prayer, eremetism. 2. Brotherly community. Charitable acts. *Brothers*: life of communal fraternity. Saint Augustin the first and key legislator."

10. Honoré de Balzac, *The Wrong Side of Paris*, trans. Jordan Stump (New York: Random House, 2003).

11. "In an author's lexicon, will there not always be a word-as-mana, a word whose ardent, complex, ineffable, and somehow sacred signification gives the illusion that by this word one might answer for everything?" *Roland Barthes by Roland Barthes*, trans. Richard Howard (Berkley: University of California Press, 1977), p. 129.

12. [Oral correction by Roland Barthes: "post-hippy."]

13. Aschenbach, the writer residing in Venice for his health, is fascinated by the young Tadzio's beauty.

14. *Moribundi*, plural of *moribundus* (Latin): dying, moribund. [Oral: Barthes translates this as "people who are going to die."]

15. The convent in *Justine*. See Sade, *The Complete Justine, Philosophy in the Bedroom and Other Writings*, trans. Richard Seaver and Austryn Wainhouse (New York: Grove Press, 1966).

16. Château de Silling. Roman Ajejandro provides a drawing of it in *Sade, Fourier, Loyola*, trans. Richard Miller (Berkley: University of California Press, 1989), p. 14.

17. The quotation is from David Amand, *L'Ascèse monastique de Saint Basile: Essai historique* (Maredsous: Éditions de Maredsous, 1948).

18. W. R. Bion, *Experiences in Groups and Other Papers*, London: Tavistock, 1961. Barthes is referring to the French translation, *Recherches sur les petits groupes*, published by PUF in 1965.

19. The group is formed as it awaits a leader.

20. *Homeostasis*: a word Barthes creates by combining two Greek words: *homoios* (sameness, similar) and *stasis* (position).

21. The initials of someone Barthes knew: André Boucourechliev?

22. [Oral: "a defense of worldliness that's far from ungenerous."]

23. [Oral: Barthes refers to the first presentation of the seminar, given by François Flahaut: "a very important theoretical presentation in the sense that he was trying to set out a linguistics of the positions occupied in speech." See also F. Flahaut, *La Parole intermédiaire* (Paris: Seuil, 1978), (preface by Roland Barthes, OC 3: pp. 849–51).

24. Joseph Rykwert, *On Adam's House in Paradise: The Idea of the Primitive Hut in Architectural History* (New York: Museum of Modern Art, 1972). Barthes is referring to the French translation, *La Maison d'Adam au Paradis*, published by Seuil in 1976.

25. [Oral: Barthes explains this allusion. In *Le Temple dans l'homme* (Le Caire: Schindler, 1950), René-Adolphe Schwaller de Lubicz describes the Egyptian temples as "diagrammatical figurations of the human body." Barthes recalls witnessing the polemics that this thesis provoked among Egyptologists firsthand during his time in Egypt (1949–1950).

26. [Oral: Barthes expands on his notes with reference to André Leroi-Gourhan. See *Le Geste et la Parole* (Paris: Albin Michel, 1964), vol. 1, *Technique et Langage*, pp. 292–93: "As we saw, the movement determined by agricultural sedentarization led to individuals becoming increasingly narrowly focused on the material world. The progressive triumph of the tool is inseparable from that of language; in fact, just as technology and society form a whole, so tools and language can be considered one and the same phenomenon."]

Session of February 16, 1977

1. In fact, a play (1905).

2. *Skene* (Greek): hut, tent and, by extension, the meal eaten in the tent.

3. [Oral: Barthes clarifies: "tent providing shelter and shade."]

4. Ezekiel 8 (prophesies the coming destruction of the city): 40–48 (vision of the new Temple).

5. Begun by Juan Bautista de Toledo for King Philippe II, the Escorial was completed between 1567 and 1582 by Juan de Herrera.

6. Juan Bautista Villalpanda established a parallel between the Escorial and the temple of Jerusalem that, inspired by Exechiel's vision, he proposed to reconstruct.

7. The writings of the Catalan theologian, poet, and philosopher Raymond Lulle (ca. 1232–1316) on the symbolic representation of divine harmony in the fields of science and architecture, which were influential in the Renaissance.

8. *Ho thalamos* (Greek): the bedroom.

9. [Oral: Barthes evokes his paternal grandmother's house in Bayonne.]

10. *Certamen anachoretale* (Latin): "the anachorite's battle." (Oral translation provided by Barthes). *Solus cum solo*: one on one. See Jean Leclercq, "L'erémetisme en Occident jusqu'à l'an mil," in *Le Millénaire du Mont Athos (983, 1963): Études et mélanges*, vol. 1 (Chevetogne: Éditions de Chevetogne, 1963).

11. *Cella continuata dulcescit* (Latin): it is pleasant to remain in one's room. Literal translation provided orally by Barthes: "Uninterrupted cell-time is calming."

12. It has not been possible to identify the source of this quotation.

13. "I have often said that man's unhappiness springs from one thing alone, his incapacity to stay quietly in one room." Pascal, *Pensées and Other Writings*, trans. Honor Levi (Oxford: Oxford World's Classics, 1995), p. 44.

14. "When the depths of agony are plumbed, Flaubert throws himself on his sofa: this is his 'marinade,' an ambiguous situation, in fact the sign of failure is also the site of fantasy, whence the work will gradually resume, giving Flaubert a new substance which he can erase anew." "Flaubert and the Sentence," in *New Critical Essays,* trans. Richard Howard (Berkley: University of California Press, 1990), p. 70.

15. Richard Rogers (an Englishman) and Renzo Piano (an Italian) are the architects of the Centre Georges Pompidou in the Beaubourg quarter of Paris.

16. [Oral: "Perhaps interiority is simply being free to fantasize."]

17. Émile Zola, *The Conquest of Plassans*, trans. Alfred Vizetelly Ernest (New York: Mondial, 2005), p. 28. Translation slightly modified.—tr.

18. See André Bareau, *La Vie et l'Organisation des communautés bouddhiques modernes de Ceylan* (Pondichéry: Editions de l'institut français d'indologie, 1957).

19. Index Card 88: "Storage space. Xenophon 76. Xenophonian hobby (cf. tidying up): to take care, to attend to, to see to: *epimeleisthai*. Those excluded from the category of being capable of attending to what they ought to (they can't be taught):

— people with a taste for drinking
— people who fall madly in love."

See Xenophon, *Conversations of Socrates*, p. 74.—tr.

20. Barthes is referring to the bedroom in *The Confined Woman of Poitiers*.

21. In the lecture Barthes uses the example of the Parthenon.

22. Both citations appear in J. Rykwert's book *On Adam's House in Paradise: The Idea of the Primitive Hut in Architectural History* (New York: Museum of Modern Art, 1972), p. 55–56.

23. *Magnificenza* (Italian): magnificence. [Oral: *magnificenza* "is the opposite of the interiority of the cell," there's "no such thing as a magnificent bedroom."]

24. "Leader," with its broader semantic range, might seem a more obvious translation of the French *chef* here. However, Barthes himself introduces a distinction between *chef* and *leader* on p. 55.

25. *Praepositus* (Latin): chief.

26. *Pater et Magister* (Latin): Father and Master.

27. *Paterfamilias*: Father of the family.

28. *Anax* (Greek): master, chief, king.

29. *Basileus* (Greek): king, sovereign.

30. [Oral: Barthes refers to Émile Benveniste's *Vocabulaire des institutions indo-européennes*, 2 vols. (Paris: Éditions de Minuit, 1969).]

31. See p. 30.

32. [Oral: "It's what prevents the chief from becoming a guru."]

33. On the subject of consensus, see book 4, chap. 2, "Suffrages."

34. See pp. 46–47.

35. [Oral: "A novel so unforgiving I wasn't brave enough to choose it."] William Golding, *The Lord of the Flies* (London: Penguin, 1960), p. 21.

36. These quotations are taken from Alan Watts's *The Way of Zen* (New York: Pantheon, 1957). The second figures in *A Lover's Discourse: Fragments*, trans. Richard Howard (New York: Farrar, Straus and Giroux, 1978), p. 234.

Session of March 2, 1977

1. Giono, *Que ma joie demeure* (Joy of Man's Desiring). The farm is in Contadour in Provence (whence the "Contadourians").

2. In his preparatory index cards, Barthes mentions *La Geste et la Parole* by André Leroi-Gourhan. No passage in the book corresponds exactly to the point Barthes is making. In the second volume (*La Mémoire et les Rythmes* [Paris: Albin Michel, 1964]), Leroi-Gourhan writes: "On the techno-economical level, human integration is essentially the same phenomenon as territorial animals seeking shelter."

3. A. Moles wrote the preface to *La Perception de l'habitat* by J. Ekambi-Schmidt (Paris: Éditions Universitaires, 1972).

4. [Oral: "large rural estate."]

5. [Oral: Barthes alludes to one of Jean Genet's characters leaving some of his excrement behind in a vase of the house he has just burgled. "At night, if it's dark, he lets down his pants, usually behind the main entrance, or at the bottom of the stairway, in the yard. This familiar gesture restores his assurance. He knows that in French slang a turd is known as a 'watchman.'" *The Thief's Journal*, trans. B. Frechtman (Olympia Press, 2004), p. 176.

6. Barthes refers throughout this lecture to Benveniste's *Vocabulaire des institutions indo-européens*, 2 vols. (Paris: Éditions de Minuit, 1969). See p. 116.

7. [Oral: Barthes makes clear that he is discussing "rural" monasteries.]

8. [Oral: "Which amounts to asking: When will it come to an end?"]

9. For Lévi-Strauss, the incest taboo is: "the fundamental step because of which, by which and above all in which, the transition from nature to culture is accomplished." *The Elementary Structures of Kinship,* trans. J. H. Ball, R. von Sturmer, and Rodney Needham (London: Tavistock, 1970), p. 24.

10. [Oral: "the incest taboo."]

11. Articulation of the "axis of selection" (metaphor) and the "axis of combination" (metonynmy) theorised by Roman Jakobson in his *Essays in General Linguistics*, chap. 2.

12. [Oral translation and remarks made by Barthes: "through the window." "a thoroughly coded expression."]

13. [Oral: theme of the forty days in the desert.]

14. [Oral: "*Stulos*, meaning the column."]

15. These details do not appear in Festugière's book *Les Moines d'Orient*, 2 vols. (Paris: Éditions du Cerf, 1961).

16. *Discretio* (Latin): discretion, reserve. Index Card 6: "*Discretio*": "Cf. Tact" Index Card 7: "*Encyclopaedia Universalis*. The Rule of Saint Benedict. Do not impose an artificial attitude, train from the inside, respect different temperaments: Benedictine discretion." Index card 8: "*Discretio*": "Discretion: *nihil asperum, nihil grave* (a tolerable, *ample* regime), Schmitz I. 33." *Nihil asperum, nihil grave* (Latin): nothing harsh, nothing heavy.

17. Léon Zander, "Le monachisme—réalité et idéal—dans l'œuvre de Dostoievski," in *Le Millénaire du mont Athos (963, 1963): Études et mélanges*, vol. 1, (Chevetogne: Éditions de Chevetogne, 1963).

18. See p. 40.

19. Logothete: a creator of language. A neologism created by Barthes in *Sade, Fourier, Loyola*, trans. Richard Miller (Berkley: University of California Press, 1989), p. 95.

20. Edmund Dantès is the hero of Alexandre Dumas's novel *The Count of Monte Cristo*. He makes a dramatic escape from the island prison the Château d'If.

21. [With a slip of tongue that makes his audience laugh, Barthes says "seminar" instead of "labyrinth" here.]

22. *Fellini Satyricon*, 1969.

23. *Eremos* (Greek), *eremus* (Latin): desert, solitary.

24. Philo the Jew or Philo of Alexandria.

25. [Barthes's oral translation: "inner space, inner calm."]

26. See J. Leclercq, "L'erémétisme en Occident jusqu'à l'an mil," in *Le Millénaire du mont Athos (963, 1963)*.

27. [*Vita eremitica* (Latin): Barthes's oral translation: "life in the desert."]

28. [Oral: "a lexicalized expression in Greek," the "absolute desert."]

29. [Oral: "Not many ideas" in this trait, "the facts are calming."]

30. In English in the text.—tr.

31. In English in the text—tr.

32. Antoine Guillaumont, "Philon et les origines du monachism" in Philon d'Alexandrie. Papers presented at the conference organized by the CNRS, in Lyon, September 11–15, 1966 (Paris: Ed. du CNRS, 1967).

33. *Melete* (Greek): taking responsibility for, looking after oneself and, by extension, practice, exercise.

34. *Agape* (Greek): affection, in the plural, *agapes*, the first Christian communal meals.

35. See p. 35.

36. Barthes uses this sign to indicate the sense of "about" or "approximately."

37. Article titled "Chartreux" in the *Encyclopaedia Universalis*.

38. [Oral: "in the Carthusians' language."]

39. [Oral: "the second room."]

40. Otium (Latin): solitary occupation.

41. Léon Zander, "Le monarchism—réalité et idéal—dans l'oeuvre de Dostoïevski," article cited.

42. [Oral: "In the strict sense: the fact of eating together."]

43. Antoine le Maître (1608–58) was the first of the Solitaires of Port-Royal. In his preparatory index cards, Barthes refers to *Mémoires pour servir à l'histoire de Port-Royal* by Nicholas Fontaine, in the 1738 edition (Cologne). A more recent edition of the *Memoires* exists, edited by Paule Thouvenin (Paris: Champion, 2001). The citation, which we were unable to identify, is not from Fontaine's book.

44. The end of this passage is crossed out in the manuscript.

Session of March 9, 1977

1. See p. 46.

2. Draguet includes and translates several chapters of *The Lausiac History* in *Les Pères du désert* (Paris: Plon, 1949).

3. In the lecture, Barthes read the extracts from *The Lausiac History* and *Swann's Way* aloud; only the page references appear in the manuscript.

4. Marcel Proust, *Swann's Way*, trans. C. K. Scott Montcrieff and Terence Kilmartin, revised D. J. Enright (London: The Folio Society, 1992), pp. 113–15.

5. [Oral: "It's a patois word that people would use when I was as a child" from "Gascony patois . . . there used to be a word, I'm not really sure if it was

a real word or if I invented it, a word for troublesome children . . . people used say: so and so is one of *chaouchoun*'s children . . . Eulogius and Aunt Léonie are *chaouchoun* subjects."]

6. [Oral: "in psychoanalytic language."] Barthes is referring to Freud's identification of the anaclitic relation and the narcissistic relation. "Freud writes in 'On Narcissism: An Introduction,' 'a person may love . . . according to the anaclitic (attachment) type: (a) the woman who feeds him; (b) the man who protects him, and the succession of substitutes who take their place.'" Laplanche and Pontalis, *The Language of Psychoanalysis* (London: Karnac Books and The Institute of Psychoanalysis, 1988), p. 33.

7. *Hesuchia* (Greek): tranquility, peace.

8. *Epoché* (Greek): interruption, suspension.

9. [Barthes, whose Latin pronunciation is "in the French style," reads the text aloud and provides a literal translation: "It is forbidden to anoint (cover, perfume) your entire body except in cases of illness. (No pomade except in cases of illness.) It is forbidden to wash your entire body in water while naked. It is forbidden to wash or anoint anyone else's body; it is forbidden to speak to anyone else in darkness. It is forbidden to hold anyone else's hand; instead, whether standing or walking, a distance of one cubit (around fifty centimeters) from others must be respected at all times."]

10. See note 6, above.

11. See "Contacts" in *A Lover's Discourse: Fragments*, trans. Richard Howard (New York: Farrar, Straus and Giroux, 1978), pp. 67–68.

12. Oral: Barthes evokes the scene where Charlus takes hold of the narrator's chin on the beach at Balbec in *The Guermantes Way* (the scene is also evoked in *A Lover's Discourse*, p. 68).

13. [Oral: "of virility and of keeping control over that virility."]

14. Sadomasochist.

15. [Oral: "symbol of non-virility," of "slackening."]

16. See Freud on the "polymorphous perverse disposition," in *Three Essays on the Theory of Sexuality*, standard ed., vol. 7, part 2, chap. 4: "Masturbatory Sexual Manifestations."

17. Wilhelm Reich, *Character-Analysis*, trans. Theodore P. Wolfe (New York: Farrar, Strauss and Giroux, 1970). The build-up of orgasmic energy gives rise to the formation of psychosomatic resistances, themselves forming a "character armor."

18. Yellow pills (in English in the original). A type of aphrodisiac fashionable in the 1970s.

19. [Oral: "To control is to punish."]

20. For Wilhelm Reich, the orgasm is the fulfillment of all successful forms of sexuality: " . . . genital gratification, decisive sex-economic factor in the prevention of neuroses and the establishment of social achievement, is in contradiction, in every respect, with present-day laws and every patriarchal religion" (*The Sexual Revolution*, p. 17).

21. *Oikia* (Greek): home/house.

22. *Famulus* (Latin): servant, slave.

23. For betraying Lord Glenarvan while he had gone to look for Captain Grant, Ayrton would be left alone on a desert island for twelve years. See Jules Verne, *The Mysterious Island*, part 2, chap. 17.

24. *Convertiti* (Latin): converts.

25. See p. 64.

26. *Famuli* (Latin): plural of *famulus*: servants, slaves.

27. The newspaper *Le Moniteur* was, under the Second Empire, a fervent supporter of the imperial regime (Zola, *Pot Luck*, trans. Brian Nelson (Oxford: Oxford University Press, 1999], p. 4).

1. See Lucien Febvre, *Le Problème de l'incroyance au XVe siècle: La religion de Rabelais* (Paris: Albin Michel, 1942), on the printing press (p. 418), on sight (p. 471).

2. [Oral: "The horizon is the line that marks the boundaries of my territory."]

3. Only the page reference appears in the manuscript, but in the lecture Barthes read the passage aloud. Franz Kafka, *The Diaries*, trans. Joseph Kresh et al. (New York: Schocken Books, 1974), November 5, 1911, p. 104.

4. Or originary scene (Freud: *Urszenen*). "Scene of sexual intercourse between the parents that the child observes, or infers on the basis of certain indications, and phantasies. It is generally interpreted by the child as an act of violence on the part of the father." J. Laplanche and J.-B. Pontalis, *The Language of Psychoanalysis*, trans. Donald Nicholson Smith (London: Karnac Books and the Institute of Psychoanalysis, 1988), p. 335.

5. [Oral: Barthes refers to Freud's article, "A Case of Paranoia Running Counter to the Psychoanalytic Theory of the Disease": a woman thinks she can hear the click of a camera when she makes love to her lover; in fact, "there had been a click in her clitoris." In *The Standard Edition of the Complete Works of Sigmund Freud*, vol. 14 (London: Hogarth Press and the Institute of Psychoanalysis, 1953–1974), p. 270. In 1972–73, Barthes devoted a portion of his seminar at the École pratique des hautes études to this particular text.]

6. [Oral: "Complex that entails discovering the nudity of the father."]

7. [Oral: "The pariah is integrated as not-integrated."]

8. [Oral: "Universal topos of wisdom, since we find the same observation made in the writings of Tao." Barthes then reads the quotation from Jean Grenier, *L'Esprit du Tao* (Paris: Flammarion, 1973).]

9. Words added by Barthes.

10. Barthes's references and citations are taken from Draguet, *Les Pères du désert* (Paris: Plon, 1949). Only the titles and page numbers appear in the manuscript. *Palladius: The Lausiac History*, trans. R. T. Meyer (New York: Newman Press, 1964), pp. 96–98.

11. See A.-J. Greimas, "Reflections on Actantial Models," in *Structural Semantics: An Attempt at Method* (Lincoln: University of Nebraska Press, 1983), pp. 196–221.

12. [Oral: "They are recognized so they can be circumscribed."]

13. "The Death of the Father would deprive literature of many of its pleasures. If there is no longer a father, why tell stories? Doesn't every narrative lead back to Oedipus? Isn't storytelling always a way of searching for one's origin, speaking one's conflicts with the Law, entering into the dialectic of tenderness and hatred? Today, we dismiss Oedipus and narrative at one and the same time: we no longer love, we no longer narrate. As fiction, Oedipus was at least good for something: to make good novels, to tell good stories (this is written having seen Murnau's *City Girl*)." *The Pleasure of the Text*, trans. Richard Miller (New York: Farrar, Straus and Giroux, 1975), p. 47.

14. *Hoi paradeisoi* (Greek): gardens, paradises.

15. [Oral: "The active symbol of for nothing."]

16. See Proust, *In Search of Lost Time*, *Sodom and Gomorrah* (part 2, chap. 2), and *Within a Budding Grove* (part 1, "Madame Swann at Home," especially the description of Odette's "winter garden"), trans. C. K. Scott Moncrieff and Terence Kilmartin, revised D. J. Enright (London: The Folio Society, 1992), p. 159.

17. *Ikebana* (Japanese): lit. "living flowers"; Japanese floral art.

18. *Bosquet* (French): a small wood, copse.—tr.

19. We were unable to identify the source of this reference.

20. As Barthes indicates in the lecture, the two anecdotes are drawn from Yve-Alain Bois' doctoral thesis on the conception of space in Lissitzky and

Malevitch (École pratique des hautes études, 1977, thesis supervisor: Roland Barthes).

21. Barthes is quoting from the French translation of Marcel Liebman's book: *Le Léninisme sous Lénine* (Paris: Éditions du Seuil, 1973), p. 31. However, this passage does not appear in the English version: *Leninism under Lenin*, trans. Brian Pearce (London: Jonathan Cape, 1975).—tr.

22. Trait crossed out in the manuscript and not read aloud in the lecture.

Session of March 23, 1977

1. Articles "Athos (Mount)" and "Monastère."

2. [Oral: "He belongs to a monastery, but lives in a small house in the vicinity."]

3. Article on "Monachisme" [Oral: Barthes translates *otium* as "leisure," "not-working."]

4. [Oral: in order to save the subject and thus return him to the symbolic, "you'd have to make him neurotic."]

5. See p. 84.

6. See p. 25.

7. See p. 9.

8. [Oral: "which carries a notation of sin."] See P. Ladeuze, *Etude sur le cénobitism pakhômien pendant le IVe siècle et la première moitié du Ve* (Frankfurt: Minerva, 1961), chap. 1, "Naissance et évolution du cénobitism sous Pakhôme et ses successeurs," p. 169.

9. See p. 181, n. 17.

10. In English in the text.—tr. [In the lecture, Barthes refers to his "unhappy experience" as a boy scout: "It didn't make much of an impression on me."]

11. Article on "Monarchisme."

12. See p. 84.

13. Jean Leclercq, "L'érémitisme en Occident jusqu'à l'an mil," in *Le Millénaire du mont Athos (983, 1963): Études et mélanges*, vol. 1 (Chevetogne, Éditions de Chevetogne, 1963).

14. [Oral: "For the Carthusians, the "desert is now simply a practice of silence."]

15. *Humanitas hopistalitatis* (Latin): lit. "hospitable humanity."

16. Jean Leclerq, "Lérémitism en Occident jusqu'à l'an mil."

17. [Oral: "which in German gave *Münch*, monk."]

18. *Singularis* (Latin): single, singular.

19. The references to Guillaumont are taken from his article entitled "Monachisme et éthique judéo-chrétienne," *Recherches de science religieuse* 60, no. 2 (April–June 1972): especially pp. 200 and 201, 207 *sq.*, 211 . . .

20. According to Mao Zedong, politics stems from the following principle: "One divides into two." Every revolutionary party necessarily comprises of a right wing and a left wing. That division is what justifies the Cultural Revolution and the constant elimination of its opponents. The reference to Lacan refers to the "mirror stage" (see "The Mirror Stage as Formative of the Function of the I" in *Écrits: a Selection*, trans. Alan Sheridan [London: Tavistock, 1977], pp. 1–7.) In the seminar on the Lover's Discourse, Barthes makes a very similar point: "*Alter*: the other component of two who is not me, but with whom I form the *dual*—grammatical entity—the *dyad* (Lacanian entity)."

21. Plato, *The Banquet*, 14.

22. *Heis* (Greek): one.

23. Plato, *The Banquet*, 15.

24. Barthes appears to have written "*comme*" {"as"—tr.} in the manuscript.

25. [Oral: "of this composite One."]

26. [Oral: "Monotropia: to invest the whole of oneself in achieving a single aim."]

27. [Oral: "passion isn't on the side of "eros" but that of obsession, "*mania*."]

28. [Oral: Barthes makes clear that he's referring to "patristic Greek."]

29. *Haplotes* (Greek): simplicity.

30. *Dipsuchia* (Greek): uncertainty, indecisiveness.

31. *Psuchè* (Greek): soul.

32. *Bios praktikos* (Greek): active life.

33. *Bios theoretikos* (Greek): contemplative life.

34. [The oral commentary clarifies the notes: Barthes is alluding to Joseph in the Old Testament, a man who is "unresolved," "torn." Genesis 30:22–24.]

35. *Poikilos* (Greek): varied, many-colored.

36. In the lecture, Barthes recalls that Paphnunce is the hermit in Anatole France's *Thaïs*, trad. Robert B. Douglas, ed. John Lane (London: Bodley Head Ltd., 1926).

37. Cited by A.-J. Festugière (*Les Moines d'Orient* [Paris, Éditions du Cerf, 1961], vol. 1:42). Barthes adapts the citation freely: "to no longer be held back by any human contact, to bond more readily with the Master—to whom he longed to be inseparably bound."

38. In English in the text.—tr. [Oral: there's a double-bind "if two equally powerful authorities simultaneously issue me with two contradictory instructions."]

39. [Oral: Barthes offers his name as an example. In "a Celtic-Iberian language" a *barthe* is a "field that is periodically flooded by rivers." Barthes remembers reading articles in the newspaper recounting "the great mystery of the *barthes*" as a child.]

40. Goupi Main-Rouges: in the lecture, Barthes refers to Jacques Becker's film (1942) based on Pierre Véry's memoirs of country life (1937). All members of the Goupi family have a nickname, relating either to physical feature (Red Hands) or a biographical fact (the colonization of Tonkin).

41. Shifter [in English in the text—tr.]: term used in linguistics to designate words belonging to both the statement and the enunciation ("I").

42. Semanteme (term used in linguistics): unit of meaning.

43. [In the lecture, Barthes recalls that he had used this example once before in a "little book." He is referring to *Roland Barthes by Roland Barthes*, trans. Richard Howard (Berkley: University of California Press, 1977), pp 165–66, and the first name Jean-Louis.]

44. The Bottin, a directory of businesses in France, equivalent to the Yellow Pages.—tr.

45. [Oral: "Roland is a shifter."]

Session of March 30, 1977

1. [At the beginning of this session, Barthes responds to a number of written questions he'd received from members of the audience. (1) The fact that there were no traits between "*Fleurs* / Flowers" and "*Marginalités* / Marginalities" is due to the doubly arbitrary nature of the alphabet: in French, the first letters are the ones most commonly used. (2) The word "symbolism" is used in a very broadly Lacanian, almost "anthropological" sense. Barthes concludes: "the impurity of words is wholly necessary"; "language," "subjects" risk "dying out" when "there are too many concepts."

2. [Oral: "It's hygiene, decency that's experienced as pollution."]

3. [Oral: "One always has to ask oneself: What, through my language, are the languages I'm rejecting?"]

4. [Oral: "A proper name is a name that refers to the incomparable."]

5. Barthes uses this symbol to mean "around," "approximately."

6. Pierre Corneille's *Médée* (1635) is based on the myth of Jason and Medea.

7. In January 1889, Nietzsche wrote in a note to Cosima Wagner, "Ariadne, I love you."

8. [Oral: "You can sometimes measure within yourself your own degree of resistance to saying 'he' or 'she' about someone you love. Or that's my experience, at least."]

9. An *escalope normande* or Normandy escalope is an escalope of veal served with fresh cream, mushrooms, and parsley.—tr.

10. *Lachana* (Greek): garden plants and vegetables.

11. See note 5, above.

12. Draguet, *Les Pères du désert* (Paris: Plon, 1949), p. 61.

13. Henri Maspero, *Taoism and Chinese Religion*, trans. Frank A. Kierman, Jr. (Amherst: University of Massachusetts Press, 1981), p. 367.

14. [Oral: "The semiology of food would be a very feasible branch of semiology; it's altogether possible to do a semiology of aliments, but it would be a complex semiology; it would not be possible to produce straightforward lists or vocabularies."]

15. [Oral: "Marking the end of the dialectic of pizza."]

16. See note 5, above.

17. The citations from Jean Anthelme Brillat-Savarin's *The Physiology of Taste* Barthes reads aloud in the lecture do not appear in the manuscript.

18. Jean Antheleme Brillat-Savarin, *The Physiology of Taste or, Mediations on Transcendental Gastronomy*, trans. M. F. K. Fisher (New York: Alfred A. Knopf, 2009), pp. 184–86. Translation slightly modified.—tr.

19. See note 5, above.

20. [Oral: "A brand."]

21. [Oral: "I imagine it's made with almonds, but that's just a guess."]

22. *La Poudre aux yeux* (1861), by Eugène Labiche and Édouard Martin: two petit-bourgeois families the Malingears and the Ratinois, pretend to be in possession of a great fortune in order to marry off their daughters.

23. Similar to a *vol au vent*, a *Bouchée à la reine* is a small pastry stuffed with a savory filling.—tr.

24. [Oral: Barthes reminisces about the time he lived abroad as a young professor: in the meals organized among colleagues, there was the culinary code, same social standing as in the Josserand's household.]

25. J. K. Huysmans, *A Vau-l'eau* (1882); *Downstream*, trans. Robert Baldick (New York: Turtle Point Press, 2005), tells the story of Monsieur Folantin, a depressed clerk who spends his evenings searching for a good meal.

26. [Seminar entitled "Inventory of systems of contemporary significations." Barthes refers to this seminar in his lecture. Wanting to establish a corpus of menus, Barthes noted a "very great resistance" among his students when asked "to recount what they ate in private, at family meals, for example . . . talking publicly about what you eat is almost like contravening a sexual taboo."]

27. The hotel-restaurant situated on Boulevard Raspail, in the sixth arrondissement of Paris. In the fragment titled "the writer as fantasy" of *Roland Barthes by Roland Barthes*, Barthes notes that he once glimpsed Gide there, "eating a pear and reading a book." *Roland Barthes by Roland Barthes*, trans. Richard Howard (Berkley: University of California Press, 1977), pp. 77–78.

28. In the lecture, Barthes evokes his stay in Romania, in 1947.

29. "The dining table," says B.-S., "is the only place where one does not get bored in the first hour." "Lecture de Brillat-Savarin," OC 3: p. 290.

30. [Oral: "A weight-loss cure is a religious act."]

Session of April 20, 1977

1. Edward T. Hall, *The Hidden Dimension* (New York: Doubleday, 1966), p. 1.

2. Cited by Jézabelle Ekambi-Schmidt in *La Perception de l'habitat* (Paris: Editions Universitaires, 1972). See Abraham-André Moles and Elizabeth Rohmer, *La Psychologie de l'espace* (Paris: Casterman, 1972).

3. [Oral: Barthes clarifies the meaning of the symbol >: "a list of the spaces that man inhabits in descending order."]

4. Cited by A. Moles in his preface to J. Ekambi-Schmidt's book. See Paul-Henry Chombart de Lauwe, *Des Hommes et des Villes* (Paris: Payot, 1965), p. 104. The exact phrase is: collection of people living "under the same key."

5. [Oral: "the territory."]

6. [Oral: "the hideout."]

7. [Oral: "the niche."]

8. [Oral: "I know I'm quite a proxemical person, someone who savors the delights of proxemics."]

9. See Jean-Leroy, article cited.

10. See p. 70. The quotation is from Proust.

11. [Oral: This isn't "a sign of laziness."]

12. In the lecture, Barthes suggests that it would be possible to establish a typology of writers according to their relation to proxemics. Index card 84: "Organization? . . . Taxonomic problems. Lévi-Strauss: 'Tell me how you classify . . .' Proxemics: *possession of one's own disorder,* in which the subject finds himself. Idiolectal order."

13. *Orego* (Greek): to extend, to stretch out.

14. [Oral: Barthes recalls the etymology of the word "*cadre*" {frame}: *quadratio, carré* {square}.]

15. See p. 190–91, note 20.

16. Full title: "*Sur quelques problèmes de sémiotique de l'art visuel: Champ et véhicule dans les signes iconiques,*" p. 843.

17. In the lecture Barthes evokes the cover of the French edition of *Fragments d'un discours amoureux* (Paris: Editions du Seuil, 1977; *A Lover's Discourse: Fragments*) that features a detail from the painting *Tobias and the Angel* (Verrocchio).

18. [Oral: "It's hard to fall in love with someone who's not doing anything." Only characters in stories are capable of falling in love with a portrait.]

19. Werther, in Goethe's eponymous novel, happens upon Charlotte giving the children their afternoon tea (Book 1, Letter of June 16).

20. "The Wolfman," "From a History of an Infantile Neurosis" (1918), in *The Standard Edition of the Complete Works of Sigmund Freud*, vol. 17 (London: Hogarth Press and the Institute of Psychoanalysis, 1953–1974), pp. 19–28. A young man experiences a powerful desire for Grusha, whom he happens across while she is scrubbing the floor.

21. See *The Banquet*, 14.

22. Bécassine, the name of a comic strip and of its heroine. First appeared in the *Semaine de Suzette* in 1905.—tr.

23. Fred, a cartoonist, was involved in the creation of the satirical revue, *Hara Kiri* in the 1960s.—tr.

24. In Homer's *The Iliad* the verb *orego* is used a number of times in descriptions of groups of horses. See, in particular, book 22 (verses 1–34).

25. [Oral: "In the monastic sense."]

26. See p. 57.

27. "'If you please sir,' said the maid, greatly excited. 'It's that dirty Adèle again. She's thrown some rabbit guts out of the window.'" *Pot Luck*, trans. Brian Nelson (Oxford: Oxford University Press, 1999), p. 9.

28. Article on "Monachisme," p. 208.

29. See p. 116.

30. Article on "Monachisme."

31. In the lecture, Barthes defines "the Grand Usage" as that form of "ready-made knowledge" that dictates everyone's behavior. In Brecht's *He Who Says No* (1930), the young invalid boy refuses to be thrown into the ravine in accordance with "the Grand Usage"; Brecht's expression has also been translated as "the Grand Custom."

32. Léon Zander, "Le monarchism—réalité et idéal—dans l'œuvre de Dostoievski." Article cited.

Session of April 27, 1977

1. [Oral: a "book inspired by Freud" on "the literary theme of excrement."]

2. "Who will write the history of tears? In which societies, in which eras, have we wept? Since when do men (and not women) no longer cry? Why was 'sensibility,' at a certain moment, transformed into 'sentimentality'?" "In Praise of Tears," *A Lover's Discourse: Fragments*, trans. Richard Howard (New York: Farrar, Straus and Giroux, 1978), pp. 180–81.

3. [Oral: "That methodology is not interested in quantity, it's concern is the oppositions between terms, it is not especially interested variations in quantity; strictly speaking the + and the –, + and – are not notions that can partake of a structural analysis; what belongs to structural analysis are yes or no, not + or –."]

4. See p. 57.

5. See A. Gide, "The Confined Woman of Poitiers," in *Judge Not*, trans. Benjamin Ivry (Urbana: University of Illinois Press, 2003), p. 153.

6. Allusion to *Psychopathia sexualis* (1886).

7. *Sade, Fourier, Loyola*, trans. Richard Miller (Berkley: University of California Press, 1989), p. 170 (OC 2: p. 1161). The extract Barthes reads aloud in the lecture does not appear in the manuscript. Index Card 35: "Initiation *Magic Mountain* 237. The rest cure (the Living-Together) as *initiation* (love). ('Up high') Hans becomes: 'capable of hearing and comprehending the unregulated, the overwrought, the namelessly extravagant key in which affairs up here were played out.' See what follows: it's basically an apprenticeship in tact."]

8. Barthes quotes this letter from Sade to his wife again on February 25, 1978, as part of his lecture course the following year entitled *The Neutral*, trans. Rosalind Krauss and Denis Hollier (New York: Columbia University Press, 2005), p. 29. See also *The Neutral*, p. 219, n. 37.—tr.

9. *Xeniteia* (Greek): a period of time spent in a foreign country.

10. *Xenos* (Greek): foreigner, stranger.

11. Guillaumont, "Philon et les origines du monachisme." Article cited.

12. See Bareau, *La Vie et Organization des communautés bouddhiques modernes de Ceylan* (Pondichéry: Éditions de l'Institut français de l'indologies, 1957), p. 63.

13. Unless otherwise indicated, the references to Guillaumont refer to his article "Le dépaysement comme forme d'acèse dans le monachisme ancien," *Annuaire de l'Ecole pratique des hautes études*, vol. 76, 1968–1969.

14. See p. 63. In English in the text.—tr.

15. *Stenochoria*: narrow space.

16. [Oral: "Wisdom that's never unrecognized, intelligence that's never divulged, the refusal of glory, etc.: these behaviors have been very well described and are highly recommended in Tao, whose fundamental principle—governing all behavior—is that you mustn't draw attention to yourself."]

17. *Thlipsis* (Greek): pressure, oppression.

18. *Thlibo* (Greek): constrict, oppress.

19. *Parresia* (Greek): to speak freely, frankness.

20. "Will-to-grasp" and "non-will-to-grasp" are expressions that Barthes uses in *A Lover's Discourse: Fragments*.

21. [Oral: "with some aspects of Samurai morality"; *bushido* is the "moral principle of the Samurai."]

22. Jacques Lacan, *The Seminar of Jacques Lacan: Book 1, Freud's Papers on Technique, 1952–54*, new ed., ed. Jacques-Alain Miller, trans. John Forrester (New York: W. W. Norton, 1997).

23. [Oral: "In the etymological sense of the term."]

24. [Oral: "It's to be incapable of substituting one image for another."]

25. *Perigrinatio in stabilitate* (Latin): traveling on the spot, immobile travel [Oral: Barthes translates the formulation as: "to go into exile while remaining in the same place."]

26. Translation slightly modified; as the translator Benjamin Ivry notes, the confined woman of Poitier's real name was Blanche Monnier. Gide changed her name to Mélanie Bastian to protect the reputation of her family: "In [Ivry's] present first-ever translation into English, the real names of individuals have been used in a uniform way." "The Confined Woman of Poitiers," p. 127, n. 1. Barthes, however, refers to Blanche as Mélanie throughout, following Gide.—tr.

27. "The Wise Man seeks neither accolades, nor riches, nor any kind of advantage. He lives for himself only: he is therefore perfectly egoistic." J. Grenier, *L'Esprit du Tao* (Paris: Flammarion, 1973),p. 107.

28. [Oral: that fit of *Xeniteia* "has to do with the particular style of that newspaper." Barthes feels like "a stranger to its language"; he experiences "an anxiety of inner fabrication" whenever *Le Monde* commissions an article from him.]

29. Lacanian expression: the great Other is of the order of language in that it structures transindividual culture and the unconscious of the subject.

30. Article on "Benedictins."

31. [Oral: Barthes adds "desirable."]

Session of May 4, 1977

1. Index card 280: "The best model for utopian Living-Together is the Buddhist monk of Ceylon. Look at Bareau again, the details."

2. *Hupar* (Greek): a waking vision.

3. Index card 64: "Pathos: it is, in sum, the (affective) Imaginary."

4. *Sophia* (Greek): knowledge, practical wisdom, then wisdom.

5. From the Greek *sophronisterion* (house of correction). See Plato, *Laws*, 908a.

6. *Sophron* (Greek): sensible, moderate, wise.

7. For a detailed discussion of "tact" see Barthes's lecture course of the following year, *The Neutral*, trans. Rosalind E. Krauss and Denis Hollier (New York: Columbia University Press, 2005), pp. 29–36.—tr.

8. [Oral: "But it's not a very good word."]

9. [Oral: "Stage fright is a hysterical phenomenon."]

10. See "How this book is constructed." *A Lover's Discourse: Fragments*, trans. Richard Howard (New York: Farrar, Straus and Giroux, 1978), pp. 3–9.

11. [Oral: Barthes adds that the list of figures isn't exhaustive.]

12. [Oral: "I don't have a philosophy of Living-Together."]

13. See Benoit Mandelbrot, *Les Objets fractals* (Paris: Flammarion, 1975), chap. 3, "Le rôle du hasard."

14. See note to p. 192, n. 1.

15. Barthes had read *Beethoven* by André Boucourechliev (Paris: Seuil, 1963). See "Les variations," p. 77.

Session of January 12, 1977

1. Barthes jotted the general plan of his lecture on a piece of paper that he then folded around his notes. An additional note appears just under "Tenir un discours": "Emergence of the notion of force within the field of method."

2. Peculiar because *École* would usually refer to primary school and *Collège* to secondary school.—tr.

3. See p. 4.

4. *To diexerchesthai* (Greek): the fact of running through, and in particular, of running through in speech, of describing in detail.

5. The source of this quotation could not be identified.

6. *Pomme de terre*: in every day usage: "potato"; when broken down into its constitutive elements: "apple of the earth."—tr.

7. The journal entitled *Première Livraison* was launched in the autumn of 1975 by the writer Mathieu Bénezet and the philosopher Philippe Lacoue-Labarthe. It ran for three years, publishing twelve editions of four pages per year. Contributors were invited to respond to two or three key words.

8. *Dielthein* (Greek): to go through, to run all over.

9. Both quotations are from Stéphane Mallarmé, *Divagations*, trans. Barbara Johnson (Cambridge, Mass.: Harvard University Press, 2007). Barthes's margin note refers to the 1945 Pléiade edition edited by Henri Mondor.—tr.

10. The fixed syntagm is a lexicalized expression that as a result belongs to the linguistic system, the code {*langue*}, and to speech {*parole*}. Example: *qu'en-dira-t-on* {what-will-people-say}?

11. See p. 148.

12. *Heuresis* (Greek), *inventio* (Latin): invention, discovery.

13. *Taxis* (Greek), *dispositio* (Latin): arrangement, ordering.

14. *Lexis* (Greek), *elocutio* (Latin): speech, elocution.

15. The spatial metaphor refers to the "common sites" of rhetoric. See Barthes' *L'Ancienne Rhétorique*, "B. 1. 18. Le lieu, *topos, locus*." OC 3: p. 959.

16. *Pronuntiatio* (Latin): declamation.

17. *Hupokrisis* (Greek), *delivery* (English), *actio* (Latin): action of playing a role, then delivering a speech. Charles Sears Baldwin, *Ancient Rhetoric and Poetic: Interpreted from Representative Works* (Westport, Conn.: Greenwood Press, 1971).

18. "Lalangue serves purposes that are all together different from that of communication. That is what the experience of the unconscious has shown us, insofar as it is made of Llanguage, which as you know, I write with two ls to designate what each of us deals with, our so-called mother tongue (lalangue dite maternelle), which isn't that by accident." *The Seminar of Jacques Lacan: On Feminine Sex, the Limits of Loves and Knowledge*, book 20, trans. Bruce Fink (New York: W. W. Norton, 2000), p. 138.

19. *De Oratore* 3: 59. Unidentified translation, possibly Barthes's own.

20. François Flahaut and Jean-Claude Milner are both linguists. In "*Présentation*," Barthes offers the following definition of "delocutionary": "For while modern linguists were initially concerned with "locution" or the "locutionary" (and rightly so: it is always a good idea to deal with questions in order), they are now beginning to raise questions relating to *inter*-locution (talking to someone else, with someone else). A final complexity remains: What happens when two or more people talk *about* someone or *about* something? It is no longer (and it is in this regard the problem is a new one) a matter of considering that someone or that something from a formal perspective (rhetoric has done so already), but of attaining to the dialectic that, in accordance with a complex play of images, brings speakers and the strategies of speech together, or in other words: locution, interlocution and delocution." OC 3: p. 1001.

21. In the Standard Edition of Freud's works James Strachey translates *Be-zetzung* as *cathexis*. See J. Laplanche and J.-B. Pontalis, *The Language of Psychoanalysis*, trans. Donald Nicholson Smith (London: Karnac Books and the Institute of Psychoanalysis, 1988), p. 65.—tr.

22. J. Laplanche and J.-B. Pontalis, *The Language of Psychoanalysis*, p. 60.

23. *Life of Galileo*. Written in 1938; the first production took place in Zurich in 1943.

24. In 1975, Barthes devoted his seminar at the École pratique des hautes études to Flaubert's *Bouvard and Pécuchet*.

25. Defoe, *Robinson Crusoe* (London: Penguin, 1994), pp. 8–12.

26. See p. 177, n. 16.

27. A village in the Basque country where Barthes owned a house.

28. " . . . if you never indulge in a single vice, you will be the unhappiest of women; either don't begin at all, or plunge deep into the abyss from the moment you have one foot on the brink." Sade, *Histoire de Juliette* in *Oeuvres*, vol. 3 (Paris: Gallimard, Bibliothèque de la Pléiade, 1998), p. 749.

29. Invited speakers: François Flahaut (linguist), Lucette Mouline (literary critic), François Récanati (linguist), Cosette Martel (literary critic), Jacques-Alain Miller (psychoanalyst), Antoine Compagnon (literary critic), Louis Marin (1931–1992, essayist).

Session of March 23, 1977

1. Index card that had been crossed out but was affixed to the lecture notes.

2. On the organization of the seminar, see p. 128.

3. Marcel Proust, *In Search of Lost Time: The Guermantes Way*, trans. C. K. Scott Moncrieff and Terence Kilmartin, revised D. J. Enright (London: The Folio Society, 1992). Barthes cites Proust in 1954 edition published by Gallimard, in the series Bibliothèque de la Pléiade, ed. Pierre Clarac and André Ferré. *Le Côté de Guermantes*, part 2: chap. 2. Pléiade, part 2: 553–61.

4. Beginning of a long passage crossed out in the manuscript.

5. *Ton-Semiotik* (German): musical semiotics.

6. "*The Case of Wagner*," in *The Case of Wagner and The Birth of Tragedy*, trans. Walter Kaufmann (London: Vintage, 1967), p. 170. Translation modified following the French.—tr.

7. *The Surrender of Breda* or *Las Lanzas* (1635).

8. End of the passage crossed out in the manuscript.

9. In the manuscript, this heading is written in felt-tip pen.

10. An *explication de texte* is a detailed examination of each element of a literary work, such as structure, style, imagery and the relation of those parts to the whole. It is method commonly used to teach literature in France.—tr.

11. *Hodos* (Greek): path, route, way.

12. *Hodoiporia* (Greek): voyage.

13. Chaim Perelman, *The New Rhetoric: A Treatise on Argumentation*, trans. John Wilkinson and Purcell Weaver (1969).

14. See Plato's *Gorgias*.

15. In French, *développement* can mean development or progression, but also, in relation to cycling, to shift gears.—tr.

16. Barthes discusses a very similar table in *L'Ancienne Rhétorique*, "A. 3.3. La division, la marque." (OC 3: pp. 906–7.)

17. See p. 97.

18. The reference is in fact to *The Suppliants*, verse 466. Barthes mentions the "*lash-word*" in *Sollers écrivain* (1979), calling it "an ancient poetic procedure."

19. Barthes quotes these passages in *A Lover's Discourse: Fragments*, trans. Richard Howard (New York: Farrar, Straus and Giroux, 1978), p. 162.

20. Barthes is referring to a point he develops around "Je-t'aime" {I-love-you} in the seminar on the Lover's Discourse:

> The holophrastic nature of *Iloveyou* . . . Relation to the act of *crying out*. On the *cry* (Freud, discussed by Safouan, Struc 36, *sq.*): cry for help: in the first instance because the child is incapable of performing the specific action himself, which can't be accomplished without outside help: voice (expenditure) . . . Freud: "It's in the cry for help that the hallucination is accomplished." In effect, *Iloveyou*: hallucinates the response: "I love you too." As a cry, *Iloveyou excludes all negativity* . . . Hallucination of a cry. It's not possible to say *Iloveyou* in the expectation of a negative response. Already that personal interpretation no longer partakes of psychoanalysis.

See Barthes, *Le Discours amoureux: Séminaire à l'École pratique des hautes études (1974–1976)*, ed. Claude Coste and Andy Stafford (Paris: Editions du Seuil, 2007), pp. 398–414. See also Moustapha Safouan, *Qu'est-ce que le structuralisme? Le structuralisme en psychanalyse* (Paris: Editions du Seuil, 1973).

21. Moustapha Safouan, *Etudes sur l'Œdipe: Introduction à une théorie du sujet* (Paris: Editions du Seuil, 1974).

22. *Interpretandum* (Latin): calling for interpretation; to be interpreted.

Session of March 30, 1977

1. Beginning of a passage crossed out in the manuscript.

2. On this distinction, see Barthes's essay "Écrivains et écrivants," translated as "Authors and Writers" in *A Roland Barthes Reader*, pp. 185–93. "The writer {*écrivant*} uses language as a means, the author {*écrivain*} uses language as an end."

3. Barthes has Lacan in mind when presenting this operation: the Other refers to culture, the other to a specific interlocutor.

4. See "Connotation: against" and "Connotation: for, even so" in *S/Z*, trans. Richard Miller (New York: Farrar, Strauss and Giroux, 1984), pp. 6–7.

5. End of the message crossed out in the manscript.

6. *Larvatus prodeo* (Latin). Barthes returns to this formulation from Descartes many times throughout his work (for instance, *A Lover's Discourse: Fragments*, trans. Richard Howard (New York: Farrar, Straus and Giroux, 1978), p. 43, which he translates as "I advance pointing to my mask."

7. See p. 189, n. 6.

8. See p. 192, n. 38.

9. In English in the text.—tr.

10. Beginning of a passage crossed out in the manuscript.

11. In the strong sense of "manifesting."—tr.

12. Jean-Paul Sartre, *Sketch for a Theory of the Emotions*, trans. Philip Mairet (London: Routledge, 1996), on fits of anger see in particular p. 46, and on fainting fits p. 50.

13. *Intepretanda* (Latin): things to be interpreted, objects of interpretation.

14. See *A Lover's Discourse: Fragments*, p. 60

15. The word *maya* has a number of different meanings. For Buddhists, the Maya veil refers to the world as an illusion; for Brahmanism, on the other hand, the Maya veil is the manifestation of the essence of the world.

16. End of the passage crossed out in the manuscript.

17. See the Combray section of Proust's *Swann's Way*.

18. See p. 19 and p. 107.

19. Barthes attached two sketches to his notes, both inspired by Y. A. Bois' thesis (see p. 114. Although difficult to make out, the sketches appear to illustrate "Oriental perspective" and "Occidental perspective."

20. See p. 161.

21. See p. 19, 107, and 168.

adunata: impossible things, extraordinary phenomena.

agape: affection; in the plural: *agapes*, the brotherly meal eaten by the first Christians.

akedia: carelessness, indifference.

akedeo: not to care for, to neglect.

akedestos: uncared for, neglected, unburied.

ana-: an upward movement.

anachorein: to move backward, to withdraw.

anachoresis: retreat.

analogon: analogy.

anax: master, king.

aphanisis: action of making something or someone disappear.

askesis: exercise, practice.

asketerion: place of exercise or meditation.

autarkeia: self-sufficiency.

basileus: king, sovereign.

bios praktikos: active life.

bios theoretikos: contemplative life.

chorein: to withdraw, to move away from.

dendrites: pertaining to trees; from *dendron*, tree.

dia thuridos: through a window.

diaita: lifestyle, way of life.

dielthein: to have gone through, to have run through.

(to) diexerchesthai: the fact of running through, of narrating something in detail (particularly in speech).

dipsuchia: uncertainty, indecision.

egkrateia: moderation.

epimeleisthai: to take care of, to manage.

epitropos: person responsible for the running or managing of something.

epoché: interruption, cessation.

eremos: desert, solitary person.

eros: love.

ethos: habit, custom.

haplotes: simplicity.

heis: one.

hesuchazein: to be calm, to keep quiet.

hesuchia: tranquility, calm.

heuresis: invention, discovery.

hodoiporia: journey, walking.

hodos: path, route, way.

homeostasis: neologism created by Barthes from *homoios*, the same, and *stasis*, condition or position.

Hulobioi: the name of members of the Garmanes tribe of India; literal meaning: living in the woods.

hupar: waking vision.

hupokrisis: act of playing a role, declamation.

idios: characteristic, particular, one's own, pertaining to oneself.

kathismata: from *khatisma*, the act of setting up, establishing.

kedeia: the care given to the dead, i.e., a funeral.

kedeuo: attend to a corpse, bury, to take care of.

kellion: storeroom, cellar.

koinobiosis: neologism coined by Barthes from *kionos*, shared, common, and *bios*, life.

lachana: vegetables, garden herbs.

lexis: speech, style, word.

mania: insanity, madness, frenzy.

melete: care, concern and, by extension, practice, exercise.

monachos: solitary, someone who lives alone.

monosis: solitude.

monotropos: living alone, a solitary person, someone who only has one way of being.

oikia: house.

onar: dream.

onoma: name.

orego: to extend, to stretch, to stretch out.

paideia: education, then training, rearing of a child.

paneremos: completely deserted, empty.

paradeisoi: parks, gardens, paradise.

pathos: affect.

peplos: tunic, veil, woven cloth.

poikilos: complicated, complex, many-colored, various.

psuchè: soul.

rhein: to flow.

rhuthmos: rhythm, measured motion.

schema: form, figure.

skene: cabin, tent and, by extension, the meal eaten inside a tent.

sophia: learning, practical knowledge, skill, then wisdom.

sophron: sensible, moderate, wise.

sophronisterion: house of correction.

stenochoria: narrow, constricted space.

taxis: arrangement, order.

telos: aim, goal.

thalamos: room.

thlibo: to oppress, to exercise pressure, to constrict.

xeniteia: a period of time spent in a foreign country.

xenos: foreign, strange; foreigner, stranger.

In his preparatory index cards, Barthes established a "bibliography of books read." Those books are marked here with an asterisk.

Works in English

Bachelard, Gaston. *The Formation of the Scientific Mind*. Translated by Mary McAllester Jones. Manchester: Clinamen Press, 2002.

Baldwin, Charles Sears. *Ancient Rhetoric and Poetic: Interpreted from Representative Works*. Westport, Conn.: Greenwood Press, 1971.

Balzac, Honoré de. *The Wrong Side of Paris*. Translated by Jordan Stump. New York: Modern Library Paperback Edition, 2005.

Barthes, Roland. "Inaugural Lecture, Collège de France." Translated by Richard Howard. In *A Roland Barthes Reader*. Edited by Susan Sontag. New York: Hill and Wang, 1982.

——. *A Lover's Discourse: Fragments*. Translated by Richard Howard. New York: Farrar, Straus and Giroux, 1978.

——. *The Neutral*. Edited by Thomas Clerc under the general direction of Éric Marty. Translated by Rosalind E. Krauss and Denis Hollier. New York: Columbia University Press, 2005.

——. *New Critical Essays*. Translated by Richard Howard. New York: Hill and Wang, 1980.

——. *The Pleasure of the Text*. Translated by Richard Miller. New York: Farrar, Straus and Giroux. 1975.

——. *The Preparation of the Novel*. Edited by Nathalie Léger under the general direction of Éric Marty. Translated by Kate Briggs. New York: Columbia University Press, 2010.

——. *Roland Barthes by Roland Barthes*. Translated by Richard Howard. Berkley: University of California Press, 1977.

——. *Sade, Fourier, Loyola*. Translated by Richard Miller. Berkley: University of California Press, 1989.

——. *S/Z*. Translated by Richard Miller. New York: Farrar, Strauss and Giroux, 1984.

——. *Writing Degree Zero*. Translated by Annette Lavers and Colin Smith. New York: Hill and Wang, 1968.

Benveniste, Émile. *Problems in General Linguistics*. Translated by Mary Elizabeth Meek. Coral Gables, Fla.: University of Miami Press, 1971.

Bettelheim, Bruno. *The Empty Fortress: Infantile Autism and the Birth of the Self*. New York: Free Press, 1967.

*Bion, Wilfred Ruprecht. *Experiences in Groups and other papers*. London: Tavistock Publications, 1961.

Brillat-Savarin, Jean Anthelme. *The Physiology of Taste or, Mediations on Transcendental Gastronomy*. Edited and translated by M. F. K. Fisher. New York: Alfred A. Knopf, 2009.

Colerus, John. *The Life of Benedict de Spinosa*. Translation anonymous. 1706; 1906.

*Defoe, Daniel. *Robinson Crusoe: Complete and Unabridged*. London: Penguin, 1994.

Deleuze, Gilles. *Nietzsche and Philosophy*. Translated by Hugh Tomlinson. London: Continuum, 2006.

Freud, Sigmund. "Three Essays on the Theory of Sexuality." In *The Standard Edition of the Complete Works of Sigmund Freud [SE]*, vol. 7. London: Hogarth Press and the Institute of Psychoanalysis, 1953–1974.

——. "On the History of the Psychoanalytic Movement" and "A Case of Paranoia Running Counter to the Psychoanalytic Theory of the Disease." *SE*, vol. 14.

——. "A Child is Being Beaten: A Contribution to the Study of Sexual Perversions." *SE*, vol. 17.

*Gide, André. "The Confined Woman of Poitiers." In *Judge Not*. Translated by Benjamin Ivry. Urbana: University of Illinois Press, 2003.

*Golding, William. *The Lord of the Flies*. London: Penguin, 1960.

Greimas, A.-J. *Structural Semantics: An Attempt at Method*. Lincoln: University of Nebraska Press, 1983.

Hall, Edward T. *The Hidden Dimension*. New York: Doubleday, 1966,

Kafka, Franz. *The Diaries*. Edited by Max Brod. Translated by Joseph Kresh et al. New York: Schocken Books, 1974.

Klossowski, Pierre. *Nietzsche and the Vicious Circle*. Translated by Daniel W. Smith London: Continuum, 2005.

Lacan, Jacques. *Écrits: A Selection*. Translated by Alan Sheridan. London: Tavistock, 1977.

——. *The Seminar of Jacques Lacan: On Feminine Sex, the Limits of Loves and Knowledge*, book 20. Translated by Bruce Fink. New York: W. W. Norton, 2000.

——. *The Seminar of Jacques Lacan: Book 1, Freud's Papers on Technique, 1953–54,* ed. Jacques Alain Miller, trans. John Forrester. New York: W. W. Norton, 1997.

Laplanche, J., and J.-B. Pontalis. *The Language of Psychoanalysis*. Translated by Donald Nicholson Smith. London: Karnac Books and the Institute of Psychoanalysis, 1988.

Lévi-Strauss, Claude. *The Elementary Structures of Kinship*. Translated by J. H. Ball, R. von Sturmer, and Rodney Needham. London: Tavistock, 1970.

Liebman, Marcel. *Leninism under Lenin*. Translated by Brian Pearce. London: Jonathan Cape, 1975.

Mallarmé, Stéphane. *Divagations*. Translated by Barbara Johnson. Cambridge, Mass.: Harvard University Press, 2007.

*Mann, Thomas. *The Magic Mountain*. Translated by H. T. Lowe-Porter. London: Vintage, 1999.

Maspero, Henri. *Taoism and Chinese Religion*. Translated by Frank A. Kierman, Jr. Amherst: University of Massachusetts Press, 1981.

Nietzsche, Friedrich. *The Case of Wagner and The Birth of Tragedy*. Translated by Walter Kaufmann. London: Vintage, 1967.

——. *The Twilight of the Idols, or How to Philosophize with a Hammer*. Translated by Duncan Large. Oxford: Oxford University Press, 1998.

*Palladius. *The Lausiac History*. Translated by R. T. Meyer. New York: Newman Press, 1964.

Perelman, Charles. *The New Rhetoric: A Treatise on Argumentation*. Translated by John Wilkinson and Purcell Weaver. University of Notre Dame Press, 1969.

Proust, Marcel. *In Search of Lost Time*. Vols. 1–5. Translated by C. K. Scott
    Moncrieff and Terence Kilmartin, revised by D. J. Enright. London:
    The Folio Society, 1992.
Reich, Wilhelm. *Character-Analysis*. Translated by Theodore P. Wolfe.
    New York: Farrar, Strauss and Giroux, 1970.
——. *The Sexual Revolution: Toward a Self-Governing Character Structure*.
    Revised Edition. Translated by Theodore P. Wolfe. New York: Octagon
    Books, 1971.
*Rykwert, Joseph. *On Adam's House in Paradise: The Idea of the Primitive
    Hut in Architectural History*. New York: Museum of Modern Art, 1972.
Sade, Donatien Alphonse François de. *The Complete Justine, Philosophy in
    the Bedroom and Other Writings*. Translated by Richard Seaver and
    Austryn Wainhouse. New York: Grove Press, 1966.
Sartre, Jean-Paul. *Sketch for a Theory of the Emotions*. Translated by Philip
    Mairet. London: Routledge, 1996,
Watts, Alan. *The Way of Zen*. New York: Pantheon, 1957.
*Xenophon. *The Economist*. Translated by H. G. Dakyns. In *The Works of
    Xenophon*. London: Macmillan and Co., 1897.
*Zola, Émile. *The Conquest of Plassans*. Translated by Alfred Vizetelly Ernest.
    New York: Mondial, 2005.
* ——. *Pot Luck*. Translated by Brian Nelson. Oxford: Oxford University
    Press, 1999.

Works in French

*Amand (dom David). *L'Acèse monastique de Saint Basile: Essai historique*.
    Maredsous: Éditions de Maredsous, 1948.
Armand, Félix, and André Maublanc, eds. *Fourier*. 3 vols. Paris: Éditions
    Sociales, 1937.
Baltrusaïtis, Jurgis. *Le Moyen Âge fantastique: Antiquités et exotismes dans
    l'art gothique*. Paris: Flammarion, 1981.
*Bareau, André. *La Vie et l'Organisation des communautés bouddhiques
    modernes de Ceylan*. Pondichéry: Éditions de l'Institut français de
    l'indologies, 1957.
Barthes, Roland. *Œuvres complètes*. 3 vols. Edited by Éric Marty. Vol 1:
    1942–1965, Vol 2: *1966-1973*, Vol 3: *1974–1980*. Paris: Éditions du
    Seuil, 1993, 1994, 1995.
Benveniste, Émile. *Vocabulaire des institutions indo-européennes*. 2 vols. Paris:
    Éditions de Minuit, 1969.
Benoit, Saint. *La Règle de saint Benoit*. Éditions d'Adalbert de Voguë. 6 vols.
    Paris: Éditions du Cerf, 1971–1972.
Bled, Victor du. *La Société française du XVe au XX siècle*. Paris: Didier, 1900.
Chombart de Lauwe, Paul-Henry. *Des Hommes et des villes*. Paris, Payot, 1965.
Casals, Pablo. *Conversations avec Pablo Casals. Souvenirs et opinions d'un
    musicien*. Paris: Albin Michel, 1955, 1992.
Cassien. *Institutions cénobitiques*. Edited and translated by Jean-Claude Guy.
    Paris. Éditions du Cerf, 1965.
Curtius, Ernst Robert. *La Littérature européenne et le Moyen Âge latin*. Paris:
    PUF, 1956; new edition, Paris: Agora, 1986, and Paris: Presses Pocket,
    1991.
*Décarreaux, Jean. "Du monachisme primitif au monachisme athonite." In *Le
    Millénaire du mont Athos (983, 1963): Études et mélanges*. Vol. 1.
    Chevetogne: Éditions du Chevetogne, 1963.

*Defoe, Daniel. *Vie et aventures de Robinson Crusoé*. In *Romans*. Vol .1.
Translated into French by Pétrus Borel, preface by Francis Ledoux.
Paris: Gallimard, 1959.

Descartes, René. *Œuvres philosophiques*. Vol. 1. Paris: Garnier, 1988.

*Desroche, Henri. *La Société festive: Du fouriérisme écrit aux fouriérismes
pratiqués*. Paris: Éditions du Seuil, 1975.

Dictionnaire de spiritualité ascétique et mystique: doctrine et histoire. 30 vols.
Under the direction of Marcel Viller. Paris: Beauchesne, 1937–1995.

Dort, Bernard. *Lecture de Brecht*, followed by *Pédagogie et Forme épique*.
Paris: Éditions du Seuil, 1960.

*Draguet, René. *Les Pères du désert*. Paris: Plon, 1949.

*Droit, Roger-Poi, and Antoine Gallien. *La Chasse au bonheur: Les nouvelles
communatés en France*. Paris: Calmann-Lévy, 1972.

Duby, Georges. *Le Temps des cathédrales*. Paris: Gallimard, 1976.

*Ekambi-Schmidt, Jézabelle. *La Perception de l'habitat*. Paris: Éditions
Universitaires, 1972.

Étiemble, René. *Parlez-vous franglais?* Paris: Gallimard, 1964, 1973.

Febvre, Lucien. *Le Problème de l'incroyance au XVIe siècle: La religion de
Rabelais*. Paris: Albin Michel, 1962.

*Festugière, André-Jean. *Les Moines d'Orient*. Vol. 1: *Culture ou Sainteté*,
Vol. 2: *Les Moines de la région de Constantinople*. Paris: Éditions du
Cerf, 1961.

Flahaut, François. *La Parole intermédiaire*. Paris: Éditions du Seuil, 1978.

Fontaine, Nicholas. *Mémoires pour servir à la l'histoire de Port-Royal*. Vol. 1.
Cologne, 1738.

——. *Mémoires ou Histoire des Solitaires de Port-Royal*. Paris: Éditions de
Paule Thouvenin, 2001.

Grenier, Jean. *L'Esprit du Tao*. Paris: Flammarion, 1973.

*Guillaumont, Antoine. "La conception du désert chez les moines d'Égypte."
Revue de l'histoire des religions, 94th year, vol. 188 (1975).

*——. "Le dépaysement comme forme d'ascèse dans le monarchisme ancien."
Annuaire de l'École pratique des hautes études 76 (1968–1969).

*——. "Monarchisme et éthique judéo-chrétienne." *Recherches de science
religieuse* 60, no. 2 (April–June 1972).

*——. "Philon et les origines du monarchisme." In *Philon d'Alexandrie: Actes
du colloque organisé par le CNRS, à Lyon, les 11–15 septembre 1966*.
Paris: Éditions du CNRS, 1967.

Jacquemard, Simone. *L'Éruption du Krakatoa ou Des chambres inconnues
dans la maison*. Paris: Éditions du Seuil, 1967.

Lacarrière, Jacques. *L'Été grec: Une Grèce quotidienne de 4000 ans*. Paris:
Plon, 1976.

*Ladeuze, Paulin. *Étude sur le cénobitisme pakhômien pendant le IVe siècle
et la première moitié du Ve*. Frankfurt: Minerva, 1961.

Lascault, Gilbert. *Le Monstre dans l'art occidental: Un problème esthétique*.
Paris: Klincksieck, 1973.

Leclercq, Jean. "L'érémetisme en Occident jusqu'à l'an mil." In *Le Millénaire
du mont Athos (983, 1963): Études et mélanges*. Vol. 1. Chevetogne:
Éditions de Chevetogne, 1963.

Leroi-Gourhan, André. *Le Geste et la Parole*. Vol. 1: *Technique et langage*,
Vol. 2: *La Mémoire et les Rythmes*. Paris: Albin Michel, 1964.

Leroy, Jean. "La conversion de saint Athanase l'athonite et l'idéal cénobitique
et l'influence studite." In *Le Millénaire du mont Athos (983, 1963):
Études et mélanges*. Vol. 1. Chevetogne: Éditions de Chevetogne, 1963.

Mallarmé, Stéphane. *Œuvres complètes*. Texte established and introduced by
Henri Mondor and G. Jean-Aubry. Paris: Gallimard, 1945.

———. *Œuvres complètes*. Vol. 1. Introduced, established, and annotated by
	Bertrand Marchal. Paris: Gallimard,1998.
Malraux, André. *Les Noyers de l'Altenburg*. In *Œuvres complètes*. Vol. 2.
	Edited by Marius-François Guyard, Maurice Larès, and François
	Trécourt with the participation of Noël Burch. Paris: Gallimard,
	1996.
Mandelbrot, Benoit. *Les Objets fractals: Forme, hasard et dimension*. Paris:
	Flammarion, 1975.
*Massebieau, Louis. "Le Traité de la *Vie contemplative* de Philon et la
	question des Thérapeutes." *Revue de l'histoire et des religions*. Annales
	du musée Guimet, Ernest Leroux éditeur. Vol. 16, 1887.
Le Millénaire du mont Athos (983, 1963): Études et mélanges. Vol. 1.
	Chevetogne: Éditions de Chevetogne, 1963.
Moles, Abraham-André, and Élizabeth Rohmer. *La Psychologie de l'espace*.
	Paris: Casterman, 1972.
*Olievenstein, Claude. *Il n'y a pas de drogués heureux*. Paris: Laffont, 1976.
*Philon d'Alexandrie: Actes du colloque organisé par le CNRS, à Lyon, les
	11–15 septembre 1966*. Paris: Éditions du CNRS, 1967.
Photo, no. 112 (January 1977).
Récanati, François. *Les Énoncés performatifs: Contribution à la pragmatique*.
	Paris: Éditions de Minuit, 1981.
Ruffié, Jacques. *De Biologie à la culture*. Paris: Flammarion, 1976; 2nd ed.,
	1983.
Safouan, Moustapha. *Études sur l'Œdipe: Introduction à une théorie du sujet*.
	Paris: Éditions du Seuil, 1974.
———. *Qu'est-ce que le structuralisme? Le structuralisme en psychanalyse*.
	Paris: Éditions du Seuil, 1973.
Schapiro, Meyer. "Sur quelques problèmes de sémiotique de l'art visuel:
	Champ et véhicule dans les signes iconiques." *Critique*, no. 315–316
	(August–September 1973).
*Schmitz, dom Philbert. *Histoire de l'ordre de saint Benoit*. 7 vols. Mared-
	sous: Éditions de Maredsous, 1948–1956.
Schwaller de Lubicz, Réné-Adolphe. *Le Temple dans l'homme*. Le Caire:
	Éditions Schindler, 1950; new edition, Paris: Dervy-Livres, 1979.
Zander, Léon. "Le monarchisme – réalité et idéal – dans l'œuvre de Dos-
	toïevski." In *Le Millénaire du mont Athos (983, 1963): Études et
	mélanges*. Vol. 1. Chevetogne: Éditions de Chevetogne, 1963.

Cézanne, Paul, 8, 116, 178n33
Chaplin, Charlie, 53
Charcot, Jean-Martin, 43, 184n7
Charlemagne, 51
Charlotte (*The Sorrows of Young Werther*), 115, 194n19
Charlus (*The Guermantes Way*), xxi, 154–57, 159–61, 164–69, 189n12
Chartreux, Monsieur de (*The Confined Woman of Poitiers*), 61
Chasles, Philarète, 17
Chombart de Lauwe, Henry, 112, 194n4
Chomsky, Noam, 148
Cicero, 148
Clarisse (*Pot Luck*), 78
Cocteau, Jean, 42
Colerus, John: *Life of Benedict de Spinoza*, 25, 108, 126
Compagnon, Antoine, 152, 172, 198n30
Corneille, Pierre, 100
Crusoe, Robinson (*Robinson Crusoe*), xxv, 14–15, 22, 33, 84, 94, 112, 115; and anachoresis, 25–26; and animals, 26–28; and domain, 116–17; and enclosure, 58–60; father's discourse to, 150; and slavery, 76
Curtius, Ernst Robert, 29
Cyran, Saint, 65

Daniel the Stylite, 122
Dantès, Edmund (*The Count of Monte Cristo*), 62, 188n20
Décarreaux, Jean, 25, 30–31, 33–35, 91
Defoe, Daniel: *Robinson Crusoe*, xxiii, xxiv, 14–15, 17, 22, 25–29, 33, 58–60, 76, 83–84, 94, 112, 115–17, 150, 171
Deleuze, Gilles, xxiii, 3, 133
Democritus, 7
Desbordes-Valmore, Marceline, 159–60
Descartes, René, 199n7
Desroche, Henri, 5
De Staël, Nicholas, 8, 178n33
Diderot, Denis, 27, 135, 142, 181n13
Dionysus (Nietzsche), 101
Donis, Comtesse de (*Histoire de Juliette*), 151, 198n29
Dorotheus (*The Lausiac History*), 60

Dostoevsky, Fyodor, 60; *The Brothers Karamazov*, 65, 90, 120, 191n2; *The Idiot*, 15, 17; *The Possessed*, p. 60
Draguet, René, 21, 29, 68, 75, 76, 102, 104, 188n2
Droit, Roger-Poi, 95, 99, 107, 125, 131
Duby, Georges, 128
Dumas, Alexandre: *The Count of Monte Cristo*, 62, 188n20
Durkheim, Émile, 148
Durtal (*En Route*), 182n33
Duveyrier (*Pot Luck*), 78

Ekambi-Schmidt, Jézabelle, 57, 111–12, 114
Eli (Bible), 63
Elias (Bible), 60, 63
Elias (*The Lausiac History*), 75
Elijah (Bible), 29
Ernst, Max, 177n18
Eulogius (*The Lausiac History*), 68–69, 71–72, 188n5
Eve (Bible), 94
Ezekiel (Bible), 51, 185n4, 185n6

Faugas, Abbé (*The Conquest of Plassans*), 53
Febvre, Lucien, 79
Félicité (*A Simple Heart*), 181n12
Fellini, Federico, 62
Festugière, André-Jean, 25, 26, 44, 60, 76, 90, 122; on food, 102, 104
Filon, Augustin, 64
Flahaut, François, 48, 148, 152, 172, 185n23, 198n30
Flaubert, Gustave, 52, 186n14; *Bouvard and Pécuchet*, 20, 149–50, 198n25; *A Simple Heart*, 27, 181n12
Folantin, Monsieur (*A Vau-l'eau*), 193n25
Foucault, Michel, xvii
Fourier, F.M.C., 4–5, 9, 35, 88, 130
France, Anatole (Jacques-Anatole-François Thibault), 96, 192n36
François (*Swann's Way*), 68, 70–72
Fred (cartoonist), 116, 194n23
Freud, Sigmund, 5–6, 18, 160, 177n16, 189n6, 189n16, 199n20; on excrement, 121, 123; and hearing, 80; on investment, 148–49; and money, 35, 183n8; and the

Thing, 43, 184n7; "The Wolfman" of, 115, 194n20
Friday (*Robinson Crusoe*), 14, 76, 83–84

Gallien, Antoine, 93, 95, 99, 107, 125, 131
Genet, Jean, 187n5
Gide, André, 109, 193n27; *The Confined Woman of Poitiers*, xxiii–xxvi, 13–14, 53–54, 60–63, 83, 86, 99–100, 107–8, 111, 121–24, 127–28, 134–35, 171, 196n26
Giono, Jean, 57, 187n1
Girard, René, 83
Gisèle (*Within a Budding Grove*), 146
Glenarvan, Lord (*The Mysterious Island*), 189n23
Goethe, Johann Wolfgang von, 24; *The Sorrows of Young Werther*, 13, 74, 115, 149, 159–60, 179n5, 194n19
Golding, William: *The Lord of the Flies*, 56, 83, 119, 187n35
Goncourt, Edmond-Louis-Antoine Huot de, 80
Gorky, Maxim, 51
Goupi family (Becker film), 97, 192n40
Gourd, Madame (*Pot Luck*), 78
Gourd, Monsieur (*Pot Luck*), 78
Gradiva, 115
Grant, Captain (*The Mysterious Island*), 189n23
Gregory, Pope, 182n24
Gregory, Saint, 30, 182n24
Greimas, A.-J., 82
Grenier, Jean, 82, 85–86, 190n8
Grusha ("The Wolfman"), 115, 194n20
Guillaumont, Antoine, 63, 64, 93–95, 124–29

Hall, Edward Twitchell, 111
Harbert (*The Mysterious Island*), 88–89
Hector (*Andromache*), 163
Hermione (*Andromache*), xxi, 161–63
Herrera, Juan de, 51, 185n5
Hollier, Denis, xviii
Homer, 52, 116, 118, 194n24
Howard, Richard, 176n3
Hugo, Victor-Marie, 159–60
Huysmans, Joris-Karl, 108, 182n33, 193n25

Ivry, Benjamin, 196n26

Jack (*The Lord of the Flies*), 56, 119
Jacquemard, Simone, 24, 33
Jakobson, Roman, 59, 187n11
Jason (*Medée*), 100
Jerome, Saint, 102
Joachim (*The Magic Mountain*), 36
John of Ephesus, 127
John the Baptist, 63
Jones, Ernest, 21
Josserand family (*Pot Luck*), 108, 193n24
Joyce, James, 179n19
Juliette (*Histoire de Juliette*), 151, 198n29

Kafka, Franz, 79–80
Karamazov, Aliocha (*The Brothers Karamazov*), 120
Kassel, Joseph, 42
Kierkegaard, Søren Aabye, 3
Klossowski, Pierre, 19
Krafft-Ebing, Richard von, 123
Krauss, Rosalind, xxviii

Labiche, Eugène, 108, 193n22
La Bruyère, Jean de, 48
Lacan, Jacques, 93, 127, 148, 160, 191n20, 192n1, 196n29, 197n19
Lacarrière, Jacques, xxii, 6, 33–35, 181n2
Lacoue-Labarthe, Philippe, 144, 197n7
Ladeuze, Paulin, 42, 73, 74, 91, 102, 118
Lao-Tzu, 85
Laplanche, J., 148–49
La Rochefoucald, François de, 48
Lascault, Gilbert, 29
Lausius, 15
Leclercq, Jean, 182n24
Le Corbusier (Charles-Édouard Jeanneret), xxiii, 114
Ledoux, François, 17
Leibniz, Gottfried Wilhelm, 135
Le Maître, Antoine, 65, 188n43
Léonie, Aunt (*Swann's Way*), xxiii, xxvi, 53, 57, 68, 70–72, 113–14, 188n5
Leroi-Gourhan, André, 57, 185n26, 187n2
Leroy, Jean, 76
Leucippus, 7

Lévi-Strauss, Claude, 59, 84, 91–92, 101, 187n9, 194n12
Liebman, Marcel, 87–88, 191n21
Littré, Émile, 88, 143, 145–46, 149
Lowe-Porter, H. T., 180n39
Lulle, Raymond, 51, 185n7
Luynes, Duc de (Charles d'Albert), 65

Magnus, Frau (*The Magic Mountain*), 98
Malingears family (*La Poudre aux yeux*), 193n22
Mallarmé, Stéphane, 4, 5–6, 145, 177n10
Malot, Hector, 5, 177n15
Malraux, André, 15, 17
Mann, Thomas: *Death in Venice*, 16, 45, 184n13; *The Magic Mountain*, xx, xxiii–xxiv, 16, 21–22, 36–37, 45, 56, 80, 83, 97–98, 109–10, 117, 171, 195n7
Mao Zedong, 93, 191n20
Marin, Louis, 152, 172, 198n30
Marivaux, Pierre de, 89
Mark (Bible), 64
Martel, Cosette, 152, 172–73, 198n30
Martha (Bible), 184n31
Martin, Édouard: *La Poudre aux yeux*, 108, 193n22
Marty, Éric, xxix, 168
Marx, Karl, 5–6, 35, 183n8
Mary (Bible), 184n31
Maspero, Henri, 104
Massebieau, Louis, 64, 132
Maublanc, René, 5
Medea, 100
Michelet, Jules, 80
Miller, Jacques-Alain, 152, 172, 198n30
Milner, Jean-Claude, 148, 197n21
Moles, Abraham-André, 57, 111
Mondrian, Piet, 88
Monnier, Blanche, 196n26
Moses (Bible), 63
Mouline, Lucette, 152, 172, 198n30
Mouret, François (*The Conquest of Plassans*), 53, 80
Mouret, Octave (*Pot Luck*), 16
Mouret, Serge (*The Sin of Father Mouret*), 16
Mouret de Plassans (*The Ladies' Paradise*), 16

Nab (*The Mysterious Island*), 88–89
Narrator (*The Guermantes Way*), 154, 164–65, 167–68
Nemo (*Twenty Thousand Leagues under the Sea*), 36
Nietzsche, Friedrich, 5–6, 19, 92, 101, 179n20, 181n43, 193n7; on active philology, 107, 170; on distance, 6, 132, 177n21; on method/culture, xx, xxiii, 3–4, 133; on music, 154–55
Noah (Bible), 49–50, 89

Oedipus, 84, 190n13
Olievenstein, Claude, 119
Or, Abba, 127
Ossian (*The Sorrows of Young Werther*), 149

Pachomius, Saint, 10–11, 17, 54–55, 66, 91–92; rule of, 42, 52, 73–74, 84, 102, 104, 189n9; successors of, 118
Palladius: *The Lausiac History*, xxiii–xxiv, 15, 60, 64, 68–69, 71–72, 75, 81–83, 135, 171
Paphnucius (*Thaïs*), 96, 192n36
Pascal, Blaise, 52, 186n13
Paul of Thebes, 29
Pécuchet (*Bouvard and Pécuchet*), 20, 149–50
Pencroff (*The Mysterious Island*), 88–89
Perelman, Chaim, 157
Philip II, 51, 185n5
Philo, 63, 188n24
Piano, Renzo, 186n15
Piggy (*The Lord of the Flies*), 83
Pinchon, Joseph, 116
Piranesi, Giambattista, 54
Pistos, Abba, 128
Piteroum, Saint (*The Lausiac History*), 82
Plato, 5, 7, 130, 142, 158; *The Banquet*, 73, 94, 109, 115
Poemen the monk, 75
Pontalis, J.-B., 148–49
Proust, Marcel, 48, 53, 113–14, 172, 179n3; *The Guermantes Way*, xxi, 145, 154–57, 159–61, 164–69, 173, 189n12; *In Search of Lost Time*, xxiii, 24, 87, 155, 163, 190n16; *Swann's Way*, 68, 70–72, 145, 168; *Within a Budding Grove*, 87, 146, 190n16
Pyrrhus (*Andromache*), 161, 163

L'Éruption du Krakatoa (Jacque-mard), 33
the Escorial, 51, 185nn5–6
Essays in General Linguistics (Jakobson), 187n11
Essenians, 34, 183n5
L'Été grec (Lacarrière), xxii, 6
ethos (habit, custom), 181n43
event (*événement*), 84–86
excrement, 121–23, 134
exile, 124–25, 127, 196n25
Experiences in Groups and Other Papers (Bion), 9, 46, 131
explosemes, xxi, 166–67

faith, 46
Familien-Roman, 5, 177n16
family, 8, 9, 97, 99, 112, 178n34
fantasy, 26, 45–46, 51–52, 72–73, 75, 113, 125–28, 186n16; of idiorrhythmic Living-Together, xxi–xxii, 4–10, 12, 19, 48–49, 81, 84, 130–32, 171–72; and idyll, 88; of irritation, 141–42, 144, 151; and teaching, xxi–xxii, 4, 141
The Fashion System (Barthes), 177n5
Fellini Satyricon, 62
flowers (*fleurs*), 86–88
folie-à-deux, 67–68, 71–72
food (*nourriture*), 101–10; connotations of, 105–9; and rhythms, 102–3; symbolism of, 101, 103–4, 106–7, 109–10
forces, 3–5, 9, 15, 17, 107, 172–73; in Charlus-Discourse, 156, 159, 162–63, 166–69; and holding forth, 142, 146–48, 151, 197n1
the frame, 114–16
France, 29, 38, 72, 93, 99, 107, 131
Franciscans, 40
François le Champi (Proust), 168
French language, xxix–xxx, 18, 93, 142–44, 148–49, 179n18, 180n39, 186n24
friendship, 65, 93
A Friend's Reunion (*Au rendez-vous des amis*; painting; Ernst), 177n18

German language, 18, 148–49, 179n18, 180n39
Germany, 38, 156
Gervais (French company), 26, 181n10

La Geste et la Parole (Leroi-Gourhan), 185n26, 187n2
gesture, 117, 133, 150, 154, 159
the Grand Custom, 120, 195n31
the Great Laura, 31
Greece, 33, 75
Greek language, 18–19, 31, 42, 142
The Guermantes Way (Proust), xxi, 145, 154–57, 159–61, 164–69, 173, 189n12
guru, 55–56, 186n32

haplotes (simplicity), 95–96
hearing (*écoute*), 79–81
hesuchazein (Lat. *hesynchastes*; to be calm, quiet), 31
hesuchia (tranquility, calm), 44, 63, 73, 95–96
He Who Says No (Brecht), 195n31
The Hidden Dimension (Hall), 111
hideouts, 14, 112–13
Histoire de Juliette (Sade), 151, 198n29
hodoiporia (journey), 156
hodos (path), 156
holding forth, 141–52, 172–73; and forces, 142, 146–48, 151, 197n1; and speech, 147–49; and theatricalization, xxi, 143, 146–51
Holland, 38
homeostasis, 47–48
How to Live Together (lecture course; Barthes), xii, xvii, xxiii, xxviii–xxix, 24, 171–72, 175n6
huit clos, 5
Hulobioi (Indian tribe), 29, 181n16
hupar (waking vision), 132, 168
hupokrisis (act of playing a role), 148
the hut, 49–51, 114

idiomatic expression, 143–44
idiorrhythmy, xxiv, xxvi, 12–13, 17, 38–41, 135, 171; and anachorites, 26, 63–66; and Athos, xxii, 9, 30–35, 63, 76–77, 90, 131, 178n23; definition of, xxii, 6–10; and desire, 75; and distance, 72; and Eros, 38; and leadership, 54–55; and marginality, 34, 40, 91–93; in novels, 24, 33, 42, 51, 57; and power, 31, 35, 40;

religious, 30–34; and *rhuthmos*, 181n2; and rule, 118, 119; and spaces, 49, 58; and *Telos*, 44, 45–46, 47; and timing, 39; and utopia, 119, 128, 130, 196n1. *See also* Living-Together
The Idiot (Dostoevsky), 15, 17
idyll (*idyllique*), 88–89, 176n1 (12/1/77), 191n22
ikebana, 87
The Iliad (Homer), 194n24
illness, 45
imagery, 7, 37, 77, 114–15, 142; and Charlus-Discourse, 155, 165, 166; false, 126–27; and food, 105, 107–8
imaginary, 4, 17, 22, 86, 106, 127, 179n14
imprinting, 28
"Inaugural Lecture" (Barthes), xvii, xxviii, 16, 18, 20, 171, 180n28; on fantasmic teaching, xxi–xxii, 4, 141
inflexemes, 164–66
In Search of Lost Time (Proust), xxiii, 24, 87, 155, 163, 190n16
intensities, 168–69
intimacy, 123
Introduction to Structural Anthropology (Lévi-Strauss), 84
"Inventory of systems of contemporary significations" (seminar; Barthes), 193n26
investment, 148–50
Ionian philosophy, 7, 178n27

Japan, xxii, 87
Jesuit, 108, 111, 193n21
Joy of Man's Desiring (Giono), 57
Judaism, 87
Judge Not (Gide), 13–14
Justine (Sade), 185n15

kellion (hermit's cells), 16, 25, 31, 49, 182n34
Kiefs (Balkans), 109
kinetics, 156–59
koinobiosis (communal life), 17

the labyrinth, 62
"Labyrinth" (seminar; Barthes), 179n3
The Ladies' Paradise (Zola), 16
"lalangue," 148, 197n19
the lamp, 112–13
language, xxi, 59, 99–101, 149, 168, 177n10, 185n26, 192n1;

solitude, xxv–xxvi, 4–6, 15, 25, 63, 94
"Someone's Discourse, the Other's Discourse" (Miller), 172
sophia (knowledge, then wisdom), 132
Sophists, 158
sophron (moderate, wise), 132
Sophronistery, 132
the sorcerer, 83–84, 91–92
The Sorrows of Young Werther (Goethe), 13, 74, 115, 149, 159–60, 179n5, 194n19
Sovereign Good, 5, 75, 130, 132
spaces, xxiv–xxv, 5, 7, 13–16, 49–54, 132, 171; and Athos, 31–32, 51; in *The Confined Woman of Poitiers*, 53–54; idiorrhythmic, 49, 58; in *The Magic Mountain*, 117; and monasteries, 39–40, 51; and monks, 31, 64; in *Pot Luck*, 117; and power, 52–54; and proxemics, 111–14
Spain, 28, 38
speech, x–xi, xxix, 131, 147–49, 155–59, 165
sponge (*éponge*), 81–84, 126
stability, 39, 54, 93
stenochoria (narrow space), 125, 126
structural analysis, 122, 155–56, 161, 169, 182n25
Studite monks (Constantinople), 123
"Style as Craftsmanship" (Barthes), ix
Stylites, 11, 60, 92, 121–22
Summerfolk (Gorky), 51
The Suppliants (Aeschylus), 198n18
The Surrender of Breda (painting; Velázquez), 155–56
Swann's Way (Proust), 68, 70–72, 145, 168
Swiss Family Robinson (Wyss), 29

symbolism, 59, 74, 87, 112, 135–36, 168, 185n7, 192n1; and dirtiness, 121–23; of food, 101, 103–4, 106–7, 109–10; and marginality, 90–91
Synanon (community), 119
Syria, 15, 29, 60, 76, 91
S/Z (Barthes), x, 155–57, 163

tact, 123–24, 132, 134, 195n7, 196n7
Tao, 38, 56, 75, 82, 101, 126, 190n8, 195n16; and egoism, 128, 196n27; and food, 104; and *stenochoria*, 125; and *Wou-wei*, 85–86
Taoism and Chinese Religion (Maspero), 104
teaching, 33, 158; of Barthes, x–xi, xxx, 21; fantasmic, xxi–xxii, 4, 141
Telos (Cause), xii, 43–49
Le Temple dans l'homme (Schwaller de Lubicz), 185n25
Temple of Jerusalem, 51, 185n6
Le Temps des cathédrales (Duby), 128
tenir (to hold), 146–47
territory, 57–59, 79–80, 112–13, 116–18, 122–23, 187n2
Thaïs (France, A.), 192n36
theatricalization, 131; and Charlus-Discourse, 156, 160, 167; and holding forth, xxi, 143, 146–51
Thelema, xxv, 132
Therapeuts, 34, 64, 183n5
thlipsis, 125, 128
timing, 39, 102, 116, 117, 128–29
traits, xii, xxiii–xxiv, 9, 13, 15, 19–21, 171–72
translation, xxvii–xxx, 17, 176nn3–4, 176n10
transparency, 52–54, 81, 102–3, 119

triggers, 159–60
Twenty Thousand Leagues under the Sea (Verne), 36
The Twilight of the Idols (Nietzsche), 6, 132, 177n21

United States, 99, 125, 131
An Unknown Masterpiece (Balzac), 13, 179n4
USSR (Soviet Union), 42
utopia (*utopie*), xxiv, xxv, 80–81, 88, 101, 130–32, 172; and daily life, 5, 138, 177n13; idiorrhythmic, 119, 128, 130, 196n1

Violence and the Sacred (Girard), 83
Visitandines, 44

wealth, 34–35, 39–40
"What is it to 'hold forth'?" ("Qu'est-ce que tenir un discours?"; seminar; Barthes), x, xxix, xxx, 172–73, 175n2
will-to-grasp, 126, 196n20
Within a Budding Grove (Proust), 87, 146, 190n16
"The Wolfman" (Freud), 115, 194n20
"Woman as Object of Speech" (Martel), 172–73
Wou-wei (non-action), 85–86, 105
writing, x–xi, xxix, 119, 130–31, 194n12
Writing Degree Zero (*Le degré zéro de l'écriture*; Barthes), ix, xxvii–xxviii

xeniteia (*xéniteia*; voluntary exile), 124–29, 151
xenos (foreign; foreigner), 124, 126

Zen Buddhism, 85

European Perspectives

A Series in Social Thought and Cultural Criticism

Lawrence D. Kritzman, Editor

Régis Debray	*Transmitting Culture*
Catherine Clément and Julia Kristeva	*The Feminine and the Sacred*
Alain Corbin	*The Life of an Unknown: The Rediscovered World of a Clog Maker in Nineteenth-Century France*
Michel Pastoureau	*The Devil's Cloth: A History of Stripes and Striped Fabric*
Julia Kristeva	*Hannah Arendt*
Carlo Ginzburg	*Wooden Eyes: Nine Reflections on Distance*
Elisabeth Roudinesco	*Why Psychoanalysis?*
Alain Cabantous	*Blasphemy: Impious Speech in the West from the Seventeenth to the Nineteenth Century*
Luce Irigaray	*Between East and West: From Singularity to Community*
Julia Kristeva	*Melanie Klein*
Gilles Deleuze	*Dialogues II*
Julia Kristeva	*Intimate Revolt: The Powers and Limits of Psychoanalysis*, vol. 2
Claudia Benthien	*Skin: On the Cultural Border Between Self and the World*
Sylviane Agacinski	*Time Passing: Modernity and Nostalgia*
Emmanuel Todd	*After the Empire: The Breakdown of the American Order*
Hélène Cixous	*Portrait of Jacques Derrida as a Young Jewish Saint*
Gilles Deleuze	*Difference and Repetition*
Gianni Vattimo	*Nihilism and Emancipation: Ethics, Politics, and Law*
Julia Kristeva	*Colette*
Steve Redhead, ed.	*The Paul Virilio Reader*
Roland Barthes	*The Neutral: Lecture Course at the Collège de France (1977–1978)*
Gianni Vattimo	*Dialogue with Nietzsche*
Gilles Deleuze	*Nietzsche and Philosophy*
Hélène Cixous	*Dream I Tell You*
Jacques Derrida	*Geneses, Genealogies, Genres, and Genius: The Secrets of the Archive*
Jean Starobinski	*Enchantment: The Seductress in Opera*
Julia Kristeva	*This Incredible Need to Believe*
Marta Segarra, ed.	*The Portable Cixous*
François Dosse	*Gilles Deleuze and Félix Guattari: Intersecting Lives*
Julia Kristeva	*Hatred and Forgiveness*
Antoine de Baecque	*History/Cinema*
François Noudelmann	*The Philosopher's Touch: Sartre, Nietzsche, and Barthes at the Piano*